INTERNATIONAL ENCYCLOPAEDIA OF ISLAM

Vol.-8

Islam and Education

INTERNATIONAL ENCYCLOPAEDIA OF ISLAM

Vol.-8

Islam and Education

Editor

A.H. Qasmi

ISHA BOOKS
DELHI-110 033

International Encyclopaedia of Islam
(*Religion*)

ISBN: 81-8205-320-X (Set)

ISBN: 81-8205-328-5

Published in 2006 in India by
Isha Books, D-43, Prithviraj Road,
Adarsh Nagar, Delhi-110 033

Printed at : Rajdhani Printers, Delhi.

Contents

Preface

Man is a social creature. It is the society where he learns how to live in this vast cosmos. Apart from society, people are divided into different castes, cultures and creeds. All these factors go in developing a man's personality. Of all the factors, mentioned above, religion is most important.

There exist about more than two thousand religions in the world today. A religion is regarded as a sacred institution, which governs a man's life here and hereafter and teaches him how to lead a happy and prosperous life.

What's unique to Islam is its endowment to humanity from the divine creator or the Almighty. It is not a set of principles and dogmas scribed by a scholar or thinker. It was sent on the earth circa fifteen hundred years ago, but its principles and preachings hold good even today. Besides showing humanity a straight way to the eternal success, it also has a say in various other walks of human life, such as economy, politics, human rights, social relations, judiciary, marriage and so on and so forth.

Another distinguished feature of Islam is that apart from being the latest religion, it is also the last one. That is to say, whatever is there in Islam, it is valid upto to the doomsday. Now, there will not come any other religion till the Day of Judgement. Therefore, it is the most powerful and as well as the most human-nature-friendly.

Given the present global scenario, there was being felt a dire need to bring out such a mini-encyclopaedia of Islam which may cater to the maximum needs of man in the least possible sheet of paper.

The present series is an humble attempt in the same direction. It comprises ten volumes which cover all the major disciplines of human life like, Prayer, marriage, justice, human rights, social justice and so on.

We are sure that the endeavour would prove to be a capsule of treasure of knowledge about Islam, prepared perfectly. Nevertheless, considering the adage 'to err is human', we would be obliged if the readers suggest some improvements for further editions.

Editor

1

Basic Concept of Education

Islam, the greatest experiment in social and cultural democracy on an essentially human and spiritual basis was a reaction against the parochial outlook of tribal life, the narrow individualism of other religions and the domination of a privileged class in Mecca who jealously preserved their vested interests in the face of an evergrowing class of paupers. The Islamic belief and observances, players and social usages, the tithe (zakat) and the fasting penance, all fostered a consciousness of corporate life among the old and created a social environment of the highest educative value for the young. It awakened among the desert Arab, the dormant desire for human association and gradually widened the sphere of their loyalties from the narrow circle of tribal life to the universal brotherhood of man.

The Roots

According to the greatest thinkers of Islam, human society is not based on the nasty and brutish individualism of Hobbes where the deeply laid instinctive suspicion of one another forced men to associate together in order to safeguard against the danger of fratricidal strife and anarchy. According to them, the origin of human association is mutual love and attraction and the Shariah has seized upon this innate tendency and has tried to foster it through religious observances. Ibn Maskwayh writes as follows while discussing the origin of human association, its recognition by the Shariah and the means by which it has attempted to place it on a sound foundation.

Basic Principle of Life : "The temporal love develops out of associating with one another.... and its origin is the innate tendency of association and company which is inherent in man's nature. Man is not unimpressionable by origin nor does he abhor company and the term Insan is derived from Uns in the Arabic language.

We should try our best that this feeling for comradeship may not be atrophied; rather we should try to foster and cultivate it as far as possible. Hence the Shariah and goodly usage have approved of the feasts and gatherings for cultivating this spirit. The Shariah has ordained all men to attend the mosque five times daily. It has enjoined prayer in company in preference to prayer in private, in order to nurture this innate feeling for association which is potential until it issues forth in action. The Shariah has strengthened it by inculcating it through religious belief and inhabitants of every street or alley can easily attend such gatherings every day.

Concept of a Cooperative Society : It is incumbent on the citizens to meet together once a week on Friday in a mosque, spacious enough to contain all of them; the inhabitants of the town and the neighbouring villages must come together twice a year in the plain outside the town in order to revive this sense of social solidarity among them and may knit themselves in bonds of unity under the influence of this integrating love.

Again it has been made obligatory that all should meet once in their life at Mecca and no specific year of one's life has been appointed for its performance in order to provide facility for the people of different lands to meet together, just as the citizens of a single town gather together and develop a sense of camraderie and sympathy of virtue and grace like those who congregate annually, weekly or daily. They flock together under the urge of the natural feeling in order to do good in common and to revive in them love of the Shariah.

***Reaction on Education*:** Such a conception of human society was bound to have a strong reaction on the system of education and the social outlook of such a system has been inspired by that religious faith in corporate life and human camraderie which is the life breath of Islamic thought and practice. A great achievement of the system was the development of a closer relation between community and education; the absence of a privileged class of the clergy precluded any possibility of knowledge degenerating into a preserve of the Elect; under the influence of this new movement of democracy. Education was primarily meant for the masses and not for the classes. The contents of education were selected from the social viewpoint and the criteria for such a selection were not determined by a ruling class or an intellectual hegemony; they were primarily chosen for their social values, social in the sense that they help the individual in the moral and intellectual regeneration of his people and along with that provide scope for his individuality and personal contribution without which all human progress is impossible.

Great Founder

A close study of the Traditions on the subject provide plenty of evidence in support of such a conception of Islamic education. The Traditions accept frankly the inherent similarity of the function of a Prophet and a Teacher, the nature of Apostlehood and the educative process. According to them, the difference lies in degree rather than in quality. The teacher is described as the rightful heir of the apostles of God; he is the caliph of the Prophet among his people; a patriarchal figure like the Prophets of the Old Testament on whose shoulders lay the responsibility of social and intellectual leadership of his people.

Great Scholar : The function of the Prophet and the scholar appears to be essentially similar in nature according to certain Traditions. They throw interesting light on the social role that a teacher is expected to play in the Islamic society. In the first place, he shares with the Divinity, the quality of Knowledge. According to the Prophet, "The Lord revealed to Abraham 'Oh, Abraham, I am 'Alim (One who knows) and I love all who have knowledge". According to another, the teacher is the Trustee of the Lord on Earth. Another set of traditions emphasise the likeness of the function of a teacher with that of an apostle.

According to a tradition, the groups nearest to the rank of Apostlehood are the teachers and the martyrs. One who offered prayers behind a teacher, gained the merit of offering prayers behind an Apostle and one who prayed behind an Apostle received absolution for all his sins. Elsewhere the Prophet declared that there are two groups among his people. In case they were sound, the rest of the people were also sound; but when they were in the wrong, the rest also were in the wrong; one of these groups, according to him was that of the teachers. Commenting on these traditions, Ghazzali remarks how closely the Prophet has associated knowledge with Prophethood. Great savants have also expressed the same idea in a similar vein. According to one, none was gifted with anything more valuable in this world than Prophethood and next to it is Knowledge. Another has said that one who desires to attend the Assembly of the Prophets should visit the Assembly of Teachers".

Teacher and Recluse : The traditions on the comparative merits of the teacher and the recluse indicate abundantly the pronounced social bias in Islamic education and the uncontested superiority of the teacher, the symbol of social good over the recluse who represents individual idealism in the religious sense. Social good and the welfare of the group as a whole outweighs all considerations of personal weal even in the field of self-edification. According to another set of Traditions, the teacher stands higher than a martyr in the estimate of the

Prophet. One is a positive and constructive force who is building up the Palace of Truth tier after tier and generation after generation until its pinnacles kiss the glorious heaven; the other is essentially a negative force under whose thundering blows the citadel of Evil is tottering to pieces.

Teacher's Status : The rank of the teacher in the Old Testament is held by the patriarch and according to the Prophet, the teacher deserves the same honoured status of social leadership and guidance in the Islamic society. "The superiority of the scholar over the recluse is that of the full moon over the rest of the stars and the learned scholars are the inheritors of the Messengers of God. Verily the legacy of the Prophets is neither gold nor silver; their legacy is knowledge and one who receives that (princely heritage) should be deemed fortunate. The simile of the full moon which bathes the whole earth in its light and makes dull and dark objects shine with her reflected glory is an illuminating symbol of the teacher while the stars, illuminous bodies in themselves, resemble a recluse who cannot shed a circle of light which may flood a world besides their own. The scholars have been aptly styled as light-houses on land.

According to another Tradition, "The learned savants among my people have the status of the Prophets among the Israelites." On another occasion, he explained in a more pointed and lucid manner the exact place of the Savant on the social ladder. "The priority of the savant over the recluse is akin to my superiority over my people." According to 'Umar, "the demise of a thousand recluses is easy to be borne than the death of a single discriminating person who knows lawful from the unlawful." The mathematical finality with which the verdict is given in favour of the teacher is a clear and indisputable indication of the social outlook of Islam and the conditions which it implies for the growth of an efficient system of education.

In fact, Islam deeply imbued as it is with the social spirit could hardly recognise much good in the individualism of a recluse who sought salvation of the self in vacuo, and not through that fuller realisation of the self which is achieved by self- surrender and sacrifice for the larger interests of the group.

Teaching and Praying : Optional prayers as distinct from the obligatory which are offered in group and gain thereby a social value peculiarly their own, aim mostly at individual salvation and are considered less meritorious than teaching as the latter involves a social process resulting in the moral and the intellectual development of the entire community. It is very important to make a pointed reference to this comparison which occurs with such a significant frequency in the Traditions and which throws light on such an aspect of the educational thought in Islam which is in the truest consonance with the social spirit of the religion.

"Teaching is praying", says Ibn Masud and when another savant was asked whether he preferred night long prayers over the writing of a single Tradition, he replied that he would certainly prefer the inscribing of a single Tradition; another would place the study of a chapter of knowledge above one thousand prostrations. According to Shafii, the illustrious founder of a school of Islamic law named after him, search after knowledge is more laudable than optional prayers (Nawafil). The superiority of the search after knowledge over optional prayers is implied in the Tradition that "search after knowledge is obligatory on every Muslim"; the author of Tadhkiratus Sami advances other arguments on the subject.

The benefit of knowledge, according to him is universal while that of the optional prayers is confined to an individual; Prayers stand in need of knowledge and are dependent on it while knowledge is independent of them; the scholars are the inheritors of the Prophets while it is not so in the case of the devotees; submission to the scholars is obligatory on all; the blessing of knowledge continues after the death of the scholar while that of the optional prayers stops with the death of the individual and in the preservation of knowledge lies the regeneration of Shariah and the protection of the symbols of the people.

Learning and Praying : The above remarks are potent with an important significance as far as the educational problems of Muslims are concerned. The Muslim backwardness in education has become a byword and there can be no more effective remedy for the propagation of knowledge among them than the wider publicity of this aspect of the teachings of the Prophet and the savants, teachings which are certainly more in harmony with the Islamic spirit than the attitude of legions of Muslims who prefer to occupy their leisure moments in religious meditation and optional prayers. Their time would be much better occupied if they devote it to the nobler task of educating the illiterate members of the community.

There is the instance of a great savant rating the pursuit after knowledge higher than obligatory prayers. It is related by Ibn Wahb that he was once studying with Malik b. Anas when the time for the noonday or the afternoon prayers approached near. He was reading and studying in his presence. Then he gathered his books and prepared to depart for prayers. Malik asked what for he was leaving. He said, "For prayers". Upon this Malik exclaimed that it was strange for his present occupation, if prosecuted in the right spirit was superior to that one for which he was departing.

Great Source

The teacher is a dynamic force for good and a quiet and silent crusader against evil. According to a Tradition, a savant is a thousand times more calamitous for the Evil One than the devotee; certainly so because he does not hide his light under a bushel like a recluse and the forces of evil recede before his radiating refulgence as the pitch black night disappears before the approaching dawn. According to a savant, the teacher can be described as a lighthouse on land which sheds its lustre far and wide. He would be seated on a pedestal of light on the Day of Judgement, a poetic reward for one who had been a radiating centre of light and learning in this world. "Three groups will enjoy the right of interceding for others on the judgement day, firstly the Prophets who would be followed by the scholars and the savants. There is an instructive legend describing the visit of the Evil One to a recluse who was easily misled by the intriguing problem whether the Lord could originate the entire universe from an egg while the savant showed the traditional ingenuity of a dialectician in evading the issue and hurling upon him a crushing rejoinder.

The teacher is a holy warrior who wages the battle for truth while the Martyr wages war against evil; the enemies of the Faith one represents the positive and the other the negative aspect of the process of moral and social progress; one acts as the surgeon and the other as the dietician of the body politic. Hence, according to Tradition, "one who enters my mosque to learn Good or impart it to others has the rank of a warrior on the path of Lord." According to another Tradition, "One who is overtaken by death during the process of learning dies a martyr."

Scholar: One Rank Higher : The nature of the service rendered by the teacher to the community is positive, comprehensive, extensive and more lasting in ordinary circumstances than the service of a martyr; also a scholar can expect to earn the merit of a martyr during his life time at any moment but the reverse cannot hold true. Hence a number of Traditions place the scholar above the martyr in merit.

The scholar stands one rank higher than martyr and on the Day of Judgment although both the groups shall have the privilege of interceding for others, the scholar will come first in priority. One who honours a teacher has earned the merit of honouring seventy prophets and one who honours a pupil earns the merit of honouring seventy martyrs. There are Traditions of rather doubtful authenticity which state that the ink of a scholar shall be weighed against the martyr's blood on the day of judgement and according to Hassan Basri the ink will outweigh the blood. When Ibn Abbas was asked about the Holy War, he replied whether they would like to know something more valuable than the Holy War and he added, "It is erecting a mosque and teaching therein the law of inheritance. Traditions and Fiqh."

Process of Socialisation : If education is defined as the self-perpetuation of culture by the younger generation, then no method of informal education can be more effective in realising the objective of education than the method adopted by the Prophet. The fundamental principle of informal education is the direct association of the young and the old through communication on a basis of equality, equality in the sense that we treat the younger members of the society as responsible beings in their own limited way who are expected to react as vigorously to external influences in their characteristic manner as any adult and are not the lifeless automations of the school whose physical and intellectual movements are controlled by the dimensions of the writing desk. The sense of responsibility is awakened by treating them as responsible persons and no persons could have a higher regard for the delicate feelings of the younger generation than the Prophet.

Faith in Childhood : He had implicit faith in the younger generation and they justified the confidence reposed in them by rising always equal to the occasion and performing in war and peace what was expected of them. His glorious confidence in man ignited in the heart of the young a spark of moral fervour and they discovered for themselves a heartening faith in personal merit and an independent outlook on life. The chief drawback of our present day social life in general and the educational system in particular is that the younger generation has lost all faith in the ideology and the experience of the older people.

Complete Loss of Faith : And there seems to be some ground for such a complete loss of faith. Somehow or other the older generation does not appear to know the younger and a proof of such a devastating generalisation lies in the fact that teachers, parents and others concerned with the training of the younger people ignore very conveniently that fundamental principle of child education which emphasizes treating the child as a responsible being and not meeting him half way condescendingly with a physical and intellectual lisp. Experiments in child psychology have proved abundantly that children when treated as responsible beings become actually responsible persons with a high sense of duty and moral vigour and those who have studied children closely and sympathetically know what a glorious spirit of idealism can be released in a young person when he learns that he is the repository of such a confidence.

***Respect for the Child's Personality*:** "Honour your progeny and educate them well," says the Prophet and like a true educator that he has, the respect for the child's personality has a precedence with him over his training. He never lost a single opportunity for bringing home to the younger people the profound regard which he entertained for them. When he saw a party of children and women returning from a marriage feast, he rose on his feet and greeted them thrice in the following words, "You are dearest to me of all humanity." When he came across young people on his way he would greet them by invoking peace on them while in the older company he had a scrupulous regard for their feelings. Once a young boy was seated on the right hand of the Prophet while some elderly persons were occupying seats on the left. He desired to treat them with a drink and preferred to start with the elder members of the company. But in deference to the usual custom of always beginning from the right, he sought the consent of the young boy to start from the left which he frankly refused. He was not prepared to waive of his privilege of partaking from the drink of the Prophet before others and the Prophet allowed him precedence over other in consideration of his feelings.

Keeping Promise with the Child : It is common for the parents to hold out petty little promises to their children, sweet nothing, never meant to be fulfilled for cajoling the child; the practice militates against a harmonious development of the child's personality, introduces a note of insincerity and is a direct insult to the self-regarding sentiment of the child. The Prophet discouraged it in undisguised terms. Once he was visiting a family when the lady of the house called her children aside and promised them something sweet. The Prophet asked what she was giving to them upon which she replied that it was a date. He approved of her action and added that if she had not given anything, the sin of telling a lie would have been entered against her in the Account.

Legally young children were given a free option of choosing the parent with which they decided to stay in case one of them had embraced Islam while the other still remained a non-believer. He would address the child who stood most probably between the two parents in benignant terms, "My dear boy, here is your mother and there stands your father; now make a choice for yourself."

Model Counselling

The confidence reposed in the younger generation by the Prophet found a faithful reflection in the thought and practice of the Companions; 'Umar would send for the younger people when faced with a crisis, took their counsel on important matters of state and availed himself of their innate intelligence in the affairs of administration. They constantly reminded the younger generation of the heavy responsibility which they were expected to shoulder in future and for which they should make preparation in right earnest from the very beginning. "Learn", said Hassan Ibn Ali to his son and nephew "because although you are the younger members of the community today, you will be their great ones tomorrow. "Ibn-al-Zubayr advised his son in the following words, "Learn from me because it would not take long when you would be the leader of the people".

No False Prestige : The spirit of mutual trust and understanding was all the more strengthened by the absence of any feeling of false prestige among the older people and their frank recognition of the merits of the younger persons when they had supplied sufficient proof of it. Hamidi, a disciple of Shafii, relates how he accompanied the great master on his journey from Mecca to Egypt and on the way he learnt from him the laws of religion (Masail) while Shafii took lessons from him on Traditions. A person describes that he saw Abu Hanifah sitting in the company of Malik as a child sits in the presence of his father and he observed all this decorum in spite of the fact that he was older than Malik.

These instances remind one of the well known episode of the intelligent boy who played the judge in the story of the two merchants and the jar of olives, in the days of the good Harun al-Rashid. The story of the Arabian Nights tells tale of a tradition of high intelligence and innate shrewdness of the Arab youth which was frequently availed of by the adults.

The children of Medina in the days of the Prophet were second to none in intelligence and shrewd repartee; they were ready witted and were gifted with a readier tongue. There exists the account of a group of children frolicking about in the street when 'Umar appeared suddenly on the scene. All the children sneaked away with the exception of Abdullah bin Zubayr who showed early signs of that undaunted spirit which brought him one day to a glorious end. When Umar asked why he did not follow the example of his companions he replied, "I have not done anything wrong that I may be afraid of thee and the path is not so very narrow as required my removal for broadening it for thee. Such boldness was the fruit of an atmosphere surcharged with educative influences of the highest order.

2

Basis of Education

The primary aim of this brief study of the Prophet's Traditions is not to justify his claim to the title of a preceptor and to discover in his teachings all the minutemen of classroom pedagogics. It will be a left handed compliment to style a Guilder of men as a pedagogue and to read into an architect of life the soul of a crack craftsman who worked out a system of classroom technique. He does not provide us with a psychoanalytical method of child study but he discovered with all the vigour of his intuitive powers and the largeness of his heart, the principle of love and sympathy, that wondrous spell which helps in opening magic casements into the heart of a child when other methods break down; which not only helps us in understanding the child but is the only secure foundation for the harmonious development of his personality. He does not posit a theory of discipline but he found out for generations of teachers and savants those genuinely human relations which could be the only bond of moral and intellectual understanding between the teacher and the taught. He did not lay down any laws for curriculum-making but he transformed the entire social life into a school and the environment into a great educative force. He did not initiate any new fangled system of formal education but he gave a practical demonstration of a method of informal education which vibrated with the spirit of joyous spontaneity, and closest association with the life of the community.

Schools at Work

One of the imminent dangers of the present-day system of formal education in this country and elsewhere is the gradually widening gulf between school and society and the consequent deadening influence on the educative process as a whole. Some of the leading thinkers of the educational world, John Dewey and others have already given a timely warning of the menace which threatens the development and growth of educational systems on account of their gradual dissociation from an intimate and intelligent contact with the needs of the community and the living problems of the day. While the rushing currents of Time march on their inexorable course, they tend boundaries of the school, as barren patches of islands in the stagnant backwaters.

The moral and social world is afflicted as relentlessly with the law of inertia as the physical world and our institutions have a tendency to lag behind times unless stimulated by new ideas and hitherto untapped sources of potential energy; some time they flower into a second spring by discovering in their living past, those nascent principles of life and activity which had made them once a dynamic factor of social progress. The new movement in education is making a serious effort to capture once more the spirit of the old informal system of education and introducing it into the formal, straight-jacketed and colourless atmosphere of the present day school.

The system of informal education employs the principle of active sharing of experiences through life-situations and the method of the Prophet as revealed in the Traditions is a shining example of such an education. He participated so joyously and spontaneously in the social life of his people and his contacts with the younger generation of the commonwealth of Islam, including the youngest, were always so rich, abundant and fruitful; therein lies a promise of hope and inspiration for those who are working for the propagation of the new ideals in more than one field of education today.

The method of informal education inherent in the Traditions has an appeal which transcends the educational frontiers of any particular caste, community or race. They are broadbased on such a conception of human association and social cooperation which has a universal application. They lend a refreshing note to the educative process and place the sharing of life-experience on a personally vital basis. This method of education, which is informal and incidental is not symbolic and abstract as in the case of formal education; it is closely linked with the everyday pursuits of life and is a natural outcome of social needs and requirements.

The greatest danger of the present day education in Indian and Pakistani schools is its tragic dissociation from the social context, both in contents of education, its method of organising those contents and handling them in the classroom. Public opinion has awakened to the graveness of the educational crisis and there is a general demand for some kind of education which may develop better social attitudes in the pupils; create in them a living sense of civic responsibility and foster a mental outlook which may enable them to repose their faith in a cooperative rather than a competitive mode of life on an intellectual and practical basis.

Social Dimensions

Our present system of education is rapidly transforming the average pupil into an egoist, a tendency all the more accentuated by the narrowly individualistic outlook of the society at large; it has awakened in him dangerous propensities, which may minister to his personal advancement and prosperity, but function nevertheless as disintegrating and disruptive forces for the society as a whole. If we are desirous of discovering some means of counteracting their influence, we will find in the system of Islamic education, as represented in the Traditions of the Prophet, an example of informal education which provides some indispensable elements for the social development of the citizen's personality. It would release the educative process from the darkening shades of the school room and would transform the business of acquiring knowledge into a vital pursuit of sharing life experiences with the adult and the older members of the society.

Climate in Society : If we make a study of the educative value of the social environment today as compared to the period of indigenous system of education in this country, we are convinced that the educative influences in the latter case were more comprehensive, deep and effective. In those days all the social institutions functioned in one way or the other for the education of the younger generation in its limited sense and every adult member of the society felt in an intensively religious way, his responsibility to function as an agent of informal education for the younger people. Western educationists and administrators who have studied this system with sympathy and understanding have appreciated this redeeming feature of the system which ensured for the school and the teacher the cooperation of the entire society. There may be no dearth of socially minded people working for the educational development of the younger generation outside the school these days, but no effective drive for mass education can be initiated through individual efforts. A study of the history of mass education reveals that large scale success has only been achieved either through religion of state. In the case of Islamic education the mainspring of inspiration was religion as represented by the Holy Quran and the Traditions of the Prophet.

The Traditions of the Prophet have been a tremendous formative influence in the growth and development of certain elements of Islamic education. The Prophet was a great builder of men, a radiating centre of influence who constantly moulded and transformed his Companions. Later on he became the inspirer of generations of teachers whose life ideals were illumined by his Teachings and whose classroom methods were coloured by his personal example. The educational conceptions of the great savants of Islam, their aims and objectives, their classroom etiquette and general behaviour in addressing lecture groups are strongly reminiscent of the chapter on social behaviour (Bab-ul-Adab) in the Books of Traditions. The Sayings of the Prophet on this subject are still a living force in the indigenous schools of this country and elsewhere in the Muslim world although they appear to have lost much of their primal vigour and vitality through the passage of time.

Tradition of Literature : The Traditions have a special significance as a literary heritage of the Islamic people, an influence which has been constantly moulding the style of generations of scholarly writers whose medium of expression was the Arabic language, the lingua franca of the Islamic world. In certain cases it helped in the growth and development of the local languages by lending them the charm of its racy, genial and human style. A study of the English and the continental languages reveals how profoundly they have been influenced by the Bible and the author of juvenile literature in Islamiat and Pakistani languages of Indian Subcontinent would do well in drawing more freely on this perennial source of literary inspiration for the Islamic people.

The educational conceptions implied in the Traditions have a special message for the social worker in the field of adult education. They determine for him in broad terms the aims and objectives of the educative process and lay down for him in clearly unambiguous terms that all education dissociated from the masses is a travesty; that all teaching divorced from moral values is hardly worth its name; it provides for him in a practical and realistic manner some highly effective means and devices of informal education for the old and the young.

Proper Planning : A careful analysis of the mainsprings of Islamic education, a survey of its inner forces, moral, social and intellectual is essential before we can appreciate its spirit or foreshadow a new scheme of education for the Muslims. The Traditions may not be able to supply us with an Educational Code or our educational programme for the future but they provide us with something more significant and valuable. They throw light on those hidden life springs which functioned as dynamic factors in the growth of an educational system, conspicuous for its intellectual vigour and socialised outlook, elements which form the only basis for a consistent and efficient system of education.

The builder of a scheme of education in future who is gifted with vision and insight would concentrate on the marshalling of the moral and social forces rather than the unravelling of the problems of Individual Psychology or the technique of teaching.

The educational research of the modern period has been mainly directed on lines essentially psychological and technical and the educationist who ought to have been more of a sociologist and moralist has been concentrating on the narrow instructional aspects of education. He has ignored the wider issues, social and human, implied in the educative process and has followed only too often the ignes fatuus of sugar coated methods and soft pedagogy, betraying at one time the misplaced enthusiasm of a specialist and at others the weakness of a publicity-monger. His insistence on his new fangled methods of teaching, apart from any consideration of the social and economic context savours of the propaganda technique of a mountebank who prescribes his patent recipe as a panacea for all human ills.

But no amount of patented stuff would do good to the suffering humanity unless it discovers once more those vital principles of social and moral life which can form the only sure foundation for the raising of a better race of men.

Philosophical Foundation

The world political crisis was preceded by a social and educational one and the second world war was a natural outcome of the moral and intellectual confusion which reigned supreme before the forces of destruction burst into a general conflagration. Thinkers in the West are realising the need of a new ideology of education in the moral and spiritual sense which may create harmony between man and man and one nation and another. This tendency would introduce a new orientation in the field of educational research as well. The Islamic education once released tremendous forces for intellectual and cultural cooperation on an international basis and the study of the inner workings of such a movement should be of some interest to all who desire to make a better world out of the old.

Al-Ghazzali has initiated a thought-provoking discussion on the problem of curriculum in the course of his commentary on the well known Tradition that search after knowledge is imposed as an obligation on every good Muslim, man and woman.

Perception of Education

He raises the issue by propounding the question – What is knowledge and who should decide its nature and contents? and he continues how the mystics, scholars, the Traditionists and the *Faqih* (legalist) differ on the fundamentals, each pushing up the claim of his particular branch of learning as the knowledge implied in the sayings of the Prophet. According to Al-Ghazzali, it does not refer to any particular branch, neither does it make obligatory all kinds of knowledge. "Every individual should learn that knowledge which is indispensable for the performance of his particular function in society. Any particular branch is not obligatory on one and all, rather the contents of education vary with the environment, the temporal and other conditions of the individual."

This Tradition is generally interpreted as dealing exclusively with religious studies but we have another Tradition on the subject with a flare of crystal crispness playing about it, and enshrining the glorious usage of distant journeying in quest of knowledge. "Seek knowledge although you may find it in China." – knowledge implied here is not obviously religious lore. China was not known for its moral teaching but for its fine arts, handicrafts and cultural refinement. Naturally the word knowledge here should be construed in the secular rather than in the religious sense. At this stage it won't be out of place to devote a few lines to the attitude of Al-Ghazzali towards this fundamental problem of education. He has based his conclusions on the Traditions and his observations on the subject are illumined by his wide scholarship, practical experience and that intuitive insight which makes him such a wonderful reconciler of cold reason and warm-blooded sentiments. His evaluation of the contents of education is utilitarian in the main wherein the social and the individualistic aims merge into one another and harmonise in the bosom of religion.

According to him, the knowledge which has been imposed as obligatory on every Muslim is the knowledge of Muamalat (Transactions), a part of experience which is vitally concerned with the relation of the individual with other members of the society. This knowledge may be classified into Farz-Ayn, and Farz-Kafaya. Farz-'Ayn is obligatory on all the members of the society without exception; they are the duties which the individual owes to himself and to the social group at large, while Farz Kafaya is obligatory in a partial sense, partial because it is imposed on a part of the society or some of its members but the partial nature of obligation does not lighten in any way its responsibility on those who have been appointed to perform that particular function in the society.

The education of the heart which includes both religious beliefs and the development of the moral sense is obligatory on all (Farz-Ayn), because none is free from such moral affections as jealousy, pride, distrust, vengeance, etc., and according to him, these common epidemics which attack the heart cannot be cured unless the individual receives training in their proper treatment.

Functional Side

He has analysed critically the kind of religious information which is imposed as obligatory on an individual. Contrary to the practice of the contemporary teachers of religion who would like to unload the entire burden of religious learning on to the pupil, he advocates a careful adjustment between the needs of the individual and the information to be imparted to him. Its nature and contents must necessarily vary with the conditions and environment of different individuals, and the knowledge becomes obligatory only when the need for such a knowledge arises in an actual life situation.

An acquaintance with the religious observances of the pilgrimage, for example, should become compulsory on the eve of its performance and not before, while a familiarity with the religious injunction on marriage should become indispensable after the nuptial ceremonies had been performed. In fact he recognises such a close inter-dependence between knowledge and action that knowledge in vacuum, even religious knowledge with all the halo of sanctity playing about it, carries no significance for him as a telling factor in the educative process. The part of knowledge styled by him as Farz-Kafaya or an optional obligation on a particular section of the society is further subdivided into religious and non-religious.

Under the non-religious branches, he includes medicine, mathematics and vocations like agriculture, weaving, blood-letting, tailoring, etc., and he derives his conclusions from a Tradition of the Prophet which makes a knowledge of Muamalat obligatory on every Muslim. Secular knowledge of such a nature when once imposed as obligatory on a particular member of the society for the furtherance of social good is as essential as

Farz-Ayn and therefore education which guarantees the maintenance of the society and ensures its continuity is an equally essential part of the scheme of education as studies of religious nature.

According to him, all the branches of learning mentioned under the general title of religious studies, are not essentially religious and he insists upon a critical analysis of the contents of curriculum prescribed for the purpose. He classifies religious studies into fundamental or principal subjects, the subsidiaries and the preliminaries. He differentiates knowledge pursued as an end in itself from that which serves only as an instrument or means for others. Fiqh is, according to him, a subsidiary subject. The third kind of knowledge, the Muqaddamat or preliminaries are language, syntax and the skill of writing.

He had observed with his own eyes the tragedy of uninspiring routine work as carried on in the schools and he was sorely grieved on seeing pupils wasting whole life time on the subtleties of law, syntax and grammar. Evidently they were chasing the *will'-o-the-wisp* of puristic gymnastics instead of setting their course towards those highlights which could illumine the personality with noble thoughts and integrity of character. His analysis was an eye opener for those who followed such a puristic form of learning in the belief of obtaining spiritual benefit and a reward on the life to come. He announced that these instruments or skills should not be confused with real knowledge and should in no way be deified as the chief objective of the educative process as they had no intrinsic value for the individual. The subjects of subsidiary importance could only bask in the reflected glory of the foundational studies and their worth would be determined by the help which they bring to bear upon the principal branches of knowledge.

In learning the Arabic language one should not make a fruitless attempt to master the entire vocabulary—but should discriminate intelligently between the working and the recognition vocabularies of the language. One should learn so much as is essential for clear comprehension and speech, while out of the rarer words one should learn only those which are indispensable for the study of the Quran and the Traditions. That much would be more than sufficient for all practical purposes.

He fought gloriously against the tendency of the scholars who professed different studies and claimed for their particular branch, the annotated sanctity of religious learning and the approval of the Prophet, thereby revelling in the glories of spiritual self-complacency. In the first place, he discredited the idea that secular education was in any way inferior to the religious; one was as essential as the other; while the one sowed the seed and prepared the harvest, the other ripened the fruit and made it luscious.

Hence some of the studies which had been raised to the pedestal of religious knowledge were relegated by him to the domain of secular learning and received their right place in a well thought out, carefully graded scheme of education. He had yet a surprise in store for the scholars, so self-complacently incensed within the stronghold of their privileges, the most startling surprise of their life when he declared that Fiqh belonged essentially to the field of secular learning, not only because it was learnt primarily for obtaining lucrative jobs under the State but also because it belonged to the field of legal administration rather than the cultivation of morals of the growth of personality.

Just as the Sultan should make laws for keeping his people in control so the legalist, a master in political administration should be well versed in the art of maintaining justice and equity among them... as a Sultan is necessary for the preservation of a Kingdom or its administration, Fiqh is essential for deciding differences among men. Just as ruling over the people by dint of political supremacy does not conform to the highest conception of religion, knowledge of the ways and means of administration which Fiqh in reality is, cannot be ranked as a religious study of the highest value.

Thus Ghazzali not only made an original contribution to the problem of evaluating different branches of learning, he rehabilitated secular knowledge into a respectable place in the scheme of education and established a carefully graded scheme of studies. His work would always be prized as a contribution of the highest value in the field of curriculum reconstruction.

His remarks sparkle with a reflected glory for the devout because they are inspired by a single Tradition of the Prophet; they stand out so sound and rational because of the clarity of his thought and the sincerity of his outlook. In fact our indigenous system and the other schools stand desperately in need of a new-birth, a renaissance in aims and ideals, contents and method of education. Once in the olden days, Al-Ghazzali touched the inner springs which constituted the foundations of the Islamic system of Education and released tremendous energy of thoughtful activity. Once through his Great work, the "Resurrection of Knowledge" or the "IHYA", he awakened the forces of the revolutionary thought and action. We hope one day some adventurous successor of his would once more galvanise the stagnant pool of our indigenous education into the rolling waters of a might current. But the original source of such a dynamic power lies hidden in its basic foundations, the Quran and the Traditions.

3

Aspects of Education

Different Disciplines

The earlier literature of the Arabs does not contain treatises providing a systematic and well-documented account of the events of the past. The historical material mostly comprised the knowledge of days, a graphic and passionate account in prose or poetry, of some historic day of a battle or a tribal catastrophe. They failed to appreciate that there was a Divine purpose running through the gamut of human affairs and that the history of mankind was not a discontinuous account of unrelated episodes; it is an integrated scheme of things unrolling into milleneums where days and months are the tiny snippets of the grand Film Roll of Time.

The Continuity : The Prophet seized upon this continuity in the history of mankind, ever emphasizing, ever reiterating the great lessons of morality in a higher sense which the catastrophe of one nation after another brought into prominence.

Divine Purpose : For him, history is not a gorgeous film roll of the past nor an intellectual amusement which may pander to imagination and love of romance. For him the entire history of Man is governed by divine purpose and is directed by the undeniable, irresistible principle that any people who did not respond to the call of Truth were doomed for ever. He allowed his Companions to study the History of the Israelites, not for the Code of Laws which it laid down for the Jews but for the sublimity of its moral teachings and great lessons in socialised living and cooperative effort.

He has permitted relating facts of Jewish history and according to another authority, once conversation about the history of Jews continued in his company upto the prayer time. According to authorities on Islamic Traditions, their history is not so reliable as that of the Prophet and his period on account of the lack of a proper chain of evidence and the passage of time.

History in the Prophet's Mosque : He had a benevolent spirit of tolerance for those who indulged in the tales of the Days of Jahiliyyah in his presence. We have it on the authority of a person who had visited his Presence hundred and odd times that his Companions would often recite poetry and talk of the Days of Jahiliyyah. The Prophet listened to them quietly and very often a smile played on his lips in the course of these narrations. (Perhaps at some pleasant anecdote, the period being so full of witticisms and bon mots).

Treasure of Knowledge

Story telling became popular in the days of the early caliphate and 'Umar was the first Caliph to allow Tamimad-Dari to relate stories. He did so in a standing posture. The story teller must have confined himself mostly to the account of the Prophets and people in the past as narrated in the Quran. In the opinion of 'Umar, the story of Joseph in the Quran was to supply the criterion for this kind of literature.

Most of the Qasis or historical stories told in the Quran deal with the people of the Old Testament and other nations who proved recalcitrant and were visited by Divine wrath in a way which was exemplary for others.

The Traditions supplement to some extent the historical information given by the Quran but they deal primarily with those episodes or aspects that have a significant moral value. For instance, the story of Joseph and his brethern occurs in the Quran but it does not find a prominent place in the Traditions. While the episode of Moses, Solomon, David, Abraham and Ismail occur frequently in moral contexts. The life story of Moses had received a detailed treatment in the Quran but his great Quest for learning as evidenced in the account of his travels presents the patriarch of the Old Testament in an extremely interesting light. The episode has been supplemented to some extent by the Traditions. According to the Traditions when Moses rose one day to address his people, he was asked, "Who is the greatest knower of all" and Moses said, 'I', and God sent him on his travels as a punishment because he had not used the saving clause of grace that the Lord was the best knower.

Three Queries by Moses : The entire story of the three queries put by Moses and answered by his Companion is narrated on similar lines in the Quran and in the Traditions, with a single addition in the Tradition. As the Moses and his Companion got into the boat, a sparrow came and sat swinging on the rim of the boat and dipped its beak in the sea. The Guide pointed to the sparrow and said, "May knowledge as compared with the Lord's is something like the small drop of water which the sparrow has taken out of the sea." The Guide is named Khizar in the Tradition.

Educative Value : Writers on education have drawn several instructive conclusions from the episode of Moses and his companion, the first being the excellence of travel for the sake of learning.

One must learn the virtue of being patient and bearing the trials and travails of the quest after knowledge in a patient manner.

It teaches the great lesson of humility to the scholar and makes him realise like Newton how limitless is the ocean of knowledge and how trivial is the amount that we acquire through our efforts. On the one hand, it teaches the pupil to be patient. On the other, it provides the lesson of forbearance for the teacher. Khizar in this story patiently answers three questions which in his opinion were unwarranted and uncalled for.

Arithmetic : The Prophet laid great emphasis on a sound knowledge of the law of Inheritance (Ilm al-Faraiz) and according to Ibn Hurayrah he had advised his people to learn the science and impart its knowledge to others because it formed one-half of the Shariah. He continued that the law of inheritance was the first branch of learning which would be taken away from his people when they fall on evil days. On another occasion, he foretold the evil times when his people would befriend riches and forget accounts (arithmetic).

The Science of Inheritance : The Science of Inheritance is defined by one of the authorities as a branch of learning which deals with the fundamentals of Fiqh and Arithmetic which determined the shares of all the claimants in the case of a particular inheritance. When the Prophet enjoined on the Faithful the learning of the law of inheritance, he was virtually pronouncing a religious decree in favour of learning Arithmetic. Elsewhere he declared that the knowledge of Religion comprised three things and the last but not the least of them is the knowledge of an equitable law of inheritance.

The Prophet entered business quite early in life and one of the caustic jibes flung at him by the unbelievers of Mecca was the claim of a person to apostlehood who ate like others and frequented the bazaar like a commoner. Most probably, he was well versed in the easier processes of arithmatic. The Books on inheritance enumerate a number of cases decided on the spot by the Prophet and they evidence a good knowledge of Arithmetic and the Rules of Ratio and Proportion.

A Feat of Mathematical Calculations : From the earliest, the Muslims have shown an uncanny alertness in problems of mathematics and some of their feats were so remarkable that they have left a mark in the annals of the period.

Khawaharzada mentions in his Sharah that Ali was wonderfully ready with numbers. Once a Christian asked him what reason he could give for the discrepancy in the period of somnolence in the case of the Seven Sleepers as stated in the Quran and the Old Testament, the period being 309 years according to the Quran and 300 years in the Bible. Without a moment's hesitation, Ali explained the discrepancy on the basis of the two different systems of measuring time in the two cases, in one case the lunar system of computation and in the other the solar.

It appears that a knowledge of the Science of Inheritance was highly prized in those days and raised an individual with such an accomplishment very high in the estimate of the people. Umar was once informed that a certain tribe had appointed an enfranchised slave as their religious chief (Caliph). He was surprised at such a preferment, but they justified the selection by explaining that he was a Reader of the Quran, a Master of the law of inheritence and a judicious person for deciding cases.

Arithmetic Enforced by Umar : Mathematical calculations were not only involved in determining the shares of the inheritors, they embraced the entire span of social and economic life; everyday business transactions, sale and purchase, security or lease, all required a knowledge of arithmetic and 'Umar was so zealous in carrying out the laws of Shariah that he threatened his people with the lash if they did not learn the religious injunctions on sale and purchase. Hence the well known saying by Ibn Dawwam, "Teach your son Hisab (Arithmetic), before putting him on to the Kitab (Book)."

Role of Language

There seems to be present a wide-spread misunderstanding that the contents of education in the days of the Prophet were only the Quran and the Traditions. There is reliable evidence to prove that the curriculum was not so narrowly circumscribed by religious considerations. The talks and discussions even in the courtyard of the Prophet's Mosque wandered frequently into the secular domain. The evergrowing contacts and conflicts of the Muslims with the neighbouring countries forced upon them the study of foreign languages and conquests abroad necessitated a more intimate knowledge of the culture and the language, the administrative and the social system of the conquered people.

The term Diwan for Audit and Accounts was borrowed early from the official terminology of the Persians and a wholesale borrowing of their system of account keeping implied a considerable amount of knowledge which was of a purely secular nature. Often the very nature of religious learning implied knowledge of secular nature. The custom of learning foreign languages had been established in the Prophet's life time and we have a tradition on the authority of Zayd bin Thabit how the Prophet received letters written in the Syriac language and he did not like to send for a Jewish scholar to read the contents of the letters. So he asked Zayd to learn the language; Zayd learnt it within the short period of sixteen days and henceforth he used to interpret the correspondence received from the Jews and wrote out replies to them.

When Prophet Spoke Words of Foreign Languages : We know on the authority of Ibn Anas that the Prophet could speak a few words of Persian and once when Salman Farsi (the Persian) visited him, he said "Darust... etc". According to Muhammad bin Amail, the words implied most probably a hearty welcome for the visitor. He is said to have used an Abysinian word also in his talk with a child. The Prophet kept a scribe named Sijl and there are traditions of rather doubtful veracity on the drying of writing with earth and using the back of the ear as a pen- holder. But there is evidence to show that there existed a class of scribes in those days who knew more than one language.

Astrology **:** The Muslims have made splendid contributions to the development of astronomy in the past. Their calendars and astronomical charts, their observatories and appliances, technical names derived from Arabic that occur so abundantly in the terminology of modern astronomy, all prove that this science was a respectable branch of learning from the earliest days. But when the spirit of scientific method was overshadowed by a superstitious belief in the influence of stars in directing human destiny, Islam stood boldly and nonchalantly and pronounced an outright condemnation of such an attitude. Accordingly it is astrology and not astronomy which has aroused the disapprobation of the Prophet. Astronomy is recognised in the Quran as a branch of mathematics which deals with the movements of the neavenly bodies. "And there is a measure for the sun and the moon." Again, "We have assigned to the moon its stages until she reverts like an old sprig."

According to al-Ghazzali, the science of astronomy deals with the relation of cause and effect and predicts the movements of the planets as a physician presages the imminent attack of a virulent form of disease from its symptoms. The Prophet has forewarned his people against the times when the Science would degenerate into astrology and the stars become the means of divination and superstitious belief. "I fear three calamities for my people in the days to come and one of them is their belief in astrology." Umar was more explicit when in his crisp and commanding tones he made a sharp reference to its practical utility and tolerated no nonsense about it. "Learn the Science of Stars only as a guidance for direction finding on sea or land and don't proceed further with it."

4

Basic Education

According to the social usage observed among the Muslims, the child started his alphabet on the fourth day of the fourth month in the fourth year of his life. According to the religious injunctions, the boy should be taught how to perform obligatory prayers from the seventh year and such an early training has been enjoined to habituate him to the individual and social discipline of Muslim prayers right from the very beginning.

The Prophet was keenly alive to the significance of education in the early years, the pliability of the young and their marvellous capacity to learn by imitation or otherwise. One who acquires I knowledge in his youth has inscribed it on the granite and one who learnt when he was advanced in age was like a scribe who tried to scribble on the surface of water.

According to Hassan, "Learning during childhood is akin to writing in stone." The history of Islamic education supplies examples of prodigies who gave wonderful demonstration of memory and intelligence in their early years. There is the account of a savant who attended the assembly of a Traditionist at such a tender age that he was actually carried in arms to the spot. Al-Ghazzali states on the evidence of Sahl Tastari how the education of the latter began in the third year and when he grew sick of attending for long periods he was allowed more freedom by teacher and he attended the school only for an hour.

Important Aspects

The importance of educating children from the earliest finds pointed expression in so many proverbs of the Arabic language during the early days of Islam. Some of them are reminiscent of the days of tribal warfare when a carefully educated son was a bulwark of strength for the tribe against a powerful enemy. "One who educates his son in childhood, cools his eye on looking upon him when he comes of age. "One who trains and educates his son humiliates his enemy thereby." In the works of the poets we come across that conception of mind which is akin to the description of tabla rasa in the history of psychology. They compare the young child to a sapling, applicable wood, a tender branch which rests so easy and graceful on its root but the grown up man is likened to a dried wood which cannot soften." "An individual may be likened to earth which receives impression only when it is moist."

Some poets have expressed the spirit of the Prophet's Tradition in rhyme. A poet writes", "I have clean forgotten all that I had learnt in childhood. There is no knowledge except that which is acquired in the morning of life and no forbearance except that which is experienced in advanced age. If you open the heart of a scholar in his early years, you will discover there, knowledge inscribed as if on stone. What is learning after one has entered upon years when the heart, the sense of hearing and sight have deteriorated."

In the words of another poet, "Education in the morning of one's life is like the watering of the roots of a plant till it springs up green and refreshing after passing through a period of drought. As for an old man, he would never renounce his style of life until he is laid in his grave and when you leave him, he relapses once more into ignorance like one who has a relapse of a malady after he has recovered from it."

The Backdrop

It appears that the social usage of putting the children early to school was not altogether unknown during the days of Jahiliyyah while the Jews and Christians had educational institutions of their own where they imparted instruction in the sacred lore, although in the opinion of the Prophet it was all de-educating the child as they were indifferent to the importance of acting upon their knowledge. Once in the course of a conversation, he mentioned that such a thing would happen after the death of knowledge and when asked to explain it, he quoted the instance of the Jews and Christians who taught and learnt the Torah and the Bible but never acted upon them, which meant the death of knowledge.

Traditions supply the case of a child of ten who had learnt the Quran and could recite it according to a recognised form and style.

Modem age is a period of inter-continental missiles and artificial satellites; it is driven by an insane desire for speed and speedy results. Its impatient spirit brooks no delay. It is impatient alike to create and to destroy. Such a world can hardly have any patience with the slow and gradual processes of evolutionary growth.

On the other hand, it is controlled and directed by extreme individualism and even the most dogmatic socialist is a believer in individualism within areas of interests which are not controlled by his political ideology.

Both these characteristics of the modern age came into a direct conflict, with the development of the child. The process of his growth is determined by the natural laws of physical and psychological development and they can no more be quickened into peace than the growth of any other organism. But the modern techniques are trying to control and direct the rhythm of organic growth while believers in the processes of an industrial world are fright fully impatient with the slow paced movement of child education and training. They would like to quicken it into an unnatural peace.

But like other arts, education of a child demands great patience, persistence and disciplined control. It demands an intense, love and sympathy with the child and an innate or acquired understanding of the child mind. It is only these qualities of dead and heart which can produce lasting results in the domain of fine arts and child education.

Power of Affection : According to a companion of the Prophet, he had never come across a person who was more affectionate towards children than the Prophet. Collections of Traditions contain chapters on his affection for children and they reveal his amazing sympathy with the child mind and a method for their informal training in daily life which persuaded the children to cooperate in a joyous enthusiasm for their training and education. Where disciplinary methods fail the dynamics of love and affection prevail and the great secret of preparing a young generation of brave souls like Imam Hussain lay in that stupendous faith that the elders reposed in the innate good that lay in children and the confidence that the younger generation entertained in the love and good intentions of the old.

A world which is being whipped into an insane drive on its mad course of speed and individualism could certainly learn a lesson or two from the technique that the Prophet developed for the training and education of young souls.

According to the Bible, "the Kingdom of Heaven belongs to children" but in the words of the Prophet "the Kingdom on earth also belongs to them".

He revelled in a sheer physical contact with children and would describe his sensuous experiences in poetic language.

He would take them in his arms and clasp them to his bosom. Then he would inhale deeply the fragrance of their fresh bodies as if they were freshly blown flowers. He described them as blossoms of earth, and fragrant blossoms into the bargain.

Whenever he went to the house of Fatima, he would invariably send for his grandsons. He would enjoy the freshness and the fragrance of their blooming personalities and take them unto his bosom.

Just as a spark kindles up a blaze, his attitude found a response in the heart of his young friends. While he discovered hidden nosegays in children, they found in him the perfumer's casket.

Once he issued forth from the mosque after the Zuhr prayers. He was accompanied by Jabir bin Samurah. On the way, he met some children. The Prophet called them to him and started caressing their cheeks; he caressed the cheeks of Jabir also. According to Jabir, there was such a coolness and fragrance in his caress as emanates from the casket of a perfumer.

The reaction of his boy servant Anas was also more or less the same. According to him he had never felt anything, not even silk, so soft as the touch of the Prophet. He had never smelt anything more fragrant than the fragrance of the body of the Prophet; not even ambergris or must as compared with it.

Process of Learning

He loved children with all the depth and richness of his great personality but his love was intensified through an allegorical interpretation of the paternal instinct in terms of Divine Beneficence for creation.

He was never moved so deeply by any spectacle as the expression of parental love for their progeny. More than once tears flowed from his eyes when he saw a parent tending a child. These occasions invariably reminded him of the immensity of that paternal affection which the Creator entertained for his creation.

He had declared on more than one occasion that God's love for his creation is more abundant than that of the parent for his offspring.

He would frequently illustrate the positive and the negative aspect of this relationship by referring to the maternal instinct for the child. Once he pointed towards a woman who was suckling her babe in his presence and said, "Can that woman throw her precious darling into the blazing fire?" Even a mare keeps her hoof off the calf so that it may not harm it. So is the case of God with his creation, and according to the Quran, God has writ large Rahmat on his Divine Self.

Casual observers from the West have often remarked about the deep attachment which parents in Islamic society evince for their children and one who is not alive to the functional purpose of the love for children and respect for elders in Islamic society has no insight into its basic foundations.

According to the Prophet, one who has no affection for the young and no regard for the old is not one of us.

It implies that such a person has derived no inspiration from the social outlook of Islam and has no understanding of the social compactness which such an outlook emphasizes upon. The Tradition encompasses both the creative and the conservative aspects of educational development.

Non-Muslims' Case : He opened out his great heart not only to the children of the Faithful but to the world of children as a whole.

He would visit Jewish children on their sick bed and had issued general instructions that children and women should in no case be put to sword during a campaign. Whenever Ibn Abbas was consulted on the subject, he decreed that the Prophet never put the children of the unbelievers to sword and they should also abstain from it.

According to a Tradition, the children of the unbelievers (Mushriks) were not denied the Grace of God.

Once the Prophet described a dream in which he saw the patriarch Ibrahim who was seated in paradise and was surrounded by a crowd of children. He remarked that they were those children who had died in the Natural Faith (Din-al-Fitrat) implying that they had died before they had reached the age of discretion, the time when they were expected to make a declaration of their faith. Then somebody asked him about the children of the unbelievers (Mushriks). He added, "And the children of the Mushriks, too!"

Elsewhere he has said, 'The Pen of the Lord has been lifted away from the children until they reach the age of discretion!

In fact in one of the rawayat, when Aishah heard of the death of the child of a companion, she said in the presence of the Prophet, 'O Messenger of God, may God bless him. He was a birdie out of the birds of Paradise. He committed no sin and he did not attain to the age of committing sin."

Programme for Children : As the Head of the state he was keenly concerned about the rights of the weak and the unprotected. In case of children he had laid down clear injunctions against the separation of the child from the mother. In his infinite sense of pity for children, he realised that no nurse could replace the mother of the child. Hence he disallowed the separation of the child from his mother in case the mother was being sold out as a slave and changing masters.

"Don't distract the love of the mother from her child", he commands and elsewhere "One who has separated the child from the mother, will be separated from his near and dear ones on the Day of Judgement." According to the Traditions, the child must be entrusted to the mother even if she is an Unbeliever because feeding the babe and nursing is permissible in the case of a woman who is an Unbeliever.

In the case of Rafi bin Sinan, when a dispute arose about the possession of his daughter who had been weaned or was about to be weaned, the Prophet decreed that the daughter should be handed over to Rafi's wife who had not embraced Islam as yet. Once he asked the husband and wife to sit in two distant corners and then asked them to call their daughter to him. At first the child turned to her mother. Thereupon the Prophet prayed to God and said, "Oh God, show her the right path," Then she went over to her father who took her away.

Disputes over the guardianship of children were decided in favour of mothers by Umar and Ali bin Abu Talib also and when the uncle of an orphan claimed the child, Umar said to the child, "The affection of thy mother is better for you than the riches of thy uncle."

The opinion of Ishaq bin Rahwayh, an early professor of law is that the child should stay with the mother up to his seventh year and should have the option of selecting either of the parent.

In fact the spirit of the Traditions and the Islamic law is protecting and safeguarding the child's right to security, love and affection.

In the case of Bint Hamzah the claims of a person like Hadrat Ali were rejected in the interest of the child. Bint Hamzah was brought up at Mecca and when Ali and Jafar were leaving Mecca after Amrat al-Qaza, she followed them calling aloud, "Uncle! Uncle!" Thereupon Ali took her along with him. There were three claimants of the child but the Prophet finally decreed that she should go to Jafar because her mother's sister was married to Jafar and a maternal aunt could legitimately claim to take the place of the mother in love and affection. Here also the decisive factor was the protection of the interest of the child.

Children enjoyed certain priorities in his assembly. The first fruit of the season when brought to the Prophet was always given to the youngest in the assembly. This simple and naive usage of his can be appreciated only by those who have observed that first flush of pleasant surprise which comes to a child when he tastes a new fruit for the first time in his life. For him it is like a new planet which has arisen on the horizon of his sensuous experience and only a person with an intense sympathy with child mind can reach to such heights and go to such details in attending to the younger generation.

He would not forget his young friends when he received presents from distant lands. Once when he received embroidered sheets from Yemen, he sent for Um Khalid who was so young that she was actually taken to him in arms. He addressed her in loving terms and pointed out the flowered design with words of impassioned delight 'Sana', 'Sana' which means beautiful in the Abysinian language. In fact the little lady was born in Abyssinia and she could understand words of that language only.

Once he received a golden necklace as a present and he declared that he would present it as a gift to that member of his family whom he loved most. Then he called Amamah, the child of his daughter Zaynab who was a great favourite of his and put the necklace in her neck with his own hands.

Relaxed Laws

He would even relax the rigour of religious injunctions for the sake of children. Women prayed along with men in the Prophet's Mosque and if he heard a baby crying while leading prayers, he would shorten the prayer so that the mother could attend to the child. The injunctions for purifying clothes soiled by the urination of a baby are less rigorous than otherwise. He would often pray with a child in his arms. Once he performed a prayer with Amamah, the daughter of Abul Ath bin Rabi in her arms. He would seat the baby on the ground when performing the prostration and take her up when he rose on his feet.

Once he got down the pulpit for receiving Hassan and Hussain who wore scarlet coloured clothes and were so young that they could hardly walk. They would stagger a few steps and then flop down. The Prophet got down from the pulpit, took them in his arms and then seated them in front of him. Then he turned to the assembly and made a frank confession of his human frailty in these words.

"How true are the words of God that your property and your progeny are a means of test and trial. When I saw them staggering and again rising to their feet, I could not help interrupting my address and taking them in my arms." He realised the great conflict which a person has to face between his duties and his family affiliations and had himself experienced the powerful instinct which created moral crises in the life of individuals. Once he issued forth from his house with a grandson of his in his arms and remarked while pointing to the child.

"You turn us into niggardly misers, plunge us into ignorance and moral apathy and make cowards of us. But there is no doubt that you are a flower modelled by the hands of the Lord."

He used to have all sorts of playful games with children. He would give them a ride on his back or on his shoulders; he would give a child a joyride on his legs. Sometimes he would seat two of them. He would seat them on his thighs, take them in his arms, kiss and fondle them. Sometimes they rode on his shoulders and when any one accosted the Prophet with the words "what a nice ride!" he would remark with a smile, "and what a rider!'

Whenever he returned from a journey, children came out with their elders to welcome him to the town. On such occasions he would take up a child or two and seat them on the ride. In this way they shared the keen pleasure of a victorious entry with the Prophet.

The liberty which the children had with them reached his very person when some of them were attracted by the Sign of Prophethood, a protuberant mark on his back. He would permit them to touch it with their fingers and when an elder discouraged them from doing so he would ask them not to interfere with their innocent pastime and let them play on.

Children undergo a feeling of measureless isolation in huge gatherings of adults and they would choose some of the most solemn occasions to initiate themselves into his presence.

Hajj at ul-Wida was the climax of the Prophet's political triumph and in those days he gave more than one addresses to huge congregations. On the day of the Sacrifice, the Prophet addressed the people while he was seated on a white mule or a camel. The scene has been well described by Rafi bin Amr who was a child in those days and had attended the function with his father. In his own words:

> "When the day advanced, I gave a slip to my father, edged my way through the huge concourse of people who surrounded the Prophet, reached his ride and put my hand in between his shoe and his foot".
>
> "The Prophet gave me a smile of recognition and said, 'Oh, is it Rafi?"

Only one who has the heart of a child can realise the great surge of love and confidence which must have thrilled the small frame of the young child. During that instance, the child must have felt that out of this seething ocean of humanity, he had discovered at least one with whom he could claim unity of the soul.

Scheme for Younger Generation: Sometimes he would enter into the spirit of their boyish pranks and direct the superabundance of juvenile energy into educative channels.

On his way back from the Battle of Hunayn, the Muezzen called for prayers. Abu Mahzurah, a young fellow who had not accepted Islam as yet along with some of his friends raised their voices and repeated the words of the call to prayers. The boys were evidently enjoying the fun. The Prophet called them to him joined in the fun like a young boy and made them repeat the call one by one. Abu Mahzurah had a good voice. The Prophet liked him immensely, made him sit before him, passed his hand over his head and prayed for him. Then he asked him to give the call of prayers regularly in the Haram.

Anyone who has some knowledge of the social status of persons attached in any way to religious service in the Haram in the Jahiliyyah and the Islamic period can have an idea of the sense of gratification which must have come to the young boy through this simple act of confidence.

His contact with children began very early. Newly born babes were often brought to him. He would bless them, perform the custom of *Tahnik* (putting something in the mouth of the infant, a chewed date or any thing else) and he selected for them a good name. He performed the Tahnik of Abdullah bin Zubayr, the first child born in Islam after the migration to Medina and that of Abdullah ibn Abi Talha, the son of Um Sulaym, the mother of Anas. He would put the newly born affectionately on his thigh and select a good name for him.

Munzar bin Abi Usayd was taken to the Prophet on his birth. The Prophet took him in his arms and seated him on his thigh. Then some other business of urgent nature demanded his attention and he was so busy that he forgot about the infant. The baby was taken away but the Prophet suddenly recalled him and once more seated him on his thigh. Then he asked for its name and when he was told the name selected by the parents he said, "No, no, his name is Munzar" and the child was named accordingly.

When a child was born to Um Sulaym, the mother of Anas

bin Malik, the boy servant of the Prophet, his mother asked Anas to take the child to the Prophet for Tahnik and the naming ceremony. The Prophet was at that time in a garden and was branding camels. He held in his hand an instrument for branding the animals. Anas says, "When I brought the child, he took him in his arms. Then he sent for the Ajwah dates, a variety of dates grown in Medina, softened it by chewing it under his teeth and put it in the mouth of the baby. The infant began to suck it. Thereupon the Prophet said, "Look how these Ansars love dates." Then he caressed his face and named him Abdullah.

His contact with children was not that of an elderly person who deigned to join their company in a half condescending, half patronising manner. He entered into the spirit of their simple joys and sorrows and like a genuine teacher gave them the feeling that he also belonged to the world of children and had the gift and vision to participate in their emotional experiences. He had the great gift of opening magic casements into their hearts and enter the Forbidden Kingdom. This was made more realistic and easy through that fund of pleasant humour which sparkled with a subdued light in his contact with children.

According to Anas, his younger brother kept a sparrow and his grief was inconsolable when the birdie died. The Prophet knew the little boy as intimately as the bird and whenever he met him after this tragedy, he would say to him, "Well my dear, what about your little birdie?"

Directive of the Holy Prophet

His admonition of children was illumined with a sense of intense sympathy with the child mind and a sense of humour.

Once a boy who robbed his neighbour's garden was brought to him. He would constantly rain stones on the neighbour's date palms and take away the fruit. The Prophet asked him, "My dear, why do you throw stones on the trees?" The child replied innocently. "For the fruit." When assured of his intention, he told him that if he wanted to take the fruit, he should take only those which fell from the trees." Then he caressed the child and said, "May God bless you with a bellyful of dates."

According to the Islamic Law, no restriction can be imposed upon taking the fallen fruit but the simple naive humour of his prayer for the child needs hardly any comment as an instructive piece of informal education.

The children would often accost him on the way, accompanied him on his walks through the streets and sometimes has a chance of taking their meals with him. On all such occasions, they were being educated in an informal way either through direct instruction or through personal observation and imitation.

Once a child was taking his meals with the Prophet and they were both eating out of the same plate.

The Prophet saw that he was not taking his meals in the proper way. He instructed him politely to begin the meals in the name of the Lord to take them with the right hand and to take only from the portion in front of him.

He has left instructions on the minutest details of every day social etiquette and has gone to the extent of determining the form of thanksgiving prescribed for a Muslim when another presents him with a nosegay. All these instructions were meant both for the old and the young. What the elders did through direct instruction the children followed through imitation.

Children attended the Prophet's assembly and sometimes a sudden fear gripped their souls when they heard him describe the great catastrophe of moral crisis that man shall have to face in days to come or when he administered punishments for the criminals. In these moments he would comfort them with a word of love or clasp them to his bosom.

Al-Mughuab bin Shubah, when a young boy would go on asking the Prophet about the Anti-Christ (Dajjal). The Prophet obviously felt that the child had a morbid interest in the subject and had developed a fear complex. Then he said to him in loving tones, "My son, never mind the Anti Christ; he won't harm you". In this case also the Prophet had affirmed the great faith which he had in the innocence of youth.

A person belonging to the tribe of Banu Harith says, "I was on the scene with my father when Maaiz bin Malik was stoned to death for adultery. Maaiz had himself openly confessed his crime and had insisted upon the extreme penalty. When the stones rained on him, the witness who was a young boy was terrified whereupon the Prophet held him in his arms and comforted him."

We find in his domestic circle a number of children whom he loved with all the depth and dignity of his great personality and the colourful modes of expression which his emotions took had a richness and variety, all his own.

These beautiful vignettes of children on the family stage include that of Usamah, the son of his freed slave Zayd and Anas bin Malik, his domestic servant. He seemed to be particularly fond of Usamah whom he would give a joy ride on his thighs along with his grandson. Usamah must have been a child of good features. He would often fondle him and say, "If Usamah had been a girl I would have bedecked him with ornaments and would have acclaimed him as a beauty in the world."

He entertained an extremely delicate feeling for this son of his freed slave. According to Aishah, once Usamah the son of Zayd, slipped on the threshold and cut his forehead. The child began to bleed profusely and the Prophet asked his young wife to clean it. Aishah demurred but the Prophet put his lips to the wound and comforted the child. Then he said, "If Usamah had been a girl, I would have dressed him in nice clothes, set him off with jewellery and would have made him famous as a beauty"

Sometimes he would tidy up Usamah with his own hands. Once he asked Aishah to clean the nose of the child which she did not. So he wiped it with his own hands and made his well known remark so often quoted in the Manaqib of Usamah, "Love him because I love those who love him."

Some of his wives had children from their former husbands and they lived with him as members of his family. In his playful moods, he would be as frolicsome with them as a child.

Um Salma had daughters by her first husband. One of them Zaynab describes how the Prophet was once taking bath in the house of Um Salma when the girl approached him.

He squirted water on her playfully and according to her belief it added to the freshness of her appearance. She always felt an air of freshness about her throughout her life.

His grand-children were the object of his love and affection out of whom Hassan and Hussain were the greatest favourites.

Books on Traditions contain special chapters on the Manaqib (praise) of the two brothers. His expression of love for them was genuine and spontaneous.

With the unquestioned privilege of a child, they would interrupt his addresses and insist on staying in his arms when he prayed.

Anas bin Malik remained in the Prophet's household for a period of nine or ten years as a domestic and he was treated always by the Prophet with a pleasant familiarity as if he was an equal. He would often address him jokingly as Unays (the diminutive for his proper name 'Anas'). He would address him as "the little boy with two ears." Once he saw Anas picking the leaves of a vegetable and he named him after the vegetable. He would often call him "sonnie."

During this long period of ten years the Prophet never addressed him with even such a mild word of reproof as 'uf'.

During this period he never took him to task for anything which he had left undone or questioned him about anything which he had done. In his own words, "He found the Prophet the kindest of all creation".

Once the Prophet asked him to go on some business but like a spoiled child he refused to go. Anas says that he never meant to disobey the Prophet but he was just being playful with him. Then he came out of the house and joined a group of children who were playing on the street. The Prophet followed him quietly and touched the nape of his neck from behind and when he turned, Anas found him laughing.

Then he said, "Unays did you go where I had asked you to go?" Anas replied, 'O Prophet of God, I am just going".

Holy Influence : His great love for children had an extremely contagious influence on his Companions. Hard hearted Beduins who never knew how to kiss their children and wondered when they saw the Prophet caressing a child, would melt and grow gentle hearted under his genial influence. Some of the Companions grew so interested in children that they would sometimes try to while away the hours of approaching death by playing with them.

There is the case of Khubayb. He had killed Harith bin Amir in the battle of Badr. Later on he was bought by the family of Harith, for satiating the demands of vendetta and was condemned to death. Khubayb prepared himself for the end and asked for a razor for removing hair. The razor was given to him inadvertantly when he was playing with a young child of the tribe who was having a joy ride on his thigh. The child's mother was alarmed about the safety of her son. Khubayb discovered her fears, went on fondling the child and said to the mother, "Do you fear that I will kill the child? I will never do so."

Then he performed two rakaat of prayers and recited those beautifully touching verses that have comforted the heart of many a man under similar conditions. These couplets were often recited by men who fought with Shah Ismail Shahid and Sayyad Ahmad Barelwi. They ran as follows:

> "And I never care on whatever side I collapse as dead so long as I die a Muslim and lie unto the Lord. If he desires he can bless every limb of my dismembered body".

The hearts of the Companions went out move abundantly towards those street urchins who were deprived of the simple and innocent pleasures of life. According to Abu Aqba, once Abdullah bin Umar was passing through a street when he came across two Abysinian children who were most probably slave boys. Thereupon he stopped gave them two Dirhams. His great love for children had a mellowing influence on those hard-headed Beduins who considered it unmanly to caress children or give them a kiss.

Once a Beduin came to visit the Prophet and was surprised to see him kissing a child. In his opinion, it was a human frailty unpardonable in a leader of the people. He told the Prophet that he had never given a caress to a child in his life. Thereupon the Prophet said, "It seems that God has deprived you of the milk of human kindness".

On another occasion when he was kissing Hassan, a bystander confessed that he had ten sons but he had never kissed anyone of them. The Prophet remarked, "One who does not treat others with affection, receives no affection in return." The spark of enthusiasm that the Prophet had ignited into the hearts of his younger followers blazed more gloriously than in the case of their elders. Once their sincerity and enthusiasm were instrumental in averting an extremely dangerous rift among the Muslims of Medina.

Abdullah bin Ubi, the chief of the dissenters (Munafiq) took advantage of a difference between an Ansar and a Muhajir during the Ghazwah of Banu al-Mustaliq, and declared that on his return, he and his party who were men of noble lineage would expel the low bred Muhajirs. On this occasion, elderly persons kept counsel for reasons which were more politic than moral.

It was a boy hero Zayd bin Arqam who defied Abdullah bin Ubi and told him that it was he who was low bred and was considered to be such by his own people. There was every danger that Abdullah would try to create mischief on his return. But when Abdullah bin Ubi returned to Medina, it was once again a boy follower of the Prophet who came out of the town and challenged Abdullah. He was Abdullah, the son of Abdullah bin Ubi himself. The boy stood nonchalantly in his way and refused his father an entry into the town until he declared openly that it was he himself who was a low bred churl while the Prophet was high and noble.

The situation created by Abdullah bin Ubi was in fact one of the most serious dangers to the internal solidarity of Islamic society at that stage and it was the implicit faith and trust which the younger generation of the Ansar reposed in the Prophet which stimulated them to stand heroically against such disruptive tendencies.

Acts of Bravery : Offering for active service was one of the usual channels through which the idealism of the younger generation often found its expression.

Asad al-Ghaba gives a long list of young people who offered themselves for active service on the eve of the battle of Badr and Uhud but were rejected by the Prophet.

Abdullah bin Umar and Bara bin Azib were both refused permission to join the ranks in Badr and they were so young that when they applied one year later to join on the eve of the battle of Uhud, their requests had to be turned down once again.

Quite a large number of young persons were rejected on the eve of Uhud. The list included the names of Abdullah bin Umar, Zayd bin Thabit, Usamah bin Zayd, Zayd bin Arqam, Bara bin Azib, Amr bin Hazm, Abu Said Khuzri, Samurah bin Jundab, Rafi bin Khudayj and several others. They belonged to the age group of 13-14.

Rafi's father pressed the request of his son on the plea that he was a good marksman with the bow and Rafi himself tried to add a few inches to his stature by raising himself on his toes when he was presented to the Prophet. He was permitted to fight.

But when Abu Said Khudri was recommended by his father because he had a well built constitution and had a strong and stout frame, he was not approved by the Prophet. According to Abu Said, the Prophet looked up on him and then lowered his eyes. He was finally rejected.

Samurah bin Jundab challenged Rafi bin Khudayj after his approval to a personal bout in which he floored him in no time. Samurah was also permitted to join.

Some of these boy soldiers performed wonders on the scene of battle.

Abu Jahl who had been described as the Pharaoh of the Age by the Prophet was killed in the battle of Badr by two young men.

According to Abdur Rahman bin Awf, "As I stood in the fighting rank on the battlefield of Badr, I looked to my left and to my right in order to find out who stood by me and I discovered myself between two young boys from Ansars who looked so tender in age. I wished that I were between more tried soldiers. Then one of them signed to me and whispered, "O uncle, do you know Abu Jahl." I said, 'And what is your business with him?' He replied, 'I have been told that he reviles the Prophet and by God who has my life in His Hand, if I encounter him to day, I will stick to him until one of us gets killed.'

> "1 wondered at these words of his. Then the other boy also said something similar to me".
>
> "Soon after I saw Abu Jahl moving about and I said, 'Don't you see, here is your man, about whom you were asking.' Upon this they advanced towards him with their swords until they killed him. Then they returned and reported themselves to the Prophet".
>
> "When he asked who had killed him, both of them claimed the credit. Then the Prophet examined their swords and said, 'Both of you have killed him".
>
> "But he allowed the Salb or the booty of Abu Jahl to Muadh. These two young men were Muadh bin Amr bin Jumuh and Maadh bin Ufra."

Inspirational Value

The supreme confidence which the Prophet had in the naive faith of children has been expressed in a number of Traditions. In one of the Traditions, he has described the True Path as the Luminous one which can be traversed easily even by the ignorant Arab of the desert and the children at school.

He has described how the innate understanding which grew out of a child's innocence would sometimes light upon truth while their elders were lost in the wilderness of their prejudices and passions. In the literature of Traditions we come across three occasions on which an infant declared the truth and averted a great moral calamity. One of them was Jesus Christ. The story has been told with magnificent restraint in the Sura Maryam.

The second was the infant born of an evil woman who charged Jurayj the pious man among the Israelites with fornication. When Jurayj prayed to God and patted the belly of the babe, he told them the name of his real father.

The third was the sucking babe who absolved a slave girl from the serious charge of adultery and theft. It is the touching story of a mother who was sucking her baby when there passed by her side a man who rode a splendid steed and was clad in magnificent garments. The mother said, "O God make my child like him" and the child left instantaneously the sucking, began to look up and when his eyes met the man, he said, "O God, don't make me like him', and once again began to suck".

Abu Hurayrah who has narrated the Tradition describes how completely the Prophet was carried away by the touching scene he was painting in words. In the course of this description, the Prophet appeared to have identified himself with the infant hero of the story. He actually put his forefinger into his mouth and began sucking it like a babe.

According to the story after that there passed a slave girl and the people were beating her black and blue. They had charged her with adultery and theft but the poor wretch protested "God is sufficient for me as an evidence and a supporter!" Upon this the mother prayed, "O God, don't make my son like that slave girl." But the baby left once more his suckling, looked at the slave girl and said, "O God, make me like her", and there ensued a discussion between the mother and the son in the course of which it became known that the infant was right in both the cases.

The babes in all these fables represent honest, straightforward, sincere humanity which speaks the truth with all the frank boldness and courage of a young child.

The fable of the boy Prophet throws light on the story of Ashab al-Khudud (the People of the Pits) as given in the Quran and describes in a moving manner the great faith with which the word of God inspires young hearts.

A tyrant who did not believe in God apprenticed a young boy to a sorcerer who had served his master, the king well and was nearing his end. The boy learnt the art of sorcery but on his way to his master, he came across a Christian monk and was initiated into the true faith. The story runs how the king came to know about the monk and got his body sawn in two. The boy was a witness to the scene and the king asked him to recant from his new faith.

The boy peremptorily refused and the king condemned him to a cruel death. He was thrown down a precipice but he escaped miraculously and when the king failed twice in his attempt, the boy suggested a way out of the difficulty. He asked him to gather the people in the market-place and impale him on the trunk of a tree or a pillar. The procedure was carefully detailed by the boy. The king must take an arrow out of the quiver of the boy and let it fly by announcing the formula, "In the name of the Lord of this boy."

The king did the same and sent the arrow flying which struck the boy on the temple. The boy died on the spot. But the moving spectacle ignited a spark of faith among the people and it was fanned into flame by the great tragedy. They rose to one man and cried out "We believe in the Lord of the boy. We believe in the Lord of the boy." And then the king ordered large pits to be dug on the mouths of the streets which were filled with glowing ambers. These pits were filled with men who did not recant from their faith. The fable which describes the heroic career of the boy Prophet is rounded up by the determined resolution of another boy. When a woman came up to the Pit, she hung back for a moment but a boy who was with her said, "Mother, be steadfast because it is all for the sake of the Lord."

It would be interesting to study how his words of love and sympathy made an undying mark on young hearts and how they were cherished as loving mementoes throughout their lives.

Anas bin Malik, his boy servant is one of the most prolific narrator of Traditions and his narrations are often richly coloured with flashes of human touches.

Usamah bin Zayd who had been described by him as only second to his father Zayd in regard and affection, has a number of Traditions to his credit.

Imam Hassan who was only seven years and some months when the Prophet died used to recall vividly his sayings. He has thirteen Traditions to his credit. He describes graphically how the Prophet asked him to spit out a date sent as a charity that he had put into his mouth by chance.

His brother Imam Hussain, who was six years and odd months when the Prophet passed away had narrated eight Traditions.

Even young children of five recalled his words and remembered even more vividly how spontaneously he joined them in their playful activities.

According to Muaẉwid bin-al-Rabi, the Prophet visited their house when he was a tiny toddler of five. He remembered vividly how the Prophet took water from a well situated in the house and spurted it on his face playfully with his mouth.

5

Scheme for Teaching

The teachers were regular in their work and demanded rigorously the same regularity from their pupils. Maula Muslihuddin Mustafa called the Red Mule for his complexion was a strict disciplinarian and if a student failed to attend his lecture, he visits him in his room in the hostel and minister to him if he was ill. If otherwise, he chastises him most severely.

Once a pupil of his, invited his uncle who was on a visit to see him, to a feast arranged in one of the gardens during college hours and when he requested the savant to grant him leave for the purpose, he flew into a passion and said 'Your entertainment programme made you stop your lesson, could not your lesson make you stop your entertainment. He further told him that the only consideration which deterred him from expelling him instantaneously was the esteem in which he held his uncle.

The same pupil related that he studied with him for a period of two years and his teacher never missed a single lecture, so assiduous was he in these matters.

But the teachers could afford to take a more lenient view when they were convinced of the urgency of their need. Abul

Ala-al-Maarri once permitted a pupil to leave his lesson in order to see a visitor from his home town.

Abu Zakariya Tabrizi had been studying with his teacher Abul Ala-al-Maarri for two years and during this period he had never once come across a single person from his native province of Azarbaijan. They were studying in a mosque when suddenly an old friend and fellow countryman came to offer prayers in the mosque. He was overjoyed to see him and Abul Ala although blind perceived his emotional excitement and asked him what had happened to him. When Tabrizi told him about his old companion he asked him to go and have a chat with him. Tabrizi demurred and told that he would prefer to complete his lesson first. But Abul Ala insisted and promised that he would wait for him till he had finished.

The assemblies of world renowned savants attracted pupils from four quarters of the Islamic world and the audience included sometimes distinguished scholars who came to hear a master discant on his favourite subject. According to Allama Zahbi, ten thousand inkpots were kept in the assembly of Abul Mutaqqai (died 251 A.H.) and the august gathering included two hundred Imams. A lecture by a traditionist Sulaiman bin Harb which was attended by the Abbaside Caliph Mamun in person drew forty thousand listeners while the record number of one hundred and twenty thousand persons came to listen Athim bin Ali discourse on traditions in the days of Harun-al-Rashid. It is said that his assembly usually comprised more than 10,000 persons.

Although lectures on religious subjects specially traditions drew the largest number, those on secular subjects like grammar were also fairly popular. A lecture delivered by Farah Nahwi was attended by eighty judges, besides students of grammar.

The management of such assemblies required a number of assistants called Mustamilis (the dictators) and some assemblies had quite a large number of such assistants.

The assembly of Abu Muslim, the well known author of the collection of traditions known by his name had seven assistants, who dictated from one to another. The assembly had 40,000 and odd persons who wrote besides others. Another had as many as 316 such assistants in his assembly."

These assistants formed a normal feature of class management in the colleges where it was not unusual to come across a class of hundreds if not thousands. The teachers were expected to group the pupils into smaller units for teaching purposes and for revision work after the lecture.

The monitorial system or the institution of a Muid or a Revisor assistant and a khalifah helped considerably in class management. The system was introduced by Dr. Bell in England in the last century and although it proved of a doubtful value in raising the standard of educational efficiency, it helped to propagate education during a period when trained teachers had not become abundantly available Seats in the class group were arranged in the form of a circle (Halqa) and the practice is traceable to the days of the Prophet. According to Zarnuji the pupil should seat himself at a bow's length from his teacher.

The pupils were expected to be properly dressed when attending lectures. The savants themselves took extreme care in matter of dress and enjoined on their pupils to follow their example. 'Make your turbans more imposing, your sleeves more widening' says Abu Hanifa. They would often expel a pupil who was improperly dressed from the class. Sheikh Abu Umar turned out of his class pupils who came without a proper headgear or whose shirt fronts were not properly buttoned up.

The seating arrangement in the class was regulated by a set of rules by which those senior in age and scholarship were given precedence over others, the front seats and those to the right hand of the teacher being given to privileged pupils. In case a pupil showed evidence of superiority over others, he was given a seat in the front rank. When Abu Hanifa attended the lecture of Hammad, he took his seat on the left of the teacher along with other freshers but a few days afterwards he was assigned a seat in the front row.

The pupils were expected to sit at their ease and listen while seated in a comfortable posture. The teachers did not approve a standing position. Imam Malik would not relate a tradition while standing, travelling or when pressed for time and used to say, "I like to feel the meaning of the Prophet's word when I repeat them to others."

Books on Education provide instructions on the manner of taking one's seat in the assembly and maintaining an attitude of attention. Class room behaviour was regulated by a formidable list of rules dealing with such minutiae as toying with a button, pulling at the beard or drawing lines on earth with the finger.

There are strictures on different postures for seating and on laughter, coughing, spitting, sneezing and yawning. The pupils would sit in the classes as if they were at prayers or as if birds had roosted on their heads and they would not change a muscle for fear of driving them away.

According to Shafii, the pupils would refrain from turning the page of a book in order to preserve the pin drop silence so incessantly enjoined on the students. But all these stringent regulations do not imply that the system was unnecessarily harsh. Its outer form was determined by the social and cultural life of the people in general, but it was essentially human in spirit. Very often the disparity between form and spirit gave rise to interesting situations. Once a student's nose tickled and he struggled hard to check a fit of sneezing. The situation tickled a fellow student who whispered in his ear that he should not be so much at pains to control it because after all he was not in the presence of God almighty.

Physical alertness is a pre-requisite of intellectual alertness and the pupils were expected to sit upright in the class. Once a son of Mahdi, the Abbaside Caliph came to attend the lectures of Sharik (died 177 A. H.) on Traditions and reclined against the wall, for support. The teacher refused to teach him and told him brusquely that he did not mean to insult him, but he could not brook an insult to Prophet's Traditions. The posture was discouraged because it signified an attitude of listlessness and lassitude on the part of the pupil.

Recitation by a pupil was a highly cherished privilege exercised by the pupils in the order of precedence in which they arrived for the day's work, and the lesson was opened by the first visitor. Pupils would often sleep overnight on the spot for availing this privilege in the morning. The right could be waived off in no case, unless the pupil himself ceded it in favour of another.

The pupils were enjoined never to demand a repetition of any portion of the lecture. According to a traditionist the repetition of a Tradition was more grievous than carrying a heavy stone. The students had to be all the more careful in this respect because in certain cases the teachers positively refused to repeat.

The pupil was expected to listen with attention a discourse even on a subject with which he was already familiar and he must feign a look of pleasant surprise on his face.

According to Ata bin Abi Ribah (died 115 A. H.) he had the patience to hear from a youngman a tradition which he had studied even before he was born, all the time showing off discreetly as if he had never listened to it before.

Mutual Relationship

Authorities on education lay great emphasis on the relations between the teacher and the pupil. They insist on an attitude of deep reverence on the part of the pupil and love and affection on the part of the teacher.

Qadi Ibn Jamaah's Views : The teacher should accost his pupils with a welcome when they visit him and when they are seated, he should make individual enquiries about their personal affairs and those of their dependants after the usual salutations. He should address them with a smiling face, and a spirit of companionship, love and sympathy so that the pupils may lay open their heart to him, be of good cheer and may be encouraged to put questions more freely.

The treatment and behaviour of the great masters and their instructions on the subject would often leave a lasting impression on the pupils. In the most depressing hours when Buwayti (d. 231) the pupil of Shafii was weighed down with an iron chain forty pounds in weight in the prison-house of Baghdad, he would experience moments when he hardly knew whether he was in chains unless he felt them with his hand. In these hours of darkest despair he had the book of his master with him in which he had taken down with loving care the parting advice of Shafii, "Be kind and sympathetic to the members of the study circle and do a good turn to the strangers"

It was common among the Arabs and other nations who came under their cultural and social influence to have more than one name for the individual, the proper name and the Kuniat : the teacher was expected to call his pupil and specially those who were distinguished from others by their scholarship by his Kunia or any other name with which he loved to be styled. In this case the savants acted as in other cases, according to the traditions of the Prophet.

Ibn Abbas used to say "Most dear to me is the person who makes his way to me by crossing over others head in order to be close to me (for listening my speech). I would hardly bear a fly sitting on him and bringing discomfort to him."

Lectures were attended as a rule by two classes of pupils, regular and irregular; those who were attached to the teacher as his pupils and casual visitors. The teacher was expected to make enquiries concerning absentees, regular or irregular and obtain information concerning the cause of absence. If he could get no information he must send some one to his house or should visit him at his residence in person, the latter procedure being the best.

According to Ibn Jamaah, "the teacher should visit the pupil if he is sick and should give expression to his sympathy and consideration for him if he is suffering from some loss or bereavement." In case the pupil has departed on a journey, he should look after his family and dependents. He should make enquiries about their needs, supply their wants and provide for them all what he can. He should help them with every thing which they seek from him.

If he has no means to help them financially or otherwise, he should express his concern for their good and pray for their well being. The teacher should in no case make invidious distinction between his pupils as regards attention and regard if they are otherwise equal in age, scholarship, love of study and singleness of purpose. But if any one of them is distinguished by his love of learning, industry or god behaviour, he may select him for special regard and give him precedence over others, but he should make it explicit that his consideration for the pupil arises out of the above mentioned reasons.

How the Teachers helped their Pupils : The economic relations between the teacher and the pupil were determined by a variety of factors, the class of the teacher as regards his special subject, the financial condition of the savant, and the traditions of the country..

As a rule the teachers of religious studies did not accept any remuneration from the pupil although exception was made in case of teachers who lived in extremely poor conditions. The teachers of Spain would enter into an agreement with their pupils for teaching certain subjects.

Imam Ghazzali does not approve that the teacher should receive any remuneration from his pupil. He was against the custom of using pupils for domestic service which was more usually practised in case of school children. In his opinion even the expression of gratitude on the part of the pupils is out of place.

According to Ghazzali instead of expecting from the pupils an expression of a sense of gratitude, "He should feel under an obligation to them because the pupils have entrusted to him the nurturing of their hearts and he has been able to gain merit in the eyes of the Lord through this service". The pupils are like the owner of a plot of land, who has surrendered it to the tenant for cultivation and harvesting purposes. In his opinion the tiller of the soil and not the landlord gets the best out of the bargain. The teacher has no right whatsoever to place his pupils under a debt of gratitude because if the pupil had not offered himself for training, the teacher could have no opportunity to earn a reward in the eyes of the Lord.

The authorities on education impose the help and encouragement of the pupil as an essential duty of the teacher and he is enjoined to use his influence and monetary resources for providing him facilities as far as possible.

According to Ibn Jamaah 'God favours the person who helps his brother in trouble and one who tries to make life easy for another in this world would enjoy an easy reckoning from the Lord in the next, the reward being richer in case the assistance was rendered to a seeker after knowledge.

The teachers of the Islamic world were essentially *loco parentis* for the pupils and helped them with all the means at their disposal in pursuit of learning.

The history of Islamic education abounds with examples of teachers helping the pupils, the tradition has been laid by the founders of the first four schools of Islamic law. Imam

Shafii was helped most generously by Imam Muhammad bin-al-Hasn and even by Imam Malik while the help rendered by Imam Abu Hanifa to his pupil Imam Abu Yusuf prevented him in giving up his studies.

Asad bin Furat relates how his teacher Muhammad bin Hasn came to know about his financial difficulties and he sent his compliments to his pupil through a servant at night. He pleaded ignorance of his condition and sent him eighty pieces of gold through the messenger. He had the courteous delicacy of feeling to send the money in the dark.

Parents in impecunious circumstances could not afford higher education for their sons and preferred that they should join an occupation which might bring a timely aid to the poor parents. In such cases a teacher with means would often come to the rescue of a deserving pupil and help him financially so that he could pursue his studies in peace.

Qadi Abu Yusuf, the pupil of Abu Hanifa was forced away from the class by his father who admonished his son not to take after his teacher, a savant who carried a rich trade in cloth, look to his interests and take to a vacation. When the savant had an opportunity to see his pupil again he came to know of his condition ; he gave him one hundred dirhams in secret and told him to inform him again when he needed money and by and by he presented him with another sum of one hundred dirhams.

Qadi Ibn Furat received a purse of eighty dinars from his teacher when he came to know that he could not pave his way with the monetary assistance which his family had provided for him.

The teachers took extreme care that the offers of financial assistance might not injure the self-respect of the pupil, a virtue which they cherished themselves so eagerly. Abu Zakariya Tabrizi, the well known grammarian relates how he used to live in a call under the minaret of the Friday Mosque at Damascus when one day his teacher Khatib Baghdadi came to see him. He started offering, profuse excuses for not visiting him more frequently. Gradually the conversation drifted to those traditions of the Prophet which extol the presentation of gifts to friends. Upon this the teacher turned to him and told that he was going to present him with a gift only to honour the behests of the Prophet on the subject so that he could provide his stationery requirements with the sum. Then he placed the money wrapped in a paper in front of him and took his leave. The paper contained five hundred dirhams. Abu Zakaria relates that he helped him in this way more than once.

Matrimonial relations were other means by which the monetary and other help rendered by the teacher was elevated from a charitable donation to something in the nature of a privilege. The pupils prosecuted their studies to quite an advanced stage of life in the early period and most of them were married. Matrimonial relations with the teachers' family became a regular feature of the educational life in the Islamic world.

There is the anecdote of Abu Wadaah who married the daughter of Said-bin-Mussayib, a gifted woman whose hand was sought by the heir-apparent of the Ommayid Caliph Abdul Malik bin Marwan without success.

The story runs that Abu Wadaah absented from the lectures of his teacher for a number of days after the death of his wife. When he made his next appearance in the class the teacher came to know of the tragedy and advised him to marry again. The pupil pleaded lack of means and asked who would marry his daughter to a person who could not pay more than two or three dirhams for marriage money. Said told that he would do it and performed the marriage ceremony of his daughter with the pupil in the same sitting. Abu Wadaah returned to his house and in the evening he found his teacher who had come to escort his daughter at the door. According to Abu Wadaah,

Said had never been observed to frequent any other path except that leading from the mosque to his house for the last forty years and he could not credit his ears when he heard Said asking permission to enter the house from without.

There were savants who did not forget to make some provision for their pupils in their will. Khatib of Baghdad sought the Caliph's permission to spend his property according to his will during his life time. His money which amounted to two hundred Dinars was distributed among the pupils.

When he was lying on his death bed an illustrious pupil of his, Nasir bin Muhammad-al-Turke, by name, who studied history with him complained against the executor of his will and told him that he had received nothing out of the money which he had earmarked for the Traditionists. Thereupon the great savant raised his head from the pillow, and told the pupil to take away his cloak which contained forty dinars. The money helped him in defraying his expenses during his educational career.

The sting was taken out of that extremely embarassing feeling which grew out of a sense of financial dependence by the refined manner in which the assistance was preferred. The teachers often tried to spring a pleasant surprise on their pupil, the joy of the moment helping to mitigate the inconvenient feeling.

Qadi-al-Laith ibn Saad, a wealthy savant of old Cairo used to have almond cakes made for his disciples and he hide gold pieces in them so that he who ate the largest number of cakes might get most of the money.

A rich savant at Herat (d. 378—988) had gold coins struck which were one and half a times worth the current coin. In his words "The poor rejoices when I make over a small packet to him for he thinks that it contains a silverpiece. On opening it he is pleased to see the yellow of the gold and more pleased still when he finds it heavier in weight than the ordinary current coin".

This sense of delicacy and sheer joy in rendering monetary help was not confined to the Near East. Even today the Delhi dialect retains the proverb *"Khankhana jis ki roti men Badana"* or Khankhana whose cakes had a stone within. Khankhana, the resplendent lord at Akbar's court and the founder of an academy, secreted gold mohurs in the cakes and distributed them anonymously. The usage reminds one of old Dr. Johnson passing through London streets late at night and placing bright new coins in the palms of street arabs sleeping on the pathway.

When a rich merchant who was a scholar sent to another man of learning a book as a present, he placed a gold leave between each two folios.

The teachers preferring help did not stop at giving the pupils the barest minimum which could keep their body and soul together. Sometimes they would arrange banquets which often stretched into regular feasting for an entire month. A teacher of the Qalandariyya College at Constantinople wrote a good hand and he used to copy out manuscripts at a great speed. Every year he would transcribe a copy of Tafsir-al-Baidhawi and sell it for three thousand dirhams. With the proceeds of the sale he used to entertain his pupils every night in the fasting month of Ramadan until the whole amount was spent up.

The teachers were more considerate and enthusiast in entertaining pupils who were themselves masters in their subject and were attending the classes of another savant in order to specialise in a different branch. Imam Shafii, the founder of one of the four schools of law proceeded to Medina in order to attend the lectures of Imam Malik, the founder of a rival school on Traditions. Malik would serve him at dinner time, and bring water for ablutions in the morning. When he expressed his desire to leave, Imam Malik went in person to hire a ride for the journey and presented him with a purse when he bade him farewell.

And all this becomes doubly significant in the light of the punctilious care which Imam Malik observed in maintaining the dignity of the profession. He had wielded the unique authority of rebuking the Caliph and the princes alike. His classes presented a rare example of decorum and orderliness.

In some cases the college was opened and maintained by a teacher and the students were also supported by the founder himself. If he could afford, he would be more generous than even the rich philanthropist Ibn Batuta describes the sumptuous meals which were served at a college in Bargi where he enjoyed the hospitality of the founder teacher. It is evident from his account that the four courses with an additional sweet dish was the regular menu of the hostel. He describes another college at Wasit which was run by the members of a learned family who belonged to the town. The pupils were supplied with free board and lodging and a suit of clothes at this institution.

Pressing Routine

The daily programme of most of the teachers even today gives evidence of a strange singleness of purpose and devotion to learning on the part of the savants which appears to belong to a different world than ours. Trimingham in his 'Islam in Sudan' gives a day in the life of a teacher in a Khalwa or School which is full of a round of educational activities from morning to morning. A resume of the daily programme is given below:

After morning prayers read the last day's lesson on Khalil, a book on Fiqh.

Corrected the tablets of the learners of Quran. Morning lesson on Khalil.

Lesson on ash-Shatibi's book on reading of the Quran.

Another class in Fiqh.

Noon day prayers.

Mid-day lesson on Khalil

Afternoon prayers.

Class on Tajwid and Fiqh.

Evening prayers.

Recited the text of Khalil from memory with Commentary.

Recitation by the students of Quran-reading while the teacher took rest in a reclining posture.

Night prayers.

The teacher took rest while the students took their supper.

The Quran students recite the *subh* of the day, retired to his Khalwa where a student read to him in the light of the fire lit in his room told the rosary.

Awakened the students for the new lesson. They washed their tablets and wrote the lesson.

Correction of their writing.

Morning prayers.

Tested the last lesson on Khalil.

On holidays he wrote legal judgements.

This programme of work was followed by a teacher who belonged to the frontier regions of the intellectual world of Islam. It might be described as devoid of joy and discovery, but it gives an indication of the selfless devotion with which the teachers pursued their professional work. It is by no means uncommon to find a teacher of indigenous education so occupied in the Madrasas of Islamic world today. In fact the determination and persistant efforts of such teachers have maintained the system under adverse conditions. The singleness of purpose with which the teachers carry on their work is the surest guarantee for the preservation and continuity of its traditions.

Relations with Non-Muslims : Great teachers were no mere pedagogues. They were spiritual and intellectual leaders of the people and they exercised considerable influence on the high and the low. This influence was mostly utilised for the general good and when the call of justice came, it was exercised irrespective of colour or creed.

Again in periods of frequent changes in ruling dynasties and princes when kingdoms were made or marred overnight, the only civic organisation which continued to exist in a more or less preserved form was the township. Like the ancient Greeks, the Muslims had a conception of citizenship which was closely associated with that of a town. The feelings of local patriotism as regards one's home town was as strong as nationalism today and Jews or Christians gloried with equal enthusiasm in the achievements of a great fellow citizen and vied with one another in doing him honour.

When Imam Abul Ala used to go from Hamadan to his native town for offering Friday prayers, the towns-people would issue forth out of the gates to receive him, the Muslims and the Jews forming two separate groups, all of them welcoming the savant home.

The funeral ceremony of a savant was largely attended and Christians and Jews of the town would come out to pay their last respects to the great dead.

Non-Muslim Students : As a rule the non-Muslim students were not enrolled as regulars in the Islamic institutions, but the restriction did not prevent them from attending classes held by teachers in private. The educational system being teacher centered, opportunities for joining these classes were abundantly available, more so when every teacher working in a college was expected to continue his work at his residence also.

A distinction was made in the case of non-Muslim pupils

between religious and non-religious studies and non-Muslims were not enrolled as a rule in the classes held for teaching religious subjects. In fact there was hardly any necessity for providing such facilities because the main interest of the Non-Muslim pupil lay in secular and professional education.

A genuine difficulty arose when a text book belonging to a profane subject included Quranic verses or other religious literature. In such cases the more orthodox teachers refused to teach the book to a non-Muslim.

It is said that a non-Muslim desired to take lessons on the well known book on Grammar by Sibwaih from Al-Mazini. He offered him one hundred dinars for his teaching, but he refused point-blank. Thereupon Al-Mubarrad asked him whether he would refuse the offer when he was actually on the verge of starvation. Mazini told that the book contained three hundred odd verses of the Quran and he did not like teaching them to a non-Muslim.

The tradition of non-Muslim pupils enrolling with a Muslim teacher go back to the earliest times and there are instances when a Christian pupil was rejected by a co-religionist and was given facilities by a Muslim savant.

Hunain Ibn Ishaq, the well-known Christian scholar attached to Bait-ul-Hikmat founded by Al-Mamun was expelled by Yuhanna bin Maswaih, the well known Christian physician of the age because he believed in preserving the science as a guarded secret for his own, people. Ibn Ishaq left the teacher in a dudgeon when the teacher had an undignified fling at his expense. He enlisted later on as a pupil of philology and prosody, Khalil bin Ahmad of Basrah gained a wonderful command of the Arabic language. Hunain introduced Kitabul Ayn, the chief work of his teacher, in Baghdad.

In fact talent and singleness of purpose on the part of the

students functioned as the open Sesame for many a pupil and helped in removing barriers other than academic. There are cases of teachers who made up their mind not to teach any Zimmi, but had to revise their opinion when they were approached by a talented pupil who showed marked eagerness for knowledge and the pressure which they brought to bear upon for enlisting themselves as his pupil.

Some, of the non-Muslim pupils showed wonderful resourcefulness in winning over an intractable teacher.

Abul Barkat of Baghdad, a Jew intended to eternal himself as a pupil of a Muslim teacher who did not take Jews as his pupils. Abul Barkat arranged with his door keeper for a hiding place in the passage leading to the lecture room where he could secret himself. After an year or so, a debatable point was raised in the class and not a single pupil could give an effective reply. At this juncture, Abul Barkat made appearance from his hide and sought the teacher's permission to join the discussion.

On receiving his assent, he began with a relevant quotation from Galens and supplied reference of the date, the tire and the month, when the teacher had made' a discourse on the subject. The aptness of his reply was a pleasant surprise for the teacher who made eager inquiries and found out his clever ruse for overhearing his lectures. He was so deeply touched by his thirst for knowledge that he declared that it would be injustice to deprive such a pupil from learning the subject. Later Abul Barkat proved to be one of his most distinguished pupils'.

Interest in non-Muslim Literature : The traditions of Muslims' interest in Jewish and Christian literature goes back to the Prophet's time. The Quran speaks highly of the Habbarin (Rabbis) among the people of the Book (Jews and Christians) while the parables and the sayings of Christ redolent as they are with a quiet wisdom and deep humanity can be traced in the Traditions of the Prophet and Islamic literature belonging to the earliest period. The Prophet had instructed one of his secretaries to learn the Hebrew language for correspondence work and the History of the Jews formed often a topic of engrossing interest in the assembly of the Prophet. History of the Jews formed an essential part of the general curriculum while there were teachers who developed further interest in the subject and made a special study of these branches.

There were teachers like Abul Fath Kamaluddin Shafii who lectured on Torah and the Bible for the benefit of his Jewish and Christian pupils. He had composed commentaries on both the books for the students'.

Place of the non-Muslim Teacher : Some of the non-Muslim teachers had extremely cordial relations with their pupils and with the student body in general.

Ibn-al-Talmiz, the chief of physicians in Baghdad treated the pupils of the Nizamiyyah college free of charge.

He kept them as indoor patients at his residence which had often served as a nursing home for ruling princes and presented them with two dinars for enjoying their recovery when they left the place to rejoin their studies.

Ibn Jazlah, the Christian physician of Baghdad who was converted to Islam later on was a great philanthropist and treated all his friends and neighbours free of charge.

During his last illness, he gave all his books as a free gift to the mausoleum of Imam Abu Hanifa.

Their verses often reveals the deep attachment which they entertained for their pupils.

Ibn Butlan the Christian physician of Baghdad who died a bachelor had composed a beautiful elegy on his supposed death expressing how there was nobody to mourn his loss but his pupils.

"And none will let fall a tear over my grave except my assembly and my books bursting in tears."

The more distinguished non-Muslim teachers who wielded considerable influence and prestige in the society of the day attracted a large number of their co-religionists.

Every student visiting the town pay a social call to these great masters. Some of them enrolled themselves as their pupils while others sought recommendations for registering with others.

Christian students continued to visit the house of Ibn-al-Talmiz even after his death and Ibn Usaibiah describes the encounter of two Christian pupils with an imbecile son of his, who had been the despair of his father during his life time.

The non-Muslim teachers used all the means of livelihood commonly open to the scholarly class and they would not allow any religious considerations to influence their usual practice. One of their leisure time pursuits was the copying of manuscripts. Manuscripts on religious subjects were specially in demand in those days and the non-Muslim teachers had no compunction in copying out manuscripts of Islamic literature.

Ibn Hamid bin Zakariyya, the Logician who had attained to the status of a Rais (chief) in his subject had made it binding on himself the incredible task of copying out one hundred pages or less in twenty four hours.

He had transcribed two copies of that compendious work, the exegesis of the Quran by Tabri for presenting it to some of the neighbouring princes.

The non-Muslim teachers had monopolised certain branches of learning as teachers during the early period. In the beginning the non-Muslims were the chief authority on Greek sciences, philosophy, logic and medicine and their great schools at Alexandria, Antioch and Junde-Sabur functioned as radiating centres of philosophic and medical learning. Furthermore the traditions of medical education took rather a long time in establishing itself among the Muslims and in most cases the profession was monopolised by non-Muslims. In fact the neglect of such an important branch of professional education by the Muslims has been marked by more than one writers on education. For these sciences, the Muslim student often resort to the non-Muslim teachers.

Some of these teachers were attached to hospitals and they examine patients and discuss important cases with the pupils on the campus.

Aminuddaulah, the Christian physician of Baghdad who was chief of the physicians and in charge of the Adhdhadi Hospital in Baghdad upto his death used to examine patients with his pupils. He had a class of fifty pupils. Ibn Usaibiah gives the account of his successful treatment of a difficult case and its discussion in the class.

Abul Farj Baghdadi, a distinguished Christian practitioner on medicine taught in the Adhdhadi hospital of his native town and Ibn Usaibiah came across a copy of Aghlotan's commentary of Galens which was read out in his presence in the hospital and was dated 496 A.H.

Teachers in medicine often hold regular assemblies at their residence which was attended by their pupils and distinguished members of the profession.

Yuhanna bin Maswaih who died in the reign of Mutawakkil used to hold an assembly for discussing all varieties of subjects specially cultivated by the ancient Greeks and its meetings attracted persons of learning and knowledge. He also used to lecture to a large number of pupils .

An exact knowledge of the Arabic language was essential for a proper comprehension of the text and the non-Muslim teachers on medicine sometimes provide special facilities for pupils who were backward in the subject.

Ibn-al-Talmiz employed two grammarians for helping those pupils who committed frequent mistakes in their recitation of medical texts, mispronounced words or stuttered in expression. He attached the pupil to one of the grammarians and the pupil was expected to pay the grammarian some tuition fee. These two persons were most probably students of the great physician. They were held in great regard by the teacher and received sometimes presents from him.

A contact with these non-Muslim teachers must have a broadening influence on the outlook of the pupil and brought home to him liberal education in a wider and truer sense.

Some teachers made special efforts in order to educate their pupils into such an outlook. Once two students came to study with Abul Farj of Baghdad and when they visited his house, they were informed that the physician had gone to the church. When they reached there, they came across a rather unexpected scene. They saw the great teacher clad in coarse woolen cloth; he was bare headed and was going round the altar with a censor in his hand. When he had done with his prayers, he issued forth, mounted a mule and rode back to his house amidst a procession of slaves.

The students presented themselves before him but there were signs of a great surprise and incredulity on their faces. He allowed them to attend his lecture. When the lecture was over he asked them whether they had ever performed the holy pilgrimage to Mecca. They replied in the negative and the teacher told them that their registration as a pupil was conditional to their performing the pilgrimage. The poor pupils had no alternative and proceeded forthwith on the journey. When they returned from the pilgrimage they were tired and out of spirits. Then he enquired them about the ceremonies of the pilgrimage and specially the flinging of the pebbles and the reason for performing the ceremony. They told him that it was a religious obligation and one could not give any reason for these injunctions.

This was exactly the conclusion which the shrewd teacher desired to impress on them and for which he had made them undertake this long and tiresome journey .

The Outcome

The association of the non-Muslims with the educational system within the Islamic bloc of countries paved the way to a closer understanding with the Zimmies and helped in the rehabilitation of these communities in the socio-political structure, but similar contacts in the countries bordering the Islamic world resulted in extremely fruitful cross-fertilisation of ideas and gave rise to scientific and literary movements which had far reaching influences. In the distant west, these contacts in Spain, Southern France, Sicily and other Mediterranian islands blossomed into a renascence in the scientific and according to some writers literary field of knowledge. The Spanish Jews were the first to avail of the new educational opportunities.

The first contact with the non-Muslims were established through the Jewish pupils who in their turn were instrumental in propagating the new learning further afield over the continent. The courts of those Christian princes who were interested in the cultivation of learning also functioned as a meeting ground for these cultural and intellectual contacts. Their patronage extended some times to the Muslim scholars who had stayed within their dominions. Some of the princes and nobles had established academies for the work of translation and adaptation and these centres provided special opportunities of contacts among the intellectual elite.

Sometimes these contacts with the alien non-Muslims were

established nearer home. The crusades gave an opportunity for a free exchange of ideas between the East and the West. Campbell mentions how Richard the Lion hearted tried unsuccessfully to secure the services of Maimonides who was attached to the court of Sultan Salahuddin (Saladin).

Maimonides, the Jewish exile from Spain became directly a radiating influence of scientific knowledge in the Middle East. The persecution of Jews in the West had driven them eastwards and Maimonides who was gifted with a rare combination of philosophic learning and knowledge of the Jewish religion became the Head of the Jewish community in Cairo and won for himself also a place of great eminence in the scientific circles of the day.

He taught Greek sciences and philosophy at his residence in Cairo, a town where he acquired a very high status. He was superb in editing books on astronomy and mathematics and two works edited by him were highly praised by discriminating scholars.

Maimonides' personality attracted a number of Jewish refugees from Spain and the North Africa and one of them was Ibn Ishaq-al-Maghribi. He had brought with him from Sabtah a copy of the astronomy of Ibn aflah of Spain and requested Maimonides to prepare an edition of the book. The work was carried out by their mutual collaboration.

The common people were more influenced by the literary traditions of Islamic learning and its universal appeal for the Christian youth is revealed in the lament of a bishop over their neglect of Latin and religious studies.

In the East, the literary curriculum had even a more profound influence in the development of local languages, literature and general education of the non-Muslims. In India it resulted in the growth of communities among the Hindus which adopted the system of Islamic education and their socio-cultural values. Some of the text books written by Hindu scholars were universally popular with students. Special schemes of curriculum were framed with a view to meet the requirements of the Hindu pupils, pursuing these courses and their literary studies included Persian translation of Sanskrit epics and other works of scientific and mathematical nature.

The lure of state service as a secretary or a tax collector also made non-Muslims pursue literary and linguistic studies under great stylists and masters of the language. In certain parts of the Islamic world, tax collection was monopolised by the non-Muslims. The demands of professional training brought all those people within the ambit of Islamic education.

6

Teacher's Role

There are good many Traditions which illustrate in figurative language the social and the spiritual significance of the teacher's role in society.

Source of Inspiration : The teacher is generally compared to a luminous body radiating light and illuminating the darkness of others' souls. They are the "light-houses of the towns and cities" they may be likened to stars and guiding lights in the darkness that covers land and ocean and when they disappear, the guides would certainly lose their way. "The teacher is a light-house for the land and a spring of fresh water for the town."

There is no end to the graceful similes which throw up realistically and forcefully the creative aspect of the teacher's function in society; he is likened to those great forces of nature whose creative efforts refreshen the world and animate it with new life and ideals. The Prophet quoted once the parting counsel of Luqman to his son that he should seek the company of Savants and listen to the words of wisdom because God resurrects the heart of the dead with the Light of Knowledge just as the barren soil begins to throb with vegetable life under the genial influence of rainfall.

Another tradition likens the Assemblies of Teachers to the flower-beds of heaven and the companions are enjoined to browse on so delectable a stuff whenever an opportunity arises.

There are teachers and teachers and the fine distinction between the grades among them is illustrated in another metaphor by Ali, according to whom knowledge may be likened to a melifluous current, while the teacher merely stroll on the banks, the thinker struggles midstream while the Arif (knower) enjoys a ride in the barge of salvation.

Mystic Qualities : The spiritual reward for teaching others is great; it is light as the rainbow coloured clouds and genial like the rainfall. In one of his accounts, Abu Hanifa describes the account of an individual whose Good and Evil actions would be weighed in the Balance on Doomsday and the Pan for evil would indicate a downwards tendency but then suddenly from some unknown quarter would appear a cloud which would turn the balance in his favour. This cloud is the grace of knowledge which he (so profusely) bestowed on the people.

We have mentioned elsewhere how the entire universe appears to be involved in the educative process, the aim of which is the social and moral regeneration of this ace of creation man; and for the teacher who is the Divine instrument for working such a transformation in man, "the angels above, the ants in their anthills and the fish in the sea send their blessings."

Such a dynamic element in human life is essential for its existence and continuity and all men are active participants in the sharing of experience either in the capacity of a teacher or a learner because life ceases to be worthy of its respectable name when man degenerates to the level of inert, static existence. According to Ali, "Men may be classified broadly into three groups, firstly, the goodly teacher, then the pupil traversing the path of salvation, while the rest of humanity are all stupid fools who take their cue from any claimant." (Naiqorerier)

Another tradition urges every man to be a dynamic factor in the educative process which works in the cyclic order of morning and evening and that every man should discover in himself the young Galahad ready to launch on a voyage of moral and intellectual adventure.

There are savants who refuse to recognise such a person as human being who has never been a teacher in his life. Al-Ghazzali quotes Ibn Mubarak according to whom "the only creation which deserves the exalted rank of Man is the teacher because only knowledge distinguishes man from animal."

The Great Trainer

The first persons who were entrusted with the duty of teaching under the Prophet were Masaab bin Umayr and Ibn Um Maktum. They had been deputed by the Prophet from Mecca on the request of the Ansar of Medina who desired some teachers of religion and Holy Quran. Masaab used to make house to house visitation and frequented suburban areas also it was through his pioneer efforts that the message of Islam was propagated in this area.

Masaab bin Umayr, a great dandy of Mecca was converted in the days when the family of the Prophet was living in exile in the defile of Abi Talib outside Mecca. He had a phenomenal success and was known as Muqarri or the teacher and he stayed in the enclosure of Asad bin Lurarai, one of the earliest Medinites to be converted to Islam.

His teaching activities aroused the suspicion of tribal chiefs like Saad bin Muad and Usayd bin Hudhayr.

Usayd actually went to Asad, the host of Masaab and complained how he was maintaining a person who was misleading the people of Medina and ensnaring the weak minded. But when he heard Masaab and his companions reciting the rythmic verses of the Quran, his naive and sensitive heart was deeply moved. He made an open confession of his faith on the spot.

Saad bin Muad followed suit. He began by abusing the host who was his cousin for lodging suspicious characters but Saad was also struck with the awful grandeur and beauty of the Quranic verses and a spark of enthusiasm for the new faith was kindled within Saad who brought his family of Abdul Shah within the fold of Islam after a direct appeal to their sense of loyalty for their chief.

Teachers were sent to the tribal areas by the Prophet from time to time. They were generally sent on the request of those deputations from the tribal areas which came to visit Medina.

Some of the companions had specialised as teachers and they continued their work of propagation of knowledge long after the Prophet. One of them Maadh bin Jabal worked in this capacity in various parts of the Peninsula. These teachers seem to have dedicated their whole life to educational work among the tribes and other distant parts of Arabia.

In Lord's Court

In the beginning, Maadh bin Jabal worked in this capacity as a judge in Yemen and would receive injunctions from the Prophet in reply to his queries. He worked as a teacher of Quran and Fiqh in Mecca when the Prophet had left for the Battle of Hunayn. Under Abu Bakr he had offered himself to go on Jihad to Syria and later on Umar I deputed him to Hims as a teacher of Quran and religious knowledge from whence he proceeded to Palestine where he met his end in the plague epidemic during the period of Umar I.

He exercised the authority of issuing legal decrees (Ifta) during the lifetime of the Prophet and Abu Bakr in Medina. Another great teacher, Ibn Masud described him as 'Amat' "Qanit" (a leader faithful to God), the attributes which are used for Ibrahim in the Quran.

According to Ibn Masud, Amat is a person who teaches people about 'Good', and 'Qanit is one who is subservient to God.

The Pioneers

The most well known scholars of Quranic readings in the days of the Prophet were Uby bin Kaab, Zayd bin Thabit, and Abdullah ibn Masud. Abu Musa-al-Ashaari was more known for his melodious voice than for the Qirat.

Uby bin Kaab was acknowledged as the greatest scholar of the Quran by Umar I and others and he was associated with its study from the earliest days.

It is related that the Prophet had told Uby that he had been ordained from above to recite to him the Quran and when Uby asked whether the Lord had named him in particular, the Prophet replied in the affirmative. Upon this, tears of joy ran down the checks of Uby whereupon the Prophet recited, "And it is due to the beneficence and grace of God. They should be happy because it (Quran) is better than what they collect".

The Prophet had trained a class of Quran Readers or Qaris at Medina. It appears that these persons who belonged in most cases to the people of the Suffa had dedicated themselves entirely to the Great Cause and had placed themselves at the disposal of the Prophet.

They used to recite the Quran and were engaged in teaching and learning the Holy Book at night.

In the day-time they were occupied with bringing water for the mosque. They would go into the jungle, bring faggots and with their sale they would provide meals for the people of the Suffa and the needy. Haram, a maternal uncle of Anas bin Malik also belonged to this group.

These Quran Readers who lived apparently in the mosque were often sent on teaching missions. Once seventy Ansars, all of whom were Qura were sent to a tribe who slaughtered them to a man.

One of the greatest authorities on the readings of the Quran was Abdullah Ibn Masud who had been described as a chest full of knowledge.

He was elder to Zayd bin Thabit, another authority on the Quranic text and according to him he had learnt seventy surats from the Prophet at a time when Zayd bin Thabit was merely a beardless youth. He kept his side tresses and used to frolick about with children. He was one of those few persons of early Islam who have been described as Allama.

The comprehensive scope of his knowledge has been described by Masruq in an impressive simile, "I would compare him to a reservoir. There are reservoirs that would satiate one or two persons. There may be others which may quench the thirst of a hundred people but Abdullah Ibn Masud was like unto a reservoir that could suffice for the whole world."

The Prophet was deeply moved by the recitation of two companions in particular; they were Ibn Masud and Abu Musa-al-Ashaari.

Once he asked Ibn Masud to recite to him the Quran and Ibn Masud replied, "How can I recite to you, O Prophet of Allah, when the Holy Book has been revealed unto you." But the Prophet insisted and Ibn Masud recited to him the Surat-al-Nissa (Women) and when he read the verse, 'And Verily we will bring witnesses out of all these people and appoint you a witness over all of them', he saw that the eyes of the Prophet were overbrimming with tears. Then he said, "If anyone desires to recite the Quran as it was revealed, he should read in the style of Ibn Um Abd (Ibn Masud)".

According to Ibn Abbas, the greatest scholar of Exegesis in early Islam, he preferred the Qirat of Abdullah Ibn Masud over the rest because the Quran was recited twice during the

Ramadan in the last year of the Prophet's life. In those day Ibn Masud says the Prophet and he came to know of the verses which had been deleted or changed.

Educational Mission

Umar Ibn Khattab had organised a well laid out plan for the propagation of learning in areas that had been recently conquered and for that purpose, he selected important centres like Kufa and Basrah in Iraq, Damascus and Hims in Syria and Jerusalem in Palestine. He selected the most outstanding scholars and teachers for this purpose. It appears that some of them received annual emoluments from the state.

Ibn Masud was sent to Kufa by Umar Ibn Khattab and he wrote to the people that he had preferred Ibn Masud to himself and they should acquire knowledge from him. It is said that Ibn Masud used to receive an allowance of 6, 000 dirhams.

The Caliphs used to keep a keen vigilance over the activities of these teachers. Once Umar Ibn Khattab had criticised Ibn Masud for relating too many Traditions to the people of Kufa. At a later period a group of Kufites who had been students of Ibn Masud came to visit Ali who cross-questioned them so closely about their teacher that they had a suspicion that the Caliph was going to give them a test. Finally Ali expressed a high appreciation of the character and learning of Ibn Masud.

Ibn Abbas and Abu Hurayrah had started their teaching work at Basrah. According to Ibn Saad, Ibn Abbas was the first teacher who acquired a great reputation in that town.

Abu Hurayrah had an extremely busy time as a teacher attending to the large concourse of students who attended his narrations. Once he was reminded of a Tradition of the Prophet when he was surrounded by a throng of pupils that a day, would arrive when people would come to him in search of knowledge from distant parts and that he should greet them with a welcome on such occasions.

Abu Musa-al-Ashaari, the golden tongued reciter of the Quran was also at Basrah during the period of Umar Ibn Khattab.

Selection Process

Umar Ibn Khattab had selected a group of three teachers for the propagation of knowledge in Syria and Palestine. They belonged to Ansars who had specialised in the compilation and presentation of Quranic knowledge. The original plan was that three teachers should start their teaching work at Hims, and should train a number of persons who had the talent and capacity to receive such a training. Later on they should proceed to Damascus and Jerusalem.

These three teachers, Maadh bin Jabal, Ubadah bin Al-Samet and Abu-al-Darda by name stayed for some time at Hims and then Abu-al-Darda shifted to Damascus where he continued his teaching work in the Great Friday Mosque of the town till the end. Ubadah stayed at Hims while Maadh went to Palestine. Their main work was the teaching of Quran and the propagation of religious knowledge.

When selecting members of missions the early Caliphs made it a point to include very often some Ansars who were considered to be very faithful keepers of the traditions of the Prophet.

Umar Ibn Khattab sent a mission of the Ansars which included Qarzah bin Kaab Ansari to Kufa for the propagation of the Traditions of the Prophet.

Umar did them the signal honour of accompanying the mission upto the mosque of Dharar on the road from Medina to Kufa. In his parting instructions he asked them to emphasize more on Traditions or Sunan and Fraiz rather than on accounts of battles.

The Most Learned : Ali was one of the greatest scholars of Quran in his days and he had great confidence concerning his knowledge about the particular context in which a verse of the Quran had been revealed. According to Ali, "Ask me about the Book of Allah because there is no Ayat (verse) about which I don't know whether it had been revealed at night or in the day, on even ground or on a hill top." He knew the reason, the place and the person about whom it was revealed.

Such an exact knowledge about the chronological sequence of the Quranic verses led him to plan the collection of the Quran on his own initiative and it appears that he was deeply engaged in this work during the period when Abu Bakr was elected to the Caliphate.

He had been late in taking the Bayt with Abu Bakr and when the latter asked him about it he told that he had taken a vow not to put on his sheet for any other purpose except offering prayers until he had compiled the Quran. It is said that he had compiled it according to its chronological order but he did not appear to have made it public.

According to Umar Ibn Khattab, Ali has been recognised as the greatest authority on Qaza (Legal judgement) in Medina. Umar Ibn Khattab would pray to God to save him from a difficult situation where Abu al Hassan (Ali) was not close at hand to give his counsel. He would seek his legal advice in personal matters and preferred it to that of others.

As a young man, the Prophet had appointed Ali once the Qadi for Yemen. It was a great distinction for a young man to be appointed a judge for this part of Arabia.

Yemen had reached a more advanced stage of social and political development because of its intimate relations with Iran and Abysinnia and Hadrat Ali was not very much in the wrong when he felt slightly diffident about the success of his office.

According to Ibn Saad he had said, "O Prophet, you are sending me to a people who are ancient and great. They are old and experienced and I fear that I may not be able to perform my duties efficiently." Thereupon the Prophet prayed for him and said, "May God give strength to your tongue and guide your heart."

According to Amir, among the early Muslims, the office of the Qadi (judge) was held with special distinction by Umar, Ali, Zayd bin Thabit and Abu Mussa-al-Ashaari.

Zaid bin Thabit, the Katib (copyist) of the Prophet was the greatest scholar of Ilm-al-Faraiz (Law of inheritance) and when he died, he was described as the 'scholar for men' i.e., the savant who dealt with the law of human rights.

He had been described as the greatest scholar of Al-Faraiz by the Prophet and Umar Ibn Khattab. He was retained in Medina and continued to hold the *Riyasat* (Headship) in Qaza, Ifta, Faraiz and Qirat till his death in 45 A.H. He was appointed an officer of judiciary by Umar Ibn Khattab and was granted an allowance. One of his distinguished followers in Qaza was Said bin-al-Musayyib, the well known savant and doctor of law who continued the legal traditions of Zaid bin Thabit in Medina.

Abdullah ibn Abbas was undisputedly the greatest scholar of Tafsir and he has been styled as Sultan-al-Mufassirin (the king of Exegesis) or Habr-al-Ummat (the savant of Ummat), and the Prophet had prayed that God may bless him with Hikmat (wisdom) and the Exegesis of Quran.

Ibn Abbas represents the cultured person of the period who had received a broad liberal education and who used his great learning for the clarification of the text of the Quran.

With Quran as the basis he would develop his lectures according to a scheme of coordinated studies, wherein Arithmetic, History, Literature and geography all would combine into a united whole, the great integrating principle for this unifying process being the Quranic text.

He would illustrate the use of a particular word or phrase occurring in the Quran by quoting the verse of a poet. He was equally sought after for the study of genealogy, accounts of battles and poetry.

He had his week days divided according to a set time-table. He would lecture one day on Fiqh, the next day on Exegesis, the third day on History of battles. Special days were appointed for the teaching of poetry and the history of Arabia.

He has been described as an Ocean of 'Ata' on account of his versatility of genius. And according to another, he overshadowed other savants as a tall date-palm overshadows the smaller ones.

He was styled as an Allama by Uby bin Kaab, and it was a signal honour to be designated with this title by one of the greatest authority on Quranic text in the days of the Prophet.

Great Genius : The educational influence of Aishah worked in favour of the most faithful rendering of Traditions and in several cases her exact knowledge of the context in which a particular comment had been made by the Prophet helped in the clarification of issues. For instance, Abu Hurayrah had related that ill lies in a women, a horse and a house but Aishah explained that he had missed to add the qualifying clause that in this case the Prophet was quoting an article of faith with the Jews.

Her intimate knowledge of the context of a particular Tradition often resolved many a controversial issue.

Once Fatima bint Qays claimed in the days of Dinar Ibn Khattab that the Prophet had abrogated the right of a divorced woman to stay at her husband's house for the period of Iddat. Umar Ibn Khattab refused to credit her statement but the ambiguity was removed only when Aishah described the circumstances under which this exception had been made by the Prophet. The husband's house in this particular case was situated in an out of the way place and the Prophet asked the divorcee to leave the house on account of its isolated situation.

Through her close association with the Prophet and her critical attitude she has been recognised as a master of the science of Istidrak, 'or the higher criticism of Traditions. Her critique has been compiled by more than one scholar out of whom the most well known study is by Sayuti under the title of '*Ayn-al-Asabah fi ma istadrak hu Aishah ala Ashabah*'.

She would lose no opportunity for imparting instruction to others and while on the pilgrimage, she had her tent on the slope of mount of Thabir, and she was accosted by a large number of persons seeking after knowledge. Sometime she would hold classes within the Haram and seat herself under the roof of Zamzam.

Another medium through which her knowledge of law was being broadcast was through Ifta (legal decrees) as she continued to exercise the authority of issuing legal decrees till the end of her life. Reference on legal points were made to her by Muawiya who would send emissaries for this purpose from Damascus. Her remarkable eloquence was a great asset to Aishah as a teacher. According to a very reliable and honest witness Ihnaf bin Qays, he had the opportunity of listening to the addresses of Hadrat Abu Bakr, Umar, Uthman and Ali but he never heard a more eloquentadness from any one in the world than that of Aishah.

Hadrat Aishah held a school for the teaching of Traditions at her residence. The place had an additional advantage as it adjoined the Prophet's mosque. Women and younger fold sat within while men took their seats in the out. She had more than 200 pupils which included 88 women. She was extremely particular about the language and expression of her pupils. Once she had criticised the language of two young persons who had come to her as pupils.

She was a great teacher of the subject, and her house was the cradle bed of a regular school of Traditions. She would take young children, maintain them out of her own pocket and give them training in this subject. Urwah, Qasim, Abu Salma, Masruq, Amrah and Saffiyah had been apprenticed to her when quite young.

Out of these Amrah acquired great distinction as an authority on Traditions and when Umar bin Abdul Aziz launched on his great task of preserving Traditional literature, he asked Ibn Hazm, the Qadi of Medina to take special care in acquiring Traditions from Amrah. He had written to Amr ibn Hazm, "Copy Traditions from Amrah because I fear the loss of knowledge and the passing away of men of knowledge."

In case of women teachers, an important group among their students always belonged to their own family. In case of Aishah, the family of Abu Bakr benefited of a great deal from her teaching.

Hadrat Abu Hurayrah, the most copious narrator of Traditions was one of the most popular teacher of the subject in his later years. He had continued his pursuit of learning with great devotion and self-sacrifice. His only rival in the field was Aishah, the wife of the Prophet and when she told him once that he narrated such traditions on the authority of the Prophet which she had never heard of, Abu Hurayrah replied, "O Mother of the Faithful, I acquired this information at that time when you were busy with your collyrium and your mirror! Aishah had criticised also the rapid speed at which he used to narrate Traditions.

Abu Hurayrah had pursued his great interest in the preservation of Traditions at great personal sacrifice. While the Ansars were busy with their daily occupations like agriculture and the Muhajirs carried on their trade in the market place, he would stick to the Prophet and acquire knowledge of Traditions. For some time, he lived with the people of the Suffa and had experienced terrible spells of starvation in those days. In his own words, "When I could scarcely move between the mosque and the residences of the Prophet's wives which were very close to the mosque without losing consciousness on the way." But nevertheless he continued his pursuit of learning in an unabated manner.

The people of Suffa used to share their meals with the Prophet or meet their needs through those charitable donations of the community which were brought to the mosque.

Abu Hurayrah had an extremely vigilant mind and he used to keep a careful note of the daily activities of the Prophet. He was often accused of being too prolific in his narrations. But it appears that he had acquired such a capacity of concentrated attention and memory that there was hardly anything which escaped his notice or passed out of his wonderful memory. Once he asked a person what Surah the Prophet had recited in the night prayers day before. The man had attended the prayers but he had no idea of the Surah. Abu Hurayrah remembered the whole of the Surah recited by the Prophet on that occasion.

A psychological treatment which helped Abu Hurayrah considerably in improving his memory was made by the Prophet when he complained of bad memory. The Prophet asked him to spread out his covering sheet. Then he sprinkled a few drops of water on it and asked him to put it on again. According to Abu Hurayrah he never forgot a single Tradition after that.

According to another version, the Prophet made a gesture of putting two or three handfuls on the sheet, as if bestowing something on him.

The Allowances : One of the main traditions which provide a sanction for monetary compensation in case of religious instruction has been related by Kharajah bin Salt, a Kufite whose uncle had visited the Prophet for instruction in the teachings of Islam. On his way back he came across a Beduin who was suffering from an attack of insanity and was bound in chains. His tribal people asked him to treat the sick person. He recited Surah Fatiha, the opening chapter of the Quran and the sick person recovered from the attack. He was offered one hundred goats as a compensation which he refused to accept. He visited the Prophet once again, and asked his opinion on the matter.

He said, "It is your right. Others accept compensation for unlawful treatment of the invalid through (sorcery or enchantment) but you have earned it through a lawful treatment."

According to a tradition, the Prophet had sanctioned payment of compensation in case of those who were engaged in religious warfare; He had compared them to Moses' mother who received payment for suckling her own child. The fighters were paid for defending the Faith.

The Hanafite school has interpreted payment in case of religious instruction as a parallel case in which the tradition is equally applicable.

Umar and Uthman had granted allowances for Muezzin, Imams and teachers and Umar bin Khattab had sent special instructions to some of his amils that those who learnt the Quran should be granted an allowance.

Umar bin Abdul Aziz had sent Yazid bin Abi Malik and Harith bin Yamjid Ashaari to the countryside for teaching purposes and granted allowances for them. Yazid accepted the grant but Harith refused it.

Great teachers who had specialised in a particular science were despatched to important centres in the dominions not only for the propagation of religious knowledge among the masses but also for the training of a class of scholars who would blaze a new trail in their special field of interest. These great teachers functioned as a great educative force for the common people also but their primary objectives was the training of teachers or scholars. For the education of the common man, Umar Ibn Khattab sent a number of Qasas (story tellers), not story tellers in the literal sense of the term but men who would present great religious truths in the form of stories as illustrated in the lives of the Prophets of old. They appealed to the imagination of the common people by their simple, direct and forceful style of teaching. The first persons to be selected for this work were Tamim-al- Dari and Ubayd bin Urnayr. They taught traditions and religion.

This class grew in popularity and their services were often requisitioned by later rulers for purposes of political propaganda. They sometimes accompanied the army and incited them to fighting on the battle-field.

Views of Experts

Great teachers were inspired by the Divine Command to the Prophet "Say, O Prophet, I don't ask for you any reward for all this."

Ghazzali affirms that the teacher should follow the noble example set by the Prophet and should not expect any compensation in the form of monetary reward, any other form of return or even the gratification of receiving thanks. On the other hand, he believes that it is the taught who lays the teacher under obligation rather than vice versa. According to him, "the pupil is like a landlord who has surrendered to the teacher the barren wastes of his soul for tilling and cultivating. As a sheer economic proposition, the cultivator of the soil stands to gain more than the proprietor. Hence the teacher has hardly any justification for making a parade of his beneficence because the teacher could not have earned the grace of God through his teaching if the pupil had not provided him with the opportunity of earning this spiritual merit.

This approach of Ghazzali which might come as a surprise to some of the teachers in our days introduces a fundamental revolution in the pupil-teacher relations, and raises the level of the professional attitude towards work from the economic to the spiritual. This outlook is indispensable in the teaching profession because the very nature of the efficiency demanded by the educative process demands an approach essentially different from that in other professions. But this does not imply that the economic aspect should be ignored altogether.

7

Teacher's Position

The teacher held an important place in the system of higher education among the Muslims, a pivotal position which determined the plan and the execution of the entire scheme of education.

Teachers for the highest kind of learning existed in the Islamic world long before the colleges came into existence. They continued to work even when that magnificent system had fallen into decay.

The study circles of the early period owed their heightened scale of intellectual effort to individual teachers and even the era of colleges failed in the regimentation of their individual traits to the dull uniformity of a college cadre; more often a college was known by the reputation of a great teacher than vice versa. Great thinkers like Ibn Khaldun, Abu Ali Sina and a host of other illustrious names owe their education to the fostering care of individual teachers rather than to an educational institution.

The teachers scaled the heights of social and moral prestige in the community, but their achievement in educational administration was something unprecedented in the history of education and all the more significant in a system which had a religious bias, but was otherwise thoroughly secular in its organisation. The system was essentially different from the education of the monasteries in Medieval Ages in the sense that there was no priestcraft or clergy among the Muslims who held an undisputed monopoly of education. Although secular in this sense the educational system was entirely in the hands of the teachers. The teaching staff exercised the right of autonomy in framing of curriculum, planning or general organisation.

The endowment system had made them more or less free of any servile dependence on the state or other patrons and the management of the endowments was also in most cases in the hands of the teachers themselves and the record of its educational history reveals that the teachers ran the system with credit to themselves and to the people.

There are certain dangers in a teacher-ridden system, but they pale into insignificance when compared to the dangers inherent in a system, which is controlled by a political or a religious group or is metamorphosed into a Government bureau by a totalitarian state.

In fact the study of the system of higher education in the Islamic world and the role played by the teacher in building up the system acquires a specific importance in a world where education has become a plaything of party politics and where its organisation is, being directed by socialistic or capitalistic planning. It is very conveniently forgotten in a world resounding with political slogans that there is one more way of planning education and it is the teachers way.

If we desire to save education from soulless uniformity and regimentation, we must concede autonomy to the teacher in organising and administering education and it is hoped that the progressive tendencies in educational administration in the democratic and the socialistic blocks will be heading in this direction.

The teacher held a key position in the system of higher education under Islam and an intimate study of the problem will have not only a historical value, it could provide us with certain organisational and administrative patterns which may help us in solving the educational tangle at present.

Teacher's Responsibility

The teacher of higher education enjoyed a specially unique status in the Islamic World. He presented a pattern of moral and social leadership, which remains unexampled in the social structure of the modern world. The social gauge by which the prestige of an individual could be measured were not so precise and prosaic as they are today. Economically the teacher did not reach the high water mark, but it was not an important measure in a world which was more open to fluctuations of fortune for the individual and wherein the value of an individual was assessed by surer and more lasting standards.

Among the people, the prestige of a teacher was known by the size of the assembly which gathered to listen to his lectures, the crowds which would go to welcome him on his arrival or accost him on his departure. The final test of his reputation was the concourse which accompanied his bier on his last journey.

In the educational world, the teacher's worth was determined in the qualitative sense and he was known by the number of distinguished scholars who had graduated under his direction. The quality of his work was also judged by the number of great teachers who attended his lectures, a custom not uncommon in those days.

The common people and the educated class determined the nature and the quality of the reputation of a teacher. It received further recognition through the ruling princes and the nobility.

The poets also provided a measure of universal respect in which a teacher was held in those days.

The teachers were held in the highest esteem everywhere, but in their assemblies they could vie with the greatest of the land in authority and prestige. It was not confined to the physical limits of the assemblies, it transcended political or racial boundaries and reached wherever their word was carried.

A witness, by no means favourably disposed towards a teacher describes how he treated the royal summons to appear before the king. The episode has been described at length by Al-Maqarri and his lively narration could bear repetition for our readers.'

When the royal slave came with a message to Abu Ibrahim, a teacher in the days of Hakam II of Spain (died. 976 A. D.) that the Caliph desired to see him he replied Go back to thy master and mine (may God pour his favours on him!) and tell him how thou hast found me in one of the houses of God, surrounded by a number of students, to whom I am recounting traditions respecting the Prophet.

Tell him that these students are attentively listening to my words and profiting by my lesson and that it behoves me not to interrupt the subject upon which I am lecturing to them until the sitting be at an end and the hour come for my dismissing them.

The royal slave returned to the palace and came back with the following characteristic reply. "The Caliph has directed me to say that he hopes God will reward thee for the good thou art doing to religion and to the Muslims who are profiting by thy lessons and that when thou has put an end to thy lecture, thou art to go to him straight."

Now Abu Ibrahim was fairly advanced in age and was too weak to ride. He requested the Caliph to order that the gate of the palace nearest to the mosque where he lectured might be opened for the occasion and the Caliph did him the signal honour and issued a royal order that the gate which was continually shut up might be opened for his reception.

The narrator tells that when he passed by the closed gate after the lecture, he saw royal slaves and attendants bustling about in order to accord a suitable reception to the savant.

Role of the Kings

There were teachers who had matrimonial relations with royalty and others who refused to maintain them. Osman, the patriarch of the Osmanides took the daughter of Maula Adah Bali, a pious savant of the age as his queen. She was the mother of Ur Khan who ascended the throne after the death of his father.

It is related that Osman Ghazi used to visit the savant at his monastery and would often stay there for a night. Once during his stay there he dreamt that a moon rose high from the residence of the savant and entered the royal citadel. Out of this moon spread out branches which covered the whole of the earth and underneath was a magnificent range of mountains out of which gushed forth springs and humanity availed of these springs, watered their beasts of burden and irrigated their gardens.

When Osman related the dream to the savant in the morning, he read into it the happy augury that the faithful would be benifited by him and his progeny and forthwith he offered him his daughter in marriage.

The daughter of Sheikh Adah Bali became the Queen of Osman Ghazi while her aunt was wedded to a minister of the state. The mother of Akbar the Great was the daughter of a mystic teacher.

There were teachers who refused the offer of a royal espouse for their daughter and preferred to marry her to a promising young member of their class who could not afford some times even a few dirhams for marriage money.

Role of the Courts

The highest offices of the state were open to the class of savants and the names of scholars who became ministers of state occur quite frequently in the annals of the Osmanides and other dynasties. There were others who acted as ambassadors and leaders of diplomatic missions and they conducted this delicate business with honour to themselves and to their country.

In spite of Ibn Khaldun's remarks on the failure of teachers in practical politics on account of their preoccupation with intellectual pursuits the ruling princes availed of the tremendous prestige which the more distinguished of the savants enjoyed in the Islamic world for diplomatic purposes.

Great scholars were more widely known than the princes and the kingdom of knowledge extended beyond the frontiers of empires and principalities. Moreover the days when political relationships were determined by personal contacts with the rulers, the social, cultural and intellectual qualities of the envoy were more important than mere diplomatic sagacity and acumen.

In the case of a prince with cultivated tastes a distinguished savant with the gift of eloquence and scholarship was sure to prove a greater success than the diplomat. When the Byzantine emperor saw the ambassador of the Omayyid Caliph Abdul Malik, he was very much impressed by his personality. He wrote back to the Caliph that he very much wondered why the Muslims elected him to the Caliphate in preference to Shaabi, the ambassador.

It was a left handed compliment which cut both ways. When the Caliph read out the epistle to Shaabi on his return to the court, the great savant replied with all the unction of a diplomat whose role he was playing that the Emperor would not have made this remark if he had seen the Caliph.

But when a great scholar was dispatched as an ambassador to a Muslim ruler, his reputation was sure to precede him and he was often given a public reception befitting the royalty. Sheikh Abu Ishaq, the first Principal of Nizamiyya College of Baghdad was sent in 475 A. H. by the Abbaside Caliph to Sultan Malik Shah at Naishapur as an ambassador. He was given grand ovations at every town which he passed on his way to the capital of the Seljuq monarch.

The towns people preserved the dust under his mule's hoof as something sacred and as he entered the town and passed through the streets, the shopkeepers thrown up their wares to the crowd in sheer ecstasy at his arrival. At Sawah, the bakers, the fruiterers and the sweetmeat sellers all distributed their wares and when last of all he passed through the cobblers street, the people had reached such an acme of emotional fervour that they flung the shoes into the air which were caught by the crowd. And when the savant stopped to rest, he was offered hospitality by such a large number of citizens that he made a polite refusal and stayed in a residence by himself.

There were occasions when they played the role of a peace-maker successfully. Allama Qushji was sent as the messenger of peace by Ulugh Beg, the ruler of Samarkand to the Osmanide Sultan, the conqueror of Constantinople. It is Sultan Ulugh Beg who was not only the patron but also the teacher of Qushji with whom he had studied mathematics and astronomy.

Ibn Khaldun had been sent to Tamerlane when he was investing Damascus in the same capacity. Sometimes a forceful address by a teacher has saved a whole town. Once the ruler of Allepo invested Marrat-ul Numan, the native place of Abul Ala-al-Maarri and fixed his war engines close to the city walls.

The siege was prolonged and the town people grew panicky. They approached Abul Ala for help and guidance. He did not speak a word in reply, took a guide, blind as he was, and passed through the gateway which was opened for him on the occasion and went straight to the king. He opened the conversation with a dignified address. The king was so much impressed by his address that he at once announced the amnesty in words eminently suitable for the occasion. He said to the blind poet, 'I present you the town and its people!

The savants were often required to deliver an address on the occasions of grand reception given to foreign missions. Al-Maqarri mentions the eloquent speech which was delivered at the court of Abdul Rahman-an-Nasir who ascended the throne in 300 A.H., when the embassy of Constantine was given a great reception at the royal court.

The great scholar Al-Qali had been specially entrusted with the duty of addressing the mission, but he failed to rise to the occasion and it was performed in a most spectacular manner by Manzar b. Said. As a recognition of his wonderful talents, Manzar was appointed Imam of the Friday Mosque of Al-Zahra and later on was promoted to be the judge of Cardova.

Sometimes diplomatic missions headed by scholars were instrumental in developing fresh contacts, cultural and intellectual between two countries and the philosopher diplomats which Akbar the Great of India sent to Shiraz caused a renaiscence of philosophical and scientific studies in India. Some of the royal courts observed a fine grade of ranks and it was scrupulously followed in the seating arrangements in case of ceremonial occasions and functions of state. The gradation of services was generally determined by the salaries received by the incumbent, but the savants and teachers were always given precedence over others without any consideration of the poor pittance which they drew from the state coffers.

A savant who taught in the days of the Osmanides relates how once Maula Lutfi went to see the minister who was closeted at the time with a high dignitary of the state. The savant went up to the minister in his simple dress and took his seat above the distinguished official and none prevented him from occupying the place. On enquiry, he was told that the savants' status was not assessed by their salary but by their learning. This set him thinking furiously and he decided to adopt the profession because although he could hardly hope to attain the status of a noble he could make an effort to win the position of a scholar

On the Indo-Pak sub-continent, the teachers were given the highest precedence at the royal court during the pre-Mughal period. Later on when Humayun drew up his weekly programme for meeting different classes of people, he assigned the first day to ahl-i Saadat, the scholarly class.

Higher Status

The teachers did not play an active part in politics yet they had the potentiality of becoming the leader of a religio-political movement any moment on account of their social status and their influence with the people. It has been said that all revolutions in Egypt had their origin in Jamia-al-Azhar and it can be affirmed with a fair degree of accuracy that most of the revolutions in the Islamic world have been inspired by religious personalities who were closely associated with education. They educated the people for the great change before it came and educated them into it when it came. Only the scholar and the savant could provide those intellectual and religious foundations which could maintain the interest of its supporters after the first wave of enthusiasm had passed over.

Hasn bin Sabbah, Ibn Tumart, Ibn Muquffah and a host of other personalities form a distinguished group who blazed a new trail in the history of religion and politics. The ruling princes kept a watchful eye over the savant whose influence was in the ascendant and sometimes they could scarcely conceal their nervousness at the spectacle of an entire people paying tribute to a savant.

As Malik Zahir Bayburs watched the funeral procession of Allama Abdul Aziz passing by, he heaved a sigh of relief and declared that for the first time in his life he felt secure because the Allama wielded such a tremendous influence with the people that he could incite them into open rebellion against him. Abu Hamid Isfraini once told the ruling prince that he owned a kingdom of knowledge from which he could not be exiled, but he could expel the prince if he wrote a slip of paper against him to the people of Khurasan.

Imam-al-Harmain, another teacher of Khurasan beard the Seljuk lion in his den and proclaimed his injunctions against the royal will in Naishapur . And when people began to throng in the assembly of Bahauddin, the father of Maulana Jalaluddin Rumi the ruling prince Muhammad Khwarizm Shah felt so nervous that he despatched the keys of the citadel and the royal treasury to the Maulana with the message that this was all that had been left to him of royal prestige and power.

The history of Islamic education abounds with instances of extremely pleasant and intimate relations between the savants and the ruling class. This great spirit of love and regard was actuated mostly by genuine motives, but sometimes political considerations also moved a prince to make a display of reverence for a teacher held in universal respect.

Ruling princes have offered themselves as a sacrifice for a savants in his sick bed. Others have composed elegies celebrating the praise of their scholarship. Some felt themselves honoured by a matrimonial alliance with the teacher while others had to suppress their sense of frustration when a teacher refused the match.

Not only princes and nobility but world conquerors did not forget the homage due to learning and scholarship in their hour of glory and amidst scenes of universal carnage and plunder.

When Amir Taimur plundered Shiraz, one of his ministers requested for an amnesty for Saiyid Sharif Jurjani and the king granted his request. An arrow from the royal quiver was stuck fast on the door of the scholar's residence and all the womenfolk of Shriaz flocked to his house and shared with him the privilege of royal amnesty.

High principled teachers would refuse to act as royal tutors for more than one reason, the primary consideration being the high educative value inherent in group teaching as compared with individual instruction. Any transgression of the classroom etiquette was checked with severity in case of the princes and the nobility. And very often a teacher refused to wind up his lecture in the face of an urgent call from the royal court.

There were others who refused to accept post of the royal tutor because they could not exercise freely their right of chastisement in case of princes. The princes and the nobility regarded good social behaviour as indispensable in case of students and insisted on a strict observation of classroom regulations. The rulers also enjoined on their progeny the maintenance of an attitude of profound reverence towards their teachers. One day Harun-al Rashid saw Asmai, his son's tutor making his ablutions while the prince was pouring water on his feet.

Harun was annoyed with the teacher and told him that he had not taught the prince good manners. The prince should have poured the water with one hand and washed the teacher's feet with another.

Status of the Poets

One of the criteria for assessing the social importance of a personality in the Islamic world is the variety and abundance of panegyrics composed in his praise during his life time and what is even of greater import, the elegies written in his honour after his demise. This form of poetry has served as a vehicle for expressing such sentiments from the days of the Prophet.

This criterion of judging the social rank of a person is a fairly sensitive means for this purpose because the eulogies written in the praise of savants were not inspired by basers motives of monetary gain or reward and when a poet eulogises a scholar or a savant, we can be fairly certain that he is giving genuine expression to his sentiments and representing also those of the people in general.

Panegyrics written in honour of scholars form a class of literature by itself and they have been preserved for posterity by historians and biographers.

They are not mere high flown, hyperbolic encomiums after the style of this kind of poetry, they have a more sincere ring about them and sometimes they throw interesting sidelight on the personality and activities of the teacher.

The inaugural function of a college provided a suitable opportunity for such panegyrics wherein after praising the founder, the poet cap the recitation by a reference to the great teacher who was expected to deliver the inaugural address and occupy the chair at the Institution. The occasion when a teacher completed the study of a particular work with his pupils was celebrated with great eclat and proved a stimulating challenge to the poetical talent of some members of the assembly.

The departure of Abdullah bin Mubarak from his native town of Marw was celebrated by a poet in memorable words. "When Ibn Mubarak departed from Marw at night, with him departed the town's beauty and light, whenever they would talk of great man in any town thou would be the new moon and the rest the stars." The poet rose to sublime heights sometimes in singing the praises of a scholar, but in most cases this type of poetry has a waddling, pedagogic air about it. Nevertheless it is an expression of genuine sentiments.

There were occasions when the atmosphere of the classroom, vibrated with the rhythm of true poetry and genuine emotion. Fakhruddin Razi was once lecturing in a mosque College when a pigeon chased by a hawk sought refuge under the cloak of the savant. A poet in the audience was deeply moved by the spectacle and he struck off a beautiful panegyric in praise of the teacher on the occasion."

According to a proverb in Arabic, the Death of Alim (Scholar) is the Death of Alam (world) and the elegies written on the death of a scholar gave a passionate expression to the widespread feeling of sorrow on the sad occasion. Sometimes the panegyrics were not actuated by a purely altruistic motive. Poets would approach sometimes a teacher for a recommendation for preferment to a prince and the request was presented in verse, its introductory lines comprising a panegyric for the scholarly patron. Even those teachers who avoided any visit to kings and courts were won over through the sweet music of poetry to intercede for others to a ruling prince.

Public Figures

The teachers were expected to maintain a reserved and dignifield demeanour and to adhere to it with the most scrupulous care in public. In this case as in others they had to make due allowance for the prevalent notions and norms concerning social behaviour in order to make their moral and intellectual influence felt as intensively as possible. More than once a great teacher had explained that his preoccupation with external appearance and behaviour was primarily actuated by his desire to maintain the dignity of knowledge and those who profess it.

While on foot, they were expected to move at a deliberate pace, more so because sometimes their educational activities continued even when on the move. For instance a pupil might be accompanying them with a book in hand or a passerby might consult them on a point of religious law or niceties of grammar, the general standard of cultural and social life being so high that such encounters were not at all infrequent in those days.

The savants would maintain this dignified behaviour irrespective of the demands of kings or their courtiers. A scholar of Spain was once invited by the king to his court and he proceeded with the dignity and decorum due to his high office. The royal messenger asked the judge to mend his pace but he took no notice of his remarks. When he arrived at the court, the king complained of his being late. The judge who had a shrewd sense of humour, took hold of his staff and began to tuck up his cloak. Upon being asked what he was about to do he told that he was trying to prepare himself for a race because it appeared that he was no longer a judge but a police official.

Family's Significance

The teachers did not belong to the order of celibates nor they were expected to lead a single life by the religion or society. Family life was a normal feature of the teaching profession and old bachelors were an exception rather than the rule. The biographers always make a pointed reference to such cases. Here as in other aspects of their life, the savants followed the precepts and the example of the Prophet.

The teachers passed a peaceful family life as a rule, but as most of his time was occupied in the pursuit of knowledge or teaching work, an irate wife would often prove as violent in temper as the wile of Socrates. Az-Zuhri's wife did not like her husband's preoccupation with books and once exclaimed in anger that his collection of manuscripts was a worse calamity for her than three rivals, implying that if he had married three other women as permissible by the Shariat, she would not have taken the stap so much to heart. Others would wreak their vengeance after the death of the scholar. The wife of a scholar was so much upset by the death of her husband that she threw the major portion of his collection in a tank because the books had not allowed him any leisure for the pleasures of domestic life.

But when an inordinate love of learning was combined with an inadequacy of the means of support, the rightful indignation of the wife would surpass all bounds. Tannukhi relates on the authority of his father that Imam Abu Yusuf the great Qadi of the court of Harun-al-Rashid was in dire circumstances in the beginning of his career and how his wife resorted to all sorts of expedients to keep the two ends together. At last her patience was exhausted and one day when he had gone to attend lectures he spent the whole day there and returned at night to ask for his meals, she produced a dish under cover. When he removed the cover he found his lecture notes within. When the astonished scholar asked her the reason for this change in the menu, she retorted that he was occupied with them the whole day, so he had better take them for his dinner.'

He returned in a dudgeon to his teacher Abu Hanifa who consoled him with the Prophetic remark that one day he would feast on almond paste mixed with shelled pistachios. Teachers were conscious of the evil effects of the lack of harmony and understanding in domestic life and its pernicious influence on the peaceful pursuit of intellectual interests and they would make an effort to provide suitable life companions for their pupils. There is an ancient tradition of students marrying their teachers daughters and it harks back to the days of the Ummayids. Some of these women were highly accomplished scholars and proved ideal companions for their espouses.

Very often the son of a teacher began his education with his father and ended by stepping into his shoes and occupying the chair vacated by the father. As a rule the teachers treated their sons and pupils alike and in most cases they did , the fullest measure of justice to the intellect and ability of students and prized a talented pupil more than the son.

Abu Jafar of Spain was one of such teachers. Once when one of the pupils recited some verses in his presence, he turned to his son who was sitting close by and said, "Here is genuine poetry so unlike the verses with which you pester me every day. If you propose to write poetry, you should better do it in this style otherwise refrain from it." Next day his son wrote two lines in the same style and he attempt was hardly better than a sorry caricature of the composition of the pupil.

The teacher quoted next day the verses composed by his son to the pupil, deprecating them in the strongest terms and indicating how his son had emphasized the form at the expense of the spirit. The pupil commented courteously that he did not agree with him and considered the lines superior to his own. This aroused the anger of the teacher who condemned his remarks as sheer sycophancy and an attempt to adorn a falsehood. But the pupils had the highest regard for the teacher's family and Ibn Jamaah lays down specific instructions for the students how they should respect and support the family of the teacher.

The Downfall

In the beginning, the better class of teachers did not wait on princes and the nobility, on the other hand the latter waited upon them. The early Caliphs had a close affinity with the common man which was all the more close and intimate with the man of religion or teacher, synonymous terms in those days. The prestige of the teacher who was a genuine leader in the social and intellectual sense was very high. Political revolutions in Islamic history have often grown out of religious movements and the instances when a prince felt nervous on account of the phenomenal rise of the influence of a savant are not infrequent in Islamic history.

The second period opened with the first foundation of the colleges by the princes and the nobility, an era which corresponds with the beginning of the system of Nizamiyya Colleges in the East and the royal foundations by Nuruddin Zangi and Salahuddin in the West.

> "The foundation of the new institutions implied certain restrictions on the appointment of teachers on grounds of personal merit. During this period the influence of the ruling class began to encroach on the intellectual life and high principled teachers would often refuse to accept the offer of an appointment in these colleges. They preferred to work in private institutions or assembly groups maintained by the teachers themselves."

The third period begins with the establishment of a system of state colleges maintained and supported by the state under the Osmanides with daily emoluments and pensions paid from the state exchequer. This era registered a marked decrease in the prestige of the teachers who could hardly be distinguished from other servants of the state; in some cases they belonged to the personal retinue of the ruling prince. The deterioration was equally marked in the social, moral, and intellectual sphere.

With the establishment of an ecclesiastical Department under a Sheikh-ul Islam as its head, the status of the teacher deteriorated still further. A teacher (d. 969 A. H.) who was overbearing in his arrogance used to criticise the Sheikh-al-Islam of the day. The sultan invited a fatwa (legal injunction) on his behaviour and the mufti decreed that he should be dismissed from service and should be banished from the town after receiving corporal punishment. He was brought to the Divan (secretariat) like a criminal and was given the required number of lashes laid down by the Mufti in the presence of a number of witnesses and expelled from the town.

After all these indignities the teacher had the patience to desire a reprieve, was pardoned by the Sultan and was reappointed to one of the eight colleges at Constantinople. Some of the teachers under the Osmanids had amassed enormous wealth and one of them helped once a minister with thirty thousand dinars. This teacher had built a bath over the hot springs near Bursa which yielded good income every year. He had presented this building also to the same minister. Notwithstanding all these rich gifts, the minister did not have a very high opinion of the man.

A teacher of Dar-ul Hadith at Constantinople was charged once with the offence of selling the posts of Muid (Reviser) and other attendants to the highest bidder and he received bribe for the allotment of residential quarters in Hostel. The teacher was finally dismissed by the ruling Sultan. He took it so much to heart that he pined away in sorrow and died.

Process of Appointment

During the early period when education had not been institutionalised, the appointment of the teacher was not governed by any strict regulations. But the wideawake interest of the people in education and specially that of the study group taught by the teacher led naturally to the selection of the most suitable candidate. In some cases the nomination was made by the retiring teacher, in others the class group and the general public selected the best of his pupils. The suitability for the post was determined by the esteem in which the retiring savant held the pupil and the candidate's public reputation.

The main factors which determined the selection was the

opinion of the class group as represented by its important and influencial members supported by public opinion. The educational system had a vital relationship with community life in those days and the keen enthusiasm of the people for education made sometimes the teachers national figures of great importance. Hence the nomination of the successor was not an election affair of an educational body, but a matter of genuine concern for the entire community.

During the early period, the ruling princes did not interfere in the appointments but they were approached sometimes to persuade a scholar in accepting a post offered to him. The demand for reappointment of Imam Ghazzali to the principalship of the Nizamiyyah College Baghdad came from the students and the staff who made their representation to the Mutawwali (Manager). When the Imam refused to occupy the post the Mutawwali approached the Abbaside Caliph to exercise his personal influence over the savant.

But the best method of appointment was through that training for apprenticeship which the teacher provided to the more promising of his pupils by appointing him as an assistant professor, or giving him a chance to officiate in his place during his absence. Another pupil of his, Ashshashi by name, who later on became a professor worked as an under tutor before his prefeıment.

The arrangement ensured continuity of pedagogical traditions after the retirement of the teacher and prevented any dislocation of work on account of unforeseen changes in the teaching staff. By the time that the system of colleges had become established, this method of teachers training had a fairly good trial. Khallikan remarks how Imam Shafii would refer persons visiting him for light on debateable issues to Buwayti, his favourite pupil and when he was approached by officers of the 'shurtah' for an inquiry, he would send them to Buwayti whom he styled as his 'Tongue'.

Abu Ishaq Shirazi the first Principal of the Nizamiyyah College of Baghdad served this apprenticeship with his teacher for more than ten years during which period he officiated for the master and also worked as Reviser assistant.

Study Circles : In the case of study circles the appointment of the successor was made very often by the savant during his life time. He would give the favoured pupil an opportunity to officiate in his place when he was indisposed or had to leave the town on business.

When Hammad the teacher of Abu Hanifa, the founder of the Hanafite School proceeded to Basra he appointed him to officiate in his place. In his absence the members of the study circle posited a number of queries on topics which had not been discussed by the teacher and Abu Hanifa gave answers on the basis of personal judgement, but he was careful to keep a faithful record of all the queries and his answers.

When Hammad returned from Basra after on absence of two months he referred his answers to him. The teacher approved forty out of a total of sixty answers and rejected the rest.

Imam Shafii had selected Buwayti to occupy his lecturing seat in the Friday Mosque after his death and he had trained him for the job during his life time. Whenever a person came to him for his opinion on a legal point or the chief of the police sought information on a legal issue, he would refer them to Buwayti adding that he was his tongue, implying his exactness in interpreting his viewpoint.

Teachers took special care in selecting the most suitable candidate for filling the post. Imam Abu Hanifa gave his parting counsel to his favourite pupil Imam Abu Yusuf and told him that if he were to certify a pupil for the teaching of Fiqh (law), he should attend his lectures in person and judge his efficiency for the post.

If the pupil committed any mistake in the course of his discourse, the teacher should point it out in the presence of the audience.

In later times, the better type of pupil served a period of apprenticeship in the capacity of a Muid or an assistant. Abu Ishaq, the first principal of the Nizamiyya College, Baghdad worked as the Muid or Reviser-assistant of his teacher for ten long years. There were often more than one Muid attached to a teacher and the experience provided good opportunity for training in educational methods in case of young teachers.

There was a keen contest among the favourite pupils for the vacant post and during the last illness of Imam Shafii two of his favourite pupils exchanged hot words on the issue. When another pupil Al-Humaidi declared that Shafii had already nominated Al-Buwayti to the job, the rival candidate called him a liar and the other retorted in a stronger language. Such language was never used in those days of genial urbanity and the episode indicates the intensity of feelings aroused on such occasions.

Thus frustrated Ibn Abdul Hakam, the vanquished candidate occupied an alcove once removed from the seat where Shafii used to lecture while Al-Buwaiti occupied the place of his master. Lecture work under the Islamic educational system was public in the truest sense of the term and when a teacher claimed to profess a subject he could be questioned by any member of the public interested in the subject, during the course of his lecture.

Under these circumstances the scholars ventured to lecture only when they had acquired a good command of the subject matter and method of exposition, otherwise they met with disastrous results.

Ibn Jinni a grammarian used to teach syntax in a mosque

at Mawsil when Abu Ali-al-Farsi whose well known text has received sanction of countless generations of teachers and pupils, chanced to attend his lecture. On questioning the teacher, he found out that he had no mastery of the subject. Abu Ali left the class with a parting fling at the novice.

He said "You have turned into a raisin before you became a fully ripened grape". Ibn Jinni came to know the identity of the learned stranger when he had left the town of Mawsil but so irresistible was the intellectual urge aroused by the remark that he gave chase, overtook him at the first stage of his journey and remained attached to him as a pupil. His educational career came to a close only with the death of his teacher. He ultimately rose to great eminence as a grammarian and a teacher of language.

8

Female Teachers

The oral expression of the Prophet had a ring of sincerity about it and the rhythmic harmony of his words haunted the memory long after they had been heard. The Traditions are inspired with a feeling of deep humanity, genuine simplicity and felicity of diction peculiarly their own. They are a natural outcome of the great rhythm of life that moved his entire frame.

It is interesting to discover that some of the women who came to see him took unconsciously after him and express themselves in a beautifully expressive language.

When a woman was divorced by her husband and she came to him for the protection of her right as the guardian of her son she said, "He is my child, my womb has been his receptacle, my breasts his water-skin and my arms his cradle."

And when he had asked Hind, the wife of Abu Jahl on the fall of Mecca to give a pledge against infanticide, she said, "We suckled them as young and you killed them when they grew old. So you and they are the better judges thereof."

Aishah who had been brought up in a family with literary traditions would often narrate a tradition in a language illumined with expressive similes and figures of speech.

While commenting on the Prophet's interpretation of dreams she said, "Every dream that he saw came true as the dawn of the day." The Prophet experienced a great psychological strain during the moments of revelation and would often perspire heavily on such occasions and she described his worked up countenance by saying, "Drops of perspiration rolled down his brow like pearls." And when she passed sleepless nights during the days of Ifk, she says, "I rarely applied the collirium of sleep to my eyes."

But when her emotions were thoroughly aroused, she presented an impressive example of an ancient woman oracle and spoke with a fiery eloquence and her bon-mots and witticisms are like unto sparks when compared to that glorious blaze of scorching eloquence with which she addressed the army in the Battle of the Camel.

The opening lines in which she recounts her claims on the regard and affection of the people seem to grip the attention and have an air of remarkable pointedness about them.

> "O Men, be quiet, be quiet. I have the privilege of a mother on you and I exercise the authority of giving advice. The Prophet died with his head in my arms. I was the most cherished of his wives. God saved me from others (she had no previous husband) and through me were distinguished the believer from the Doubter (the accident of Ifk). It was for my sake that God revealed the injunction on Tayammum."

After summing up in one glorious repertory her claims to be listened, she speaks about her father.

"When the string of religion was set atremble after the Prophet, it was my father who held its ends in both his hands. He controlled the reins of dissension, he dried up the sources of renegacy. He extinguished the fiery plans of the Jews. He took those who had been watered to their resting place, and brought those who were thirsty to the water side and watered again those who had slaked their thirst before.

And when he had nipped the dissension in the bud and had blazed the mighty conflagration of battle for the unbelievers and had secured the bundle of provisions with a string he was called away by God."

With such remarkable gifts of eloquence women could very well help the Prophet in his great work.

Some of the women companions rendered services as teachers of the new cause and they did so at a great personal risk to themselves.

Um Shank Dawsiyyiah started her secret propaganda among the women of Mecca during those days when the Muslims were still a persecuted minority and she was ejected from the town by the Quraish. At Medina her residence was the rendezvous of the visitors from outside who came to learn about the new religion. And there was such a crowd of them always coming in and going out of her place that the Prophet did not permit Fatima bint Qays to prolong her stay when he had quartered her with Um Sharik after her divorce.

Another woman Ghuziyyah who worked among the women of Quraish was evicted from Mecca under appalling circumtances. She was secured tightly with cords on the naked back of a camel and was kept without food and drink for three days during the journey. It is said that the Quranic verse: In Wahabat Nafsaha linabi – if she has offered herself for the Prophet – had been revealed to commemorate her great sacrifices in the cause of truth.

Women in the days of the Prophet served on the battlefield and were responsible for a variety of duties. They would prepare meals on the way and in the camps on field service they supplied drinking water, attended to the wounded and looked after the injured and the sick. In some cases they were entrusted with the responsibility of carrying the dead to Medina.

Some of the more outstanding among those who accompanied the Prophet on his military operations were Um Sulaym, the mother of Anas bin Malik, and Um Atiyyah. Um Sulaym was an extremely courageous woman and was never daunted by the most grievous reverses. She had served with Aishah bint Abu Bakr on the battlefront of Uhud.

According to an eye-witness, they had tightened up their garments a little so that their anklets were visible. They would carry skinbags full of water on their back poured water into the mouths of the people and again hurried back to fill them up again.

Services like these were highly prized and Umar gave precendence to Um Kalthum bint Ali because she had taken part in the supply of water on the day of Uhud.

Um Sulaym kept always a cool mind under extremely trying conditions. When Muslims received a setback in the first encounter on the day of Hunayn, she was seen going about with a dagger and when the Prophet asked her what purpose it could serve, she replied that she would tear open the belly of the first unbeliever who would approach her with evil intentions. Um Atiyya another lady companion took part in seven campaigns with the Prophet and proved extremely useful on such occasions.

Um Umariyyah, a woman belonging to the Ansar was an early convert to Islam. She had embraced the new faith with the third group of Medinites who had embraced Islam at Aqabah. She served in the fighting ranks in the battles of Uhud, Hudaybiyyah, Khaybar, Hunayn and Yamamah.

A description of the part played by her in the Battle of Uhud reveals the great spirit of service and sacrifice which the Prophet had awakened among his women followers. She was performing at the same time the duties of First Aid to the injured and acted as a personal bodyguard of the Prophet.

She had a water skin and took drinking water to the wounded. She had rolls of bandages kept in a piece of cloth that was secured to her waist.

She experienced a narrow scrape when she attempted to ward off the enemy who were heading towards the Prophet. She formed one of the trusted band of followers with Musab bin Umayr and others who defended the Prophet at a great personal risk when he was beset by tried and determined warriors like Ibn Qamiyyah and others. She received twelve or thirteen wounds in the affray.

One of them which she had received on her shoulder took more than one year to heal. She gives herself an interesting description of her fighting technique. According to her, "We were fighting at a great disadvantage. The enemy fought on their rides and we were mostly on foot. Whenever a soldier attacked me, I would check the onslaught with my shield and when he retreated I would give a sword thrust on the legs of the horse and make it rear and fall. Then the Prophet who was close by called out my son to help and we finished him between ourselves."

Um Umariyyah had joined the battle with her whole family, her husband and two sons serving in the ranks. She followed her military career with equal zeal after the death of the Prophet.

And when Muslims fought the great battle of Yamamah against the renegades she took an active part in actual fighting. She received eleven wounds and one other arms was severed on the occasion.

This was not an isolated example of women joining a battle, with her whole family.

Khansa, the great elegist fought in the battle of Qadisiyyah in 1 A. H. along with four sons all of whom met their end in the sanguinary fight. The brave mother offered thanksgivings when she heard of their martyrdom?

Examples of personal bravery on the part of women were not uncommon in the Prophet's family. There is the case of Safiyyah, an aunt of the Prophet on the paternal side who killed a Jew with a tent peg during the Battle of the Ditch when she could not find a more handy weapon.

Hassan bin Thabit, the poet who was staying behind with the ladies in those perilous days when the Muslims were seriously threatened by the Jews of Medina could not gather up his courage to meet the man who was approaching the fortified retreat with evil intentions. When she had killed the man, she asked him to go and despoil him. But he refused to go and bring the armour of the victim which was a legitimate right of the victor. Thereupon Saffiyah issued forth once again, severed the head and threw it amidst the Jewish melee who had gathered below.

In addition to these brave women who were more known, there were several unnamed heroines who served with equal zeal and self-sacrifice. An unnamed woman took part in six battles out of twelve acting with her husband and performed duties of nursing and first aid.

Although there had been no sea campaign during the lifetime of the Prophet there is one distinguished instance of a lady companion who participated in naval engagement. She was Um Haram, the wife of 'Ubadah bin Thamar, the companion who was described as 'Kamil' or the perfect man in the language of the Jahiliyyah, one of the qualifications for earning the title being skill in the art of swimming.

She was a sister of the redoubtable Um Sulaym. It is interesting to know that Ubadah was the first companion of the

Prophet who had joined maritime warfare and was accompanied by Um Haram.

One of the chief traditions, in fact the main tradition on the blessings of sea warfare, is related on her authority. She gives a graphic picture of the whole scene. 'The Prophet visited my house and took his meals.

Then I began to massage his head and he dozed off. He woke up all of a sudden and laughed out. I said 'What makes you laugh, O Prophet of Allah', and he said 'A group among my people were presented to me (in the dream). They were fighting on the path of the Lord and they had mounted the waves of the sea as kings mount their thrones.' Thereupon Um Haram said, 'Pray for me O Prophet of Allah, that I may be one of them'. So he prayed for her.

Um Haram had accompanied her husband in the sea campaign against Cyprus during the reign of Muawiya. As she was disembarking from a boat she slipped down from her mount and was drowned in the sea.

Social Responsibility

The position of women in some of the Muslim countries today raises the important question how far the state of affairs is directly inspired by the Traditions of the Prophet.

A careful study of this literature brings us evidence of an overwhelming nature which proves that the deterioration in the status of women set up with the capitalistic society of a later age which believed in the proprietorship of woman as a commodity rather than treating her as a conscious being.

According to the Traditions, woman has an extremely important role to play in society. Although her primary duties lay in the creation of a rich and fuller life in the family, she was in no way barred from participating in the life outside home whenever there was a demand for such help on social or personal grounds.

Woman's place in the Muslim society of subsequent periods in no way reflects the spirit of those traditions which determined her role in society. They provide rich and abundant opportunities for the development of her personality within the framing arch and outside it. They provide means for the growth of healthy moral attitude and variegated modes of expression for her social, economic and even physical aspirations. And the annals of Islamic history reveal a rich variety of social, educational and spiritual occupations through which womanhood of Islam expressed itself under changing times and climes.

The perennial source of information for this freedom of expression can be traced out to the original teachings of the religion.

In this context, it would be interesting to make a critical study of two problems of an extremely controversial nature and see how far his teachings accorded with the eternal verities of human nature and moral and social good and how his injunctions provided ample facilities for a colourful variety in their modes of expression so long as they preserved the basic principles on which these injunctions had been framed. They are purdah and birth control.

The problem of purdah or the segregation of the sexes has been made a highly controversial issue for more than one reason. It is difficult to discover the origin of the so called harem life in the injunctions or the practice of the Prophet. It was the growth of a later stage that was far removed from the genuine democracy of early Islam. It developed during a period of kingship supported by a landed and commercial aristocracy that seriously jeopardised the freedom of the common man and woman. Started as a symbol of social prestige by the higher classes, it percolated down to the lower strata and recognised as a social institution was given the sanction of a religious institution by the clergy who tried to discover religious injunctions for it.

In its essence it was the product of a society that was essentially oligarchical and which tried to justify its undemocratic institutions by invoking the support of religion.

The Quran and the Traditions are fairly clear on the subject. They provide injunctions for regulating the life of men and women in a democratic society and establishing their relationship on an equable basis.

In fact the issue has been complicated by the two sets of injunctions, those for the wives of the Prophet and for the rest of women.

In fact social conditions of the town and the unfriendly intentions of the dissenters demanded special precautions for the preservation of the dignity of the Prophet's household.

Hence certain restrictions had been imposed on the Mothers of the Faithful and the Sura of Hijab had been primarily revealed with specific reference to the Prophet's wives.

The Sura was revealed on the occasion of the marriage of Zainab bint Jahsh with the Prophet. According to Anas after this event the wives of the Prophet began to observe Hijab. The injunction forbids the believers from entering the Prophet's residence without permission.

It appears that before this event visitors entered the Prophet's house without permission and would sometimes prolong their stay indefinitely. Henceforth they were to seek permission for admission. This specific injunction was further implemented by the Prophet's wives by taking the Hijab.

But the practice cannot be interpreted as a general commandment for the entire womanhood. This is not an isolated example when the Prophet had imposed restrictions exclusively on himself and his family. He had denied to his family any right of inheritance to his worldly possessions. The restriction had no force for others.

The women of Medina continued with their routine share in the normal life of the community, and did so without purdah, at least purdah as understood today.

There is abundant evidence to prove that women addressed the Prophet with uncovered faces.

Once in the course of his address to women on the Eid day the Prophet declared that most of them were faggots for hell. This was a device to set their moral frames atremble. On this occasion it was a woman belonging to the masses described as Saflat Annisa, Safal Khadayn (lowly woman with black spots on her cheeks) who stood up and cross questioned him on the subject. According to the traditions, she was marked with dark spots on her cheek. Obviously the woman could not be described by an eyewitness in these words if she was veiled.

On another occasion, in the words of the tradition (a woman had raised herself on her knees so that the Prophet might see her.)

The books on Tafsir mention the episode of a fair complexioned woman who used to join the prayers in the Prophet's mosque and how there was a larger rush in the back rows than the front rows.

Instances where women attended mixed gatherings without a veil during the lifetime of the Prophet can be multiplied indefinitely. The very nature of the work performed by women on the battlefield, in the gardens and the field, the pastures and the grazing grounds of Medina precluded the possibility of the use of a veil.

A fairly large number of women worked in the fields and engaged themselves in agricultural operations. These included both women belonging to the Ansar and the Muhajarin. In the early days the Prophet had granted tracts of lands to the poorer section among the Muhajarin. These grants had been made out of the landed property of Banu Nadhir.

These persons were helped by their women folk. Women living in the desert must have led even a more free life. They looked after the flocks and attended to guests in the absence of menfolk. During the Prophet's time one comes across women who looked after goats transacted petty business like selling of milk to the travellers. The Prophet and his fellow traveller had been entertained by such a woman on their way from Mecca to Medina.

It would be interesting to make a study of the Traditional evidence on the subject in greater details.

Holy Prophet's Assembly : Women attended his assembly along with men and he would discuss very intimate topics like that of sex in such mixed gatherings.

Once he addressed the people about a person who let out his bed chamber secrets to others. There were present on that occasion both men and women and they were seated in separate groups.

He asked them frankly whether there was any one who behaved like that. All kept quiet. Then one of the women raised herself on the knees so that the Prophet might be able to see her and listen to her. She said, "There are persons like that both among-men and women." This incident throws light on the frankness with which women used to discuss things and how they addressed the Prophet and the people with uncovered faces.

Women would come to him for clarification of legal points concerning all sorts of matters including their conjugal relations and some of them would express their views in a language which might be considered too frank. Questions like these don't indicate any morbid curiosity about sex affairs.

For the Arabs, these matters had no air of morbidity about them. They were as normal as other features of their every day life. What stimulated them to ask such questions was the great desire to learn the Prophet's injunctions on all matters and to preserve them for future generations.

There is the case of a woman who demanded separation before she had performed coitus with her husband. And when she preferred her case, she raised the edge of a piece of cloth and told the Prophet that her husband's limb was as supine as the cloth. On another occasion a woman had actually put him a question on bed pollution in case of women and when Um Salma, the Prophet's wife expressed displeasure on the question he told that there was no harm about the query.

Attending Prayers : During the life time of the Prophet, women enjoyed considerable freedom in their movements and they attended the Prophet's mosque regularly for morning and for other prayers. According to Aishah women used to join the morning prayers that were led by the Prophet. They used to have their sheets on them.

The Prophet was extremely considerate for children and he would often cut short his prayers if he heard a child crying for its mother who had obviously joined prayers led by the Prophet.

The chapters on Salat as given in the authentic collection of Traditions contain instructions as regards the participation of women in prayers with men. According to Ibn Umar no woman should be disallowed from visiting a mosque and elsewhere he has said that she should be permitted to visit the mosque even at night and when a son of his refused to accept the statement he grew so violent that he abused him.

According to another source, he struck his fist against his chest and said, "I am telling you a command of the Prophet and you have the facetiousness to say that I won't accept it." According to Ibn Umar, a wife of Umar bin Khatib attended the mosque regularly for morning and night prayers. Umar was rather over strict as regards movement of women as evidenced from the episode of Sawdah, the wife the Prophet. He did not like it personally that his wife should join the night prayers in the mosque but he did not prevent her from attending the mosque out of his great regard for the Prophet's injunctions on the subject. Atikah, a wife of Zubayr had married him on the express condition that he won't check her from attending night prayers in the mosque.

Certain other injunctions are concerned with the actual act of praying.

According to a Tradition in Bukhari, women are not permitted to rise from prostration until men had seated themselves. A number of chapters in books on Salat deal with injunctions concerned with women praying along with men.

Women used to join Eid prayers and other prayers like those offered during a solar eclipse. According to Um Atiyyah, the Prophet ordered us to take unmarried women or married and even those in menses to the Eid prayers.

They were not silent spectators on such occasions but would call out the Takbir also.

Maymunah used to call out Takbir on the prayers for the Eid of Sacrifice and women would recite Takbir when they joined prayers with men under the leadership of Aban bin Uthman and Umar bin Abd-al-Aziz during the nights of Tashriq.

The Prophet insisted that women both married and unmarried and even those in their menses should go forth out of their houses on the Eid day and join the prayers. He enjoined on them to lend scarfs to one another for dressing properly for the occasion.

Women attended the addresses of the Prophet on Fridays

and the Eid days and on other occasions along with men. But as they sat at a distance, apart from men he had sometimes the feeling that he was not easily audible to them.

For a number of years he used to address men and women together and afterwards he would come down from the pulpit and address the women separately. It was also necessitated by the appeal for the poor relief which the Prophet would make to them on the spot.

A ready collection was always possible in case of women because they would donate their ornaments on such occasions, a form of contribution not possible in case of men. On such occasions Bilal or some other person was always at hand to collect the donations in a piece of cloth.

Sometimes he would appoint a particular day for addressing women alone. Once a representation was made that men had an easier access to him than women so he named a special day for them on which he gave them spiritual counsel and told them about the commandments of God. He gave a special address to women on Eiḍ days also.

The Obligations

The Prophet visited some women at their homes too. They were either women like Um Sulaym the mother of Anas bin Malik who used to accompany him on his military campaigns and Um Haram her sister, a brave woman who met her end in a naval campaign during the period of Muawiyyah. She belonged to the family that had fostered the Prophet in his early years, and was a sister of his foster mother.

She lived at Kaaba, quite a distance from the Prophet's mosque and whenever he visited Kaaba he would make a point to visit her and take his noon day siesta there. Um Haram would scurry his hair and he would go to sleep.

It was in her house that he saw in a dream how some of his followers rode the waves of the ocean as kings mount their throne. This had occasioned the well known tradition on the excellence of naval warfare.

He would often take his siesta in the house of Um Sulaym also who would collect his perspiration as a sacred memento in a phial.

The Prophet used to pass his noon day hours some times at the residence of Shifa bint Abdullah, a learned lady of those times who had taught writing to Hafsah, the wife of the Prophet.

Women would often visit him at his residence and discuss things, obviously without any purdah restrictions as interpreted today and even the presence of the Prophet did not deter them from raising their voices to the loudest pitch. It is interesting to note that women exercised such a freedom only in the presence of the Prophet. They would take every precaution for more decorum if Umar bin Khattab appeared on the scene.

Once Umar sought permission to see the Prophet who had with him at that time some women from Quraish who were talking with him and they would often shout at the highest pitch of their voice. When Umar bin Khattab sought admission (from outside) they hastened to cover themselves (Yabdarun al Hijab). When Umar entered the house he found the Prophet laughing.

Thereupon Umar said, "May God keep you laughing", and the Prophet explained, "I was tickled by these women who were with me. When they heard your voice, they hastened to cover themselves."

Upon this Umar said, "O Prophet of God, you have a better right to be feared by them than myself and then he turned to the women and said, "O enemies of your souls, do you fear me and do not fear the Prophet". They replied, "Yes, because you are more strict and harsh."

The phrase 'Yabdarun al Hijab implies that the women were sitting without any Hijab.

Women in Action

In the case of a town like Medina which was the settlement of an agricultural community it was natural that some women should have engaged themselves in agricultural operations. They were not essentially Ansars, some of the Meccan emigrants had also taken to this profession when they were allotted pieces of land out of the property of Banu Nadhir after their exile.

One such piece was allotted to Zubayr, the father of Abdullah that brave and redoubtable claimant for the Caliphate under the Umayyids. His wife Asma bint Abu Bakr describes how she used to go often to the land and bring fodder for the horse carrying it all the way on her head. She would often mend the leather bucket for drawing water for her husband. This piece of land was situated three quarter of a Farsakh (league) from her house.

It is interesting to learn that Asma belonged to the highest of the high. She was the daughter of Abu Bakr and one of the most courageous and renowned women of early Islam. She had revealed an amazing sense of loyalty to Islam even during the Meccan period as a young girl and she must have enjoyed all the social prestige and precedence she deserved. But all these things did not prevent her from following an occupation which belonged essentially to out of door life.

A large number of unnamed women occupied themselves with agricultural operations. Sahl describes how a woman used to sow beet root along the channels of her field and would give them a treat by making a preparation of the beet root mixed with flour every Friday.

Women used to look after herds of animals, specially goat and sheep both at Mecca and Medina. Um Ayman, the freed slave girl of the Prophet's family used to look after goats.

Once the master of a slave girl who used to tend his flock of goats gave her a beating because she had lost a goat. The Prophet had asked the man to set her at liberty as a compensation for his harsh treatment.

Some of the women at Medina followed professions involving operations which could in no way be performed with a covered face.

Rufaydah was a surgeon and she used to perform minor operations in a tent like structure adjacent to the mosque.

Shifa bint Abdullah was a scholarly woman of the age who knew reading and writing, she dabbled in medicine and was often put in charge of supervision work in the market place by Umar.

The Prophet's injunctions on birth control revealed an extremely objective outlook on an issue which can hardly be 'discussed in this scientific age of ours without arousing considerable feelings. For him it does not seem to have any moral significance, good or bad, it is 'a moral' to all intents and purposes.

Birth control was practised in the days of the Prophet for more than one reason, its chief reason in the earlier years being scarcity. It was practised under war conditions too. Sometimes it was practised in case of a woman during the suckling period.

One of the chief traditions on the subject has been narrated on the authority of Jabir bin Abdullah who had married after the death of his father in Uhud. His father had left a rather heavy debt which the Prophet helped to pay off. But he had left a more burdensome legacy of seven or nine daughters and it was not easy for Jabir to feed so many mouths.

Jabir took a widow for a wife and the news reached the Prophet after the marriage had been celebrated. When Jabir saw him next, the Prophet said, "You should have married a virgin. She would have proved more playful with you," Thereupon Jabir told him that he had married a widow so that she might look after his sisters.

Now according to Jabir, birth control or Azl was commonly practised in those days. In his own words "We used to practise Azl during the days that the Quran was being revealed. It may be any time before A.H., the year of Hajj al Wida. It was represented to the Prophet that some of companions practised birth control but the Jews objected to the practice and described it something in the nature of burying a child alive. The Prophet said, "They lie. When God intends to create, nothing can stand in His way."

According to a tradition by Abi Said, "When birth control was mentioned in his presence, the Prophet said, 'Why does anyone practise birth control.' He did not make any further comments and he did not prohibit it."

According to Muslim, the Permission for the practice is negative in nature. According to Abu Said al Khudzari when they practised Azl during the battle of Bani Mustalaq and the opinion of the Prophet was sought on the matter he said, "There is no harm if you don't do it because a soul that God has ordained to be created any time till Doomsday will be created."

According to Iman Malik, it is essential to obtain consent for its practice in case of a free woman.

Female Education

The Prophet had a soft corner of his heart for the girls who had suffered most from that callous indifference to human life and dignity which was the darkest spot in the social life of the Pre-Islamic Arabia. An inordinate feeling of tribal pride led to the cruel custom of infanticide.

The Prophet once wept like a child when one of his companions related to him the pathetic description of an infanticide he had committed before he had accepted Islam; the memory of the innocent voice crying out from the bottom of the pit where he had heartlessly buried her calling upon the departing parent to reclaim her from a living grave, set his moral fibre atremble.

Any expression of motherly feeling had always a profound influence on him and when a widow visited Aishah with two other daughters and on receiving a single date from the Mother of the Faithful, divided it equally between them, the Prophet was evidently overwhelmed with emotion and called out his blessing on all who tended their daughters because verily they were a covering of protection from the consuming fire of Hell."

There is a tradition on the authority of Shaabi that "one who has imparted good education to his daughter, trained her on sound lines and provided for her a matrimonial alliance, verily for him there lay a reward in God." Again according to Abi Said al Khudri, one who has brought up three daughters, educated them, married them and acted otherwise handsomely towards them has won his title to heaven.

We have made a passing reference already to the fact how the Prophet had relaxed the formal discipline of the prayers when a child chanced to approach him on such occasions with the privilege that its naive and unconventional nature gave him.

According to Abu Qatadah, he prayed while Amamah, the daughter of Abi-al-Ath bin Rabi rode on his shoulders; the Prophet would place her gently on the ground when performing the prostration and lifted her up after completing it. Innocent hands played with his mighty frame.

They rollicked and frolicked about him boldly and freely and he always beamed into smiles. Once the tiny daughter of Khalid bin Said played with the Mark of Apostolate a scar-like formation on his back and he permitted her benevolently to continue with her innocent mischief uninterrupted. He won't forget his little friends amidst more respectable company and even when engaged in important affairs of state.

Once he was presented with a black 'cheddar' and he sent for Um Khalid who was so small that she was actually carried to him. When the child arrived he pointed out to her lovingly the flowered embroidery of the piece and called out, 'Sana, Sana, ('Beautiful' in the Abysinian language) and he spoke the word because the little lady was born in Abyssinia and it was the only language which she understood. She began to play with the Seal of Prophethood, a purple coloured protuberance on his back. Thereupon her father tried to check her rudely, but the Prophet requested him not to prevent her from doing so.

It appears that the shades of gloom had lifted from the girlhood of Arabia on the advent of Islam and we have evidence that they sang, played on musical instruments, revelled in joy rides on the swings and shared with the girlhood of all ages the pastime of doll playing and had toys as fantastic and grotesque as found in any other country of the world.

Women enjoyed more freedom and liberty to move out in the days of the Prophet than the orthodox Muslim women of today and naturally women who accompanied warriors on the battlefields and rendered First Aid service must have had ample opportunities for playing and physical exercise in order to train them for such an arduous duty. There is the instance of Aishah running a race with the Prophet in the earlier years of their married life and winning it. She lost the second race which she arranged with him in later years.

Aishah's house appears to be an educative and a playing centre for girls in the earlier years and the rendezvous of scholars and intellectuals during the later period. The pleasure of her company and the attractive display other playthings of the days of childhood must have brought to her the girls of the neighbourhood in numbers who had a chance to benefit by her talk and experience.

A breath of joyous life appeared to have passed over the house when they joined company with Aishah and they were not daunted by the presence of the Prophet in their merrymakings.

We have it on the authority of Aishah that once two girls were singing war songs of the battle of Badr in her house and the Prophet came and lay on bed for some time. At this stage, Abu Bakr arrived on the scene and reprimanded the girls. Thereupon the Prophet asked him to let the girls alone and they continued with their songs for some time.

A group of Abyssinians had arranged a display of war games and probably war dances on an Eid day, and Aishah stood behind the Prophet with her chin resting on his shoulder while the Prophet urged them on with encouraging words. Such displays and public performances must have been a good training ground for instilling in women a spirit of discipline and physical agility.

Women were taught reading and writing and we have it on the authority of Shifa bin Abdullah, a scholarly woman of the period, whom the Prophet visited frequently and often had his siesta at her house. Once the Prophet visited her and she was with Hafsa; thereupon he said, "Why did not you teach Hafsa the incantation for Namlah (minor swellings on the sides) as you had taught her writing."

It is remarkable that more specific injunctions and promises of higher rewards were held out specially in case of girls education. The Education of the boys was most probably a normal feature of the social life and the Prophet was more solicitous about women's Education because it was one of the most neglected spheres of social and cultural activity during that period.

The Companions of the Prophet were equally solicitous for the education of girls and Jabir stated in the presence of the Prophet that Abdulla his father, died leaving behind daughters of tender age and that he had married a widow for their instruction and training.

That the objective of women's education was not merely the raising of the social prestige of womanhood but it derived its sanction on account of an intense faith in human worth in general, is revealed by the traditions containing instructions on the education of the slave girls.

The chapter on Slaves of the same book contains instructions to one who owns a slave girl and how she should be educated and trained into an exemplary behaviour.

9

Appointment Procedure

As a rule teacher of established reputation did not apply for a post but they were approached with all the deference due to their high position with the offer of the vacant chair. Sometimes the Mutawalli (Manager) or a patron of the college had to marshall all his persuasive powers in order to win over a teacher. When Imam Ghazzali was invited a second time to resume his work at the Nizamiyya College of Baghdad he was supplicated by Ahmad bin Nizam-al-Mulk, the son of the illustrious founder of the college and a minister of state in those days. When he failed to create any impression on Al-Ghazzali who was at that time staying at his native town, the people of Baghdad approached the Abbaside Caliph Mustazhar Billah to persuade the savant to rejoin his post at Baghdad. An invitation was drafted under the signatures of all the dignitaries of state, and sent to the savant.

But Ghazzali would not come. He thanked them cordially for the offer but replied that he could not leave those one hundred and fifty pupils whom he was teaching in a private college of his own in his native town. Again he had taken a vow not to participate in a debate and he was certain that he could not keep that vow in the metropolis. Another formidable obstacle was the economic one. In Tus he had his family property which yielded him sufficient income for making both ends meet while he could not do without monetary remuneration at Baghdad and this he had foresworn to accept for the rest of his life.

The founders of institutions, their managers and sometimes even the ruling princes were always on the lookout for savants who chanced to visit the country and availed of the first opportunity to offer them a post in a college. Teachers who had distinguished themselves in a particular branch of learning were specially in demand for occupying the chairs in the colleges.

When Shatibi, the famous authority on Qirat (recitation) of the Quran came to Egypt from Spain, he was given a-cordial welcome by Qadi-al-Fazil and appointed a professor at the Faziliyyah College founded by him at Cairo where he composed his well known poems, the Lamia and the Raiyah on Qirat. Qadi-al-Fazil was not only a great patron of learning who saved a considerable number of books from the palace library of the Fatimides when it was despoiled during the period of orthodox reaction under Ṡalahuddin, he was also generous in extending his patronage to great scholars and teachers without any consideration of caste and creed.

He had a soft corner of his heart for the scholars from foreign countries. He befriended Maimonides who had been hunted out of Spain and not only saved him from further persecution at the hands of religious fanatics but helped in safeguarding his interests in other ways.

Royal Foundations : In case of royal foundations the appointment of the teacher was commonly made by the ruling prince. It appears that no person could teach in the Friday mosque raised by Mansur at Baghdad without royal permission. Khatib-al-Baghdadi whose life long ambition was to relate traditions from its historic pulpit had to approach the Caliph

Al-Qaim-bi-Amrillah with the request and it is interesting to learn that the very nature of his favourite subject provided him an opportunity to win the royal consent.

It appears that Khatib came across a book on traditions which comprised a particular tradition that had been related by the Caliph himself. Khatib sought the royal audience in order to verify the authority and when he approached the Caliph with the request the latter made a shrewd guess that the renowned traditionist had some secret motive for the audience. On discovering that his desire was to dictate traditions in the mosque of Mansur, the Caliph instructed the chief of the Naqibs, the official in charge of organising the assemblies in the mosque to arrange for him an assembly in the mosque.

Later Period : So long as the profession exercised a high prestige in national life, the savants were sought after for occupying the jobs, but in the later period the tables turned, it was the scholar who gave a hot pursuit to the posts which often proved a wild goose chase. The appointments in the later period were not made after the implicit desire of the people whose tacit selection was endorsed by the ruling prince indirectly. Under the Osmanides, the authority was exercised by the judge of the armies (Qadi-ul-Asakir) who had to obtain the final sanction of the prince in case of all recommendations made by him and would often incur the displeasure of his master if he acted on personal initiative.

It appears that although the judge of the armies was the chief authority for the appointment of the teachers, powerful ministers exercised influence in certain cases and a weak judge could hardly refuse the recommendation of a minister.

These judges could very well exercise their authority against the expressed desire of a minister because ministers and judges were recruited from the same class and they frequently interchanged places. But the regalia of the ministerial power had tamed the spirit of the savant and he had learnt in some cases to compromise with the demands of the powers that be. A minister asked a Qadi to appoint the tutor of a personal slave of his to a college and the poor Qadi had no alternative but to pray for divine help in order to seek protection from a misuse of his authority.

State of Affairs

The appointments were generally open to all persons qualified to occupy the post without any consideration of the race and nationality of the teacher. This usage was a legacy of the democratic spirit of religion and that cosmopolitan spirit which conceived the intellectual world of Islam as a whole. Certain restrictions were laid on the appointment of the teacher of law, who should belong to that particular School of law, for which the endowment had been specifically made. There were state colleges which had four *iwans* for the four Schools of laws and the professorship in each department was held by a savant belonging to that particular School. In some cases the post was held by a Qadi who decided the cases of those litigants who belonged to his sect and he held his court in the department. This practice afford practical training of considerable value to the students of *fiqh*.

But in colleges with a single chair for law, the post was occupied by the teacher belonging to the school, professed by the founder of the institution. This had an indirect influence in the selection of the teachers. Under these circumstances as the foundation had been made in favour of a particular school the majority of appointments in other departments besides Law went as a rule to those savants who followed that particular School.

Abdullah bin Hussain of Baghdad was once approached by a group of Shafites who promised to him the chair of Grammar in the Nizamiyya College of Baghdad if he changed his creed. The savant spurned the suggestion and told that if they were to shower on him so much of gold that he was covered from head to foot he would not play the role of a renegade.

But there were teachers and the instance of Wajihuddin Ibn-al-Dahan indicates how the prospects of a college appointment could transform a teacher into a weather cock.

Ibn-al-Dahan who was a Hanbalite changed over to the Hanafite sect and when he started his career as a teacher at the Nizamiyya College of Baghdad he changed his creed once again. A poet satirized him in the following verses.

> You became a Hanafite after being a Hanbalite.
>
> And it was because you needed rich food,
>
> You would have never accepted the faith of Shafii
>
> If you had not been sure of gaining all that you desired.
>
> A day will come when you would certainly change over
>
> To the Malikites, so beware of my prophecy.

It appears that reputed masters of their subjects had no difficulty in obtaining recognition of their worth or an appointment even in a foreign country, their reputation often preceding them into distant lands. When Ibn Khaldun went to Egypt he relates how students flocked to him in search of knowledge notwithstanding his insignificant acquirements and would accept no excuse on his part. During his stay in Cairo he received the privilege of lecturing at the Al-Azhar.

In his days the colleges in Egypt were mostly state institutions and the Sultan granted to Ibn Khaldun an allowance usually sanctioned in the case of savants because he held no appointment in a college and when a professorship was rendered vacant at the Qamahiyya College on account of the death of a teacher, Khaldun was appointed to the post by the Sultan.

Inaugural Address : The first day of a newly appointed

principal at the college was a red lettered day and his first lecture was more or less an ordeal which he had to stand in the presence of a representative gathering of scholars and savants who were specially invited for the occasion. The function introduced the teacher to a larger audience than the class group specially his professional brotherhood and provided an opportunity for a test of his mettle and scholarship by others.

The inaugural address of the teacher was an outcome of considerable thought and preparation and he marshalled up all his erudition and his literary talent in order to make it imposing and effective. The lectures were often cherished by teachers as valuable mementos of their old glory in later years. Ibn Khaldun for instance records his inaugural addresses ad verbatim in his autobiographical sketch.

In his first address he spoke of the merits of Ulama in supporting a Muslim state, of the rise of states and the patronage of learning by the dynasties of Egyptian Sultans. He invoked blessing on the ruling monarch and praised his justice and sagacity. The address was garnished with pieces of poetry composed by the savant in which he described his voyage from the West to the East, the greatness of Islam and the nascent intellectual movement of those days.

When appointed a professor at the Sarghatmash College for lectures on the Muwàttah of Imam Malik he opened his address by an account of the life of Malik, his origin and the diffusion of his doctrines.

The inaugural address introduced the teacher to a selected gathering of savants. Some times the inaugural address was criticised by a member of the audience and the lecturer had to marshall all his intellectual talent in order to satisfy the critic.

A representative gathering of savants attended the function when Muhammad Shah, the son of Maula Fannari was installed as the chief professor of the Sultania College at Brusa during the life time of his father and on the first day he was successful in rebutting the objections of one and all except those of a person who was notorious for his irreligious tendencies.

When his father visited him after the lecture, Maula Fannari told him that he was never so nonplussed as on that day. His father told him that his critic was really a good scholar. Thereupon he remonstrated that an irreligious person could not achieve true scholarship. But his father told him that if the man had not lacked faith, his excellence would have been even greater than he had experienced on that day.

Scales for Salary

There were various sources for the payment of teachers salaries. The main source was the income of the endowment, the amount and nature of the teachers salaries and allowance being indicated in the original deed of the foundation.

Another important source was the public exchequer and this system of grants in aid by the state could be traced to the earliest times.

Umar bin Abdul Aziz was the first Caliph who sanctioned allowances for the teacher in the Empire. Once he despatched two persons to the desert for teaching the Bedouins the Traditions of the Prophet. One of them Yazid by name accepted the monetary award made for the service while the other refused it.

But it seems that the monetary assistance given to the learned profession in the earliest days was not liberal.

Khaldun had an opportunity to study the salary registers of this class under Al-Mamun and was successful in discrediting the general notion that the learned class received princely help from the state.

The monetary aid from the state took various forms according to the custom or usage of different parts of the

Muslim world. The Osmanides had a regular system of salaries paid on a daily basis followed by superannuation allowances in some cases. The payments were made either directly from the public treasury or made payable from the proceeds of a particular tax levied on a particular town.

In countries like India, there was an Ecclesiastical Department under the chief Divine called Sadr as Sadur who sanctioned monetary assistance to the learned profession. It took the form of grants of landed property free from taxation.

There was a country wide system of free land (Muafi) granted not only to the distinguished members of the profession who were associated with higher learning, but also to the teachers of the Maktabs (Elementary school). Dr. Leitner came across a number of such grants in Punjab as late as the second half of the nineteenth century.

Shahjahan had styled the Eastern part of the United Province (India) as the Shiraz of India, because this tract of land was dotted all over with seats of higher learning and its towns and villages were peopled with scholars and savants who received stipends or '*Madad-e-Maash*' and held free lands granted by the state.

The princes often examined the applicants for monetary assistance in person. During his reign, whenever a scholar applied for a maintenance allowance Madad-e-Maash, Sher Shah examined them personally on Hashiyah-i-Hindi for even then he had much liking for books of history and dynasties of ancient kings.

Besides grants and salaries, the teachers received sometimes munificent rewards from the rulers in lump sum. Mulla Abdul Hakim of Sialkot the well-known scholar and teacher was weighed in gold and received the amount as a present. According to another version he was weighed in silver and received six thousand rupees as a present.

The teacher was expected to maintain the dignity of his profession by not frequenting the presence of the rich without a proper excuse. He was permitted to visit them in case of financial necessity or for some religious purpose. Writers on education defend such visits on the authority of Imam Shafii; Al-Zahri and others. Shafii had intimate relations with the House of Banu Abdul Haq in Egypt and they had presented him once with one thousand dinars and acquired another contribution of two thousand from a merchant and their other friends for him . These exceptions are made on the basis of urgent financial need of the savant. Public subscriptions were an important source specially in the case of the Elementary school (Maktab) teacher who was entirely maintained by the local community by the payment being made in cash or kind. He was provided free meals by the parents and received gifts and presents on festivals.

In some cases the townspeople subscribed to the salary of a college professor also. Marwzi, the Traditionist who founded a study circle in his native province of Khurasan received annually four hundred dirhams from the governor of Khurasan, four thousand from his brother and an equal amount was contributed by the townspeople of Samarkand.

A trader relates how he came across Imam Fakhruddin Razi in one of the lesser known colleges of Bukhara and he was not keeping good health. The savant sought from him monetary help and he collected for him some money from the Arab traders in the town who contributed their tithe to the help of the indigent scholar.

The establishment of a regular system of colleges provided facilities of professional work for those teachers who were retiring in nature and not so well-known. According to Wakhshi 'After an arduous educational career I returned to my native village and nobody had any idea of my worth and no conception of the rich treasure of learning which I had amassed in the course of my travels. I feared that I would fade away in oblivion and none would invoke blessing on me after my death. But God made Nizamul Mulk lay the foundation of this College of Balkh and he got me appointed as the professor of traditions.'

The establishment of colleges provided the additional facility of relieving financial worries of the teachers. Wakhshi for instance had seen terrible times in his educational career. There were days when he was too poor to purchase bread and he would often seat himself beside the baker's shop and inhale the flavour of the steaming bread in order to give a momentary satisfaction to the pangs of hunger.

Oldage Pensions : Sometimes the savants retired from college service and stayed permanently at home where they continued their professional work. Generally they had a chamber for study attached to their residence. Under the Osmanides, the teachers were granted a pension in some cases. Usually there was no appreciable reduction in pay and the savant continued to enjoy the same salary which he received when he was at the college.

Retirement did not depend so much on reasons of age or efficiency. It was left in most cases to the choice of the teacher. He could be dismissed or forced to retire earlier only because of serious defalcations or sometimes on account of the vagaries of royal temperament.

There are instances when the progeny of the savant also benefited through the generosity of the ruler specially in the case of a family which was reputed for its traditions of learning. Muhammad, the Osmanide was told that his kingdom would last as long as a single descendant of Maula Fanari stayed in the realm. The sultan thereupon granted an allowance of fifty dirhams daily for Maula Alauddin, the grandson of Maula Fanari, fifty dirhams for his elder and forty for his younger son. He issued orders that the post of the judge at Ibnah Kol was to be held permanently by a descendent of the savant.

Another member of the family was granted an allowance of thirty dirhams daily from his very birthday.

The grants of land made to the scholarly class usually passed from father to son. On the Indo-Pakistan subcontinent Madad-e-Maash, or stipends were granted to individuals on a personal basis while *jagirs* and *Muafies* became a part of the family inheritance.

Some of the more distinguished savants of the Osmanides received annual grants in addition to the daily allowances. Maula Alauddin the grandson of Maula Fanari received fifty dirhams daily and 10,000 dirhams annually under Muhammad which was raised to 70 dirhams daily and 12,000 dirhams annually under Sultan Rayazid.

Teachers' Agreements : In the teachers agreements common in Spain one comes across the first example of an attempt to emancipate education from its bondage to religion and its establishment on a comparatively secular basis. This great achievement of Spanish teachers must have gone a long way in bringing financial security to a class of teachers who were not attached to a well established institution and who earned their livelihood by means of running private schools.

In Spain teachers entered into agreement with another member of the profession for opening a school on a cooperative basis, sharing the fees and taking turns at teaching. Each partner would hold office for a month by turns.

Agreements were also drawn up between parents and teachers specifying clearly the subject to be taught and the payment to be made to the teacher.

The payment was to be made monthly or annually, as specified in the deed. In some cases the teacher was to receive a specified amount of flour, oil, fresh water. He could demand gifts on the two festivals of Eid and presents on the completion of education if they were included in the terms of agreement.

Authorities disagree on the legality of specifying a period within which the pupil was to complete the reading of the Quran, because it did not conform to the spirit of genuine educational principles.

The teacher was to receive payment for the free day of the week which was Friday. and he could enjoy leave within reasonable limits. He continued to enjoy his payment in case the pupil did not attend on account of a brief spell of illness or if his father or guardian withdrew the child from the school for reasons of their own.

These agreements form part of a book on legal documents and such transactions seem to be a normal feature of professional life in Spain. The usage was fairly widespread and master artisans took over apprentices on agreements of a similar nature.

These business relations between the teacher and the taught hardly detracted from the quality of the work. According to the observation of Ibn Khaldun, the standard of teaching in Spain was higher as compared with that obtaining in North Africa. Teachers agreements were all the more necessitated on account of the absence of a well organised system of colleges in Spain, a country where educational system was maintained mostly by individual teachers holding classgroups on a personal and private basis.

Low Economic Return : The teaching profession was not so lucrative as others and Khaldun gives more than one reason for its low economic returns. In the first place, the common people did not count education and learning as something indispensable. Only those occupations which met more universal and immediate demands yielded good returns. Again self-abasement and adulation was the very secret of success in life and men of learning and religion did not approve of these methods. Another reason for their economic failure in life was their preoccupation with intellectual pursuits which permitted them hardly any leisure for waiting upon kings and nobles.

In his opinion the learned class is compensated to some extent by the honour and consideration which they receive from the people and their states and dignity prevents them from stooping to means adopted by others.

Elsewhere Khaldun rightly emphasizes that the teachers prove signal failures in life because they are so much engrossed in theoretical studies that they are unsuccessful in correlating their knowledge to the needs of practical life.

This affects their economic prospects in an adverse manner.

Other Means of Income: Handicraft provided some teachers with a precarious means of livelihood and it would be intriguing to know how they could adjust their teaching hours in case of such occupations. The specialised nature of work, in which a teacher taught only a particular book or subject and the common usage of the pupils attending in person at the teacher's residence might have provided facilities for time table adjustments in such cases.

It is related about Abdul Wahid-al-Baji that he worked as a watchman in Baghdad and on his return to Spain he became a gold beater in the bazar. He used to copy documents, also his pupils related that he came to teach them with the marks of working with a hammer still visible on his hands.

There were scholars who worked as cabinet makers. Abul Fazl the engineer of Damascus was extremely skilful in the art, some of the gateways of the Kabir-Shahi hospital have been prepared by him. He was incharge of the clock-tower of the Friday mosque in Damascus and used to receive a regular allowance for this service. As most of the teachers carried on some kind of art or craft for earning a livelihood, the authorities on education realised the necessity of laying down certain regulations about the selection of vocations. The teachers were expected to maintain their status by abstaining from vocations which were not considered worthy of their status and dignity.

According to Ibn Jamaah the unsuitable vocations included hair dressing, tannery, money exchange, dyeing etc.

Role of a Judge

When Imam Abu Hanifa refused to be appointed a judge, Ibn Hubairah the minister gave him ten lashes daily for eleven days but he could not force him to revise his opinion. The Imam was again invited to be a judge by the Abbaside Caliph Al-Mansur who swore a royal oath to appoint him a judge while the savant took an equally determined oath not to succumb to the temptation. He persisted in his refusal after repeated requests and was ultimately sent to the prison cell where he met his end in 150 A.H.

And when Ibn Idris refused the offer, Harun said in anger, "I wish I had never seen your face." The savant replied with quiet dignity, "And so was my desire."

When a savant of the Osmanide period refused to accept the post of a judge at Damascus, his friends mustered strong to persuade him to accept the offer. They found him adamant in his resolution, but they were not discouraged. They were determined not to be defeated. The savant owed money to some of his friends and they declared that if he did not accede to their request he must clear all the debt to the last penny. According to some doctors of law, a person in debt could not occupy the post of a judge.

The poor scholar preferred the judge's chair to the debtor's cell, but not without a passing taunt flung at his friends, " I am only exchanging known debts for the unknown", said he, implying the account of his record as a Qadi which he shall have to render to his Creator after death.

But the fear of pronouncing incorrect decisions was not the only obstacle in accepting the post. There were savants who considered salary for state service to be illegal.

When the Abbaside Caliph Mansur expressed a wish to appoint a person, a governor, he told him that his family people had declared that if he became a governor they wont accept from him even a paltry gift costing two dirhams. So he besought the Caliph not to appoint him to the post.

Role of an Authority

Besides working as a judge, the teachers very often performed a number of other functions which were closely allied to the legal profession, for instance every teacher of Fiqh was expected to perform the duties of a Mufti. They issued decrees on the legal aspect of everyday problems with which the average citizen was confronted in his daily transactions. Only the teachers who had received an Ijazah (Certificate) for issuing decrees were permitted to function as a Mufti.

As the function of issuing legal decrees was an important duty of the teachers, the writers on education have contributed special chapters on the subject.

The Mufti had to fulfill certain stringent conditions as regards character and knowledge. According to Imam Malik, he did not begin to perform the function of a Mufti until seventy persons testified that he was suitable for the job.

The teachers took a great care in issuing their verdict and would make a frank avowal of their ignorance when they were not sure about it. Once a woman questioned a teacher in the Shahid College at Mardin on religious injunctions concerning menses and the teacher pleaded ignorance. The woman fired up and said, "You flourish the tasselled end of your turban up to your waist and you cannot reply the query of a woman." The teacher retorted with quiet dignity, " If I could answer every question the length of my turban's loose end would have equalled the horn of a bull."

The functions of the Mufti, sometimes interrupted the educational activities of the teachers and they invented interesting devices in order to secure themselves from such distractions. A teacher who stayed in the upper storey of a building received the slip of paper on which was inscribed the debatable point for opinion, in a bucket and draw it up to him and he send back the reply in writing in the same way.

There were a number of other vocations which were closely allied to the above. Some professors acted as witnesses to law papers.

One of the teachers of Ibn Khallikan who lectured in a College used to act in this capacity. This teacher had a pleasant sense of humour which found its expression in his daily contacts with persons who came to him for witnessing the law-papers.

The chancery and the correspondence office provided work for many a teacher. Persons employed in these departments were expected to be good stylists and calligraphists. A good linguist with a flare of literary style had excellent chances for a rise in this line. Ibn Khallikan mentions a scholar Ibn Bari by name from whose pupils he had procured certificates of license. He was a supervisor of chancery and he used to revise the state correspondence despatched to the rulers of foreign states.

Although the job of the secretary was a lucrative one it was not popular with the teachers and it was rare to find a person who carried the functions of the secretary and the teacher side by side.

Art of Copying : Some teachers did an incredible amount of copying. Ibn Jawzi had been preserving the savings of his red pen whenever he was engaged in the writing of the Prophet's traditions and he left instructions that they should be used for warming the water for washing his body after his death. It is amazing to learn that they sufficed for the purpose.

When the total amount of writing work by Tabari, the historian was estimated after his death, it worked out at the rate of fourteen folios daily in his hand and forty folios daily in common type.

For some teachers copying formed a normal feature of their daily programme. It is related of Ahmad bin Abu Daim that he copied manuscripts both for personal use and for payment. When free he could strike away nine Kurasas or more daily, but if otherwise busy he would copy out two or three Kurasas in twenty four hours. It is said that he used to copy out the whole of Al-Qaduri in a single night, but Safdi very much doubts it .

Another savant Abu Said Nahwi used to copy out ten folios before proceeding to the court where he acted as a judge in an honorary capacity. He used to maintain himself entirely by copying manuscripts . Some teachers spread their copying programme over an year and copy one important work or more annually which they would send to a prince or a noble for sale.

The reputation, the scholarship and the aesthetic skill of the copyist determined the price of a manuscript.

In the case of distinguished scholars, the manuscripts copied by them were highly prized for the accuracy of the text.

Copying was adopted as a leisure time occupation on account of sheer economic necessity in most cases, but in certain instances it provided the teachers with spare money for innocent pleasures which they shared with their pupils. The author of Shaqaiq remarks how a scholar used to copy out manuscripts and from the proceeds of the sale they gave feasts to their students during the month of Ramadan.

The Dress : Authorities on education often lay down rules and regulations concerning the dress of the teachers. In a society which observed great punctiliousness in matters of costume because of its vital and symbolic relationship with the social status of the person, the teachers had to maintain certain decorum in dress, speech and general behaviour. The formality of court life might have influenced the teachers also to some extent in this case, but their primary motive in keeping a good standard in sartorial matters was to maintain the dignity of the profession.

Imam Abu Hanifa used to say, "Make your turbans more imposing, your sleeves more ample so that learning and those who profess it might not be looked down upon."

Hammad, the son of Imam Abu Hanifa relates that his father was fond of using scent. When he proceeded on his way he was known by the fragrance which preceded him. He uses a costly cheddar which was once priced at thirty dinars.

Shaikhul Islam Harwi used to issue forth from his house clad in splendid raiments and mounted on a noble steed and he used to say that he did all this in order to maintain the prestige of religion.

In fact teachers whose assemblies were visited by the ruling princes and the nobility must have devoted some attention to their dress and general arrangement of their assembly. Such was the case with Imam Malik whose class had been attended by two Abbaside Caliphs who had travelled from Baghdad with the express desire to study his great collection of Traditions with him.

Imam Malik maintained the dignity of his high status by keeping an impressive assembly and richly equipment. Once a savant criticised his practice of employing a door keeper. Malik quoted in reply the following verse of the Quran, "Tell O Prophet, who has the authority to make unlawful what God has bestowed on his creation and fragrant delicacies" implying thereby that there was no religious injunction against the use of fine raiment and enjoying a good meal.

Tilsan which is considered by some writers to be the precursor of the academic gown was not the distinctive mark of the scholarly class in all parts of the Islamic world. In Iraq and Spain, it was a popular style of dress for the common people, only in Spain the styles in which it was worn by the savants and the laity were different.

According to Ibn Khallikan, Qadi Abu Yusuf, the chief judge of Harun-al-Rashid was the first savant to order a special kind of dress for the scholarly class, and this dress has been the hallmark of this class since those days. It included a cloak in addition to a Tilsan.

It appears that this additional cloak was a special contribution of the great Qadi to the fashion of the scholarly world otherwise Tilsan was the usual robe of honour with which the scholars were invested by princes and the nobility in those days. It was also the usual dress of a scholar in the days of early Abbasides.

Asmai for instance used to visit the nobility in his old Tilsan and he relates how he received it as a gift from an Abbaside noble.

It appears that while Tilsan or a cloak was worn by one and all, the rank of a scholar was often known by the cut of his cloak, its colour, his head veil and sometimes by the accoutrement of his ride.

The common dress of scholars and judges in Egypt according to Sayuti was a loose longish cloak opening on the shoulders and a shash or piece of cloth with its teaselled end between the shoulders and in the direction of the left shoulder, others wore a Farjiah while some used a Tilsan. The Khatib's cloak was black in colour with a black Shash and a black head-veil. They used a cloak round in form.

The robes of honour conferred on the scholars and judges were made of wool and were without any Taraz (ornamentation). They were invested with a head-veil also.

The chief judge of the Shafite sect was distinguished by his Tarhah (head gear).

Although the Ijazah ceremony was a private business between the teacher and the taught and it was not accompanied by any investiture function like the convocation in a modern university, it appears ,that the teacher authorised the pupil to wear the Tilsan, the distinguishing mark of a scholar. It was a rather unusual sight to come across a person with a Tilsan attending lectures because he was considered to have completed his education.

Ibn Khallikan remarks that four hundred persons with Tilsan used to attend the lectures of Imam Baud Zahiri. It implies the universal esteem in which he was held even by those who had already graduated and received their academic gown.

Headgear : The teachers used a simple and light turban for every day use while a more imposing one for ceremonial occasions. But different usages were observed in various parts of the Islamic world. Al-Maqarri saw a savant of Mereia, in Spain appearing bare headed before the king.

Social etiquette demanded that the ministers and the king should be visited in proper uniform and the small turban (Shamlah) which most of the teachers usually wore was not the proper dress for such ceremonial occasions ; nevertheless there were savants who would visit the ministers with the little turban on. When once Maula Yusuf bin Hussain-al-Karmasani was asked by the minister to see him immediately when the Maula issued forth from the mosque after offering prayers, he went straight to him without changing his little turban for another more worthy of the occasion and when the minister objected to it, he replied brusquely that he had presented himself to his Creator in the same dress and did not consider it undignified if he appeared before the minister in the same.

There were teachers who wore a crown on their head which was capped by a small turban. The savants borrowed the fashion most probably from the mystics who very often gave evidence of remarkable ingenuity and taste in inventing various styles of headgear, it being an essential part of the dress of mystical orders.

Academic Gown : The scholarly class, both teachers and students had their academic uniform with the distinction that the graduate's dress was the same as that of the teacher's uniform. Ibn Khallikan has mentioned Thiabah Ahi-ul-ilm (the uniform of the learned) and he ascribes the fashion to Qadi Abu Yusuf, the famous courtier and judge of Harun.'

As a rule teachers and pupils were expected to maintain the professional dignity by dressing themselves in a suitable manner. Imposing turbans, long flowing garments and loose sleeves were the hallmark of the scholarly class in those days.

It is not known whether the academic uniform was supplied by the college although there was a rich abundant of endowments for specific purposes, but there is evidence to show that vestments suitable for the dignity of a scholar were given to him in case of special merit.

When Shahabuddin Suhrawardi went to Allepo, he stayed in the Halawiyyah College. He was clad in coarse garments, but when the Head of the institution discovered his pre-eminence among the scholars he ordered for him the '*anabiyyah*' over garment, an undercloth and a bodice without sleeves. It seems that the anabiyyah was a special mark of the scholars in those days.

The colleges did not hold a convocation for investing the pupils with the academic dress but the mystics used to celebrate an investiture ceremony and every disciple received a Khirqa or Dalq (cloak) of a form and colour befitting his attainments in the spiritual and moral sense.

According to Shahabuddin Suhrawardi, 'The Khirqa is presented to one who has a good report with the Sheikh'.

The choice of the colour and form of the disciple's garments depended upon Sheikh's vision, 'If he sees that his inclination is for splendid and soft raiments he awards him the coarse variety of Khirqa, but if he sees that his inclination is for the coarse by way of hypocrisy and pretension, he clothes him in soft silk.'

According to Haneburg the Western Universities have borrowed their academic gown from the Islamic world. His opinion has been criticised, but there is no doubt that the academic costume in the Islamic world had been established long before the beginning of the first universities in Europe. It cannot be laid down with certainty how far the colleges influenced the West in this respect, but it is possible that the costume and the investiture rituals of the mystics might have set the vogue in this direction.

These fads and fashions were equally popular in the East and the West and everywhere they carried a prestige characteristic of the particular form of dress.

When a Christian doctor came to see Ibn Mitran of Damascus (died 587 A.H.) a Christian convert and personal physician to Sultan Salahuddin, the visitor had on him a tightly fitting suit of brocade, blue in colour with wrapper for the head. Ibn Mitran told him not to move about so often in the dress of a European doctor ; he advised him to change it for one more acceptable to the Muslims as he was not following the fashion of the Muslim physicians and forthwith he ordered for him a long flowing anabiyya cloak and a bodice without sleeves.

10

Funds for Education

One of the chief sources of income for the maintenance of these institutions was the monetary assistance by the state, which was offered without any restriction of code rules or grant-in-aid regulations ; this help was rendered in a rich variety of forms.

There were rulers, who had allocated a certain percentage of their annual revenue for educational purposes. For instance Nur-ud-Din Zangi used to spend the entire revenue of the town of Damascus on its colleges and mosques, half of the proceeds went for the maintenance of the Friday mosque while he divided the other half into eleven parts, two of which were allocated to the Shafiyya and Hanafiyya colleges. Ibn Batuta mentions the ease of a Sultan in Asia Minor, who devoted one-third of his revenues to the maintenance of colleges and monastries in the realm.

There were others, who made grants in a lump sum for education and works of public welfare. The grand Vazir Nizam-ul-Mulk had earmarked 700,000 Dinars annually from the public exchequer for his college in addition to an equal amount of grant which came from his privy purse. He had settled one-tenth of his private income on educational institutions.

It is related that once Malik Shah, his master criticised the lavish expenditure which he had made on the college. In his opinion, he could raise such an army with the help of that money, which would have razed Constantinople, the stronghold of the Byzantine Empire to the ground. The great Vazir was deeply moved by his remarks and told the king that the blade of his soldier's sabre did not exceed two yards in its swoop while their arrows could not reach beyond three hundred footsteps, but he was rearing up an army the shafts of whose prayers will scale the very heavens.

Ibn Zubayr visited Egypt during the reign of Salah-ud-Din and has supplied instructive details of the patronage of learning by the king. According to him, the Sultan defrayed the entire expenses of the colleges of Misr and Cairo from the public treasury and the total budget came up to 2,000 Egyptian Dinars or 4,000 Momina per mensem. In addition to this, the expenses of the wandering scholars and the aliens who visited Egypt in pursuit of learning were met from the state coffers. Every person, who came to Alexandria in search of knowledge was supplied well furnished residential quarters and was provided with a generous allowance. He had the facilities of Turkish bath and medical attendance at home or in the hospital, free of charge.

Fiscal Sources

According to a royal decree, any person founding a college in the town of Damascus was to be paid the bill for its total expenditure from the royal treasury. The salaries of the teachers, who taught in the institutions within his kingdom amounted to 300,000 dinars annually and the amount was paid from the public exchequer.

Nur-ud-Din Zangi, his able successor, who was renowned for his love of learning went one better. In addition to earmarking a portion of the revenue for educational purposes he made rich endowments from his privy purse. He spent eighteen thousand

Suria Dinars per mensem on the college teachers of Damascus and Allepo and twenty two-thousand Dinars on the mosques and colleges of Himat and Hims. These endowments were maintained long after he had passed away. In certain cases, the ruling princes allocated salaries to the teachers and in others assigned to them the proceeds of the property given in endowment. Sultan Salah-ud-Din had sanctioned a monthly salary of eleven Dinars for the principal of Sayufiyya College. The Qamhiyya College or "the College of the Wheat" received its name from the proceeds in kind which came from the property endowed by Sultan Salah-ud-Din for the purpose of teachers' remuneration.

While the average philanthropist, so common in the Middle ages founded a college or two, there were large hearted benefactors like Nizam-ul-Mulk, who laid the foundation of a whole network of such institutions and there is at least one instance where another Maecena of the age planned a whole town for the advancement of learning.

Rashid-ud-Din Fadhlullah, the Prime Minister of the Mongol ruler Ghazan Khan founded at Tabriz a city named Rab-i-Rashidi and his bounty attracted the greatest scholars and most eminent professional practitioners. There were 200 Quran readers with fixed salaries for reciting the Holy book and they had forty selected acolytes for training. The scholar's street provided accommodation for four hundred savants with suitable salaries and allowances, who directed and supervised the studies of one thousand students, who had flocked from distant lands for education and instruction. There were fifty skilful physicians, renowned practitioners in various systems of medicine, who resided in the street of the Healers and had ten students assigned to each with definite duties in the hospital.

The endowments made by the rulers from the public exchequer or their privy purse took various forms, according to the popular usage in the country or the conditions under which the endowment was made. A common practice was to assign the proceeds of income from arable lands or other property to a particular foundation and when Caliph Mustansir Billah opened his college, he endowed it with a number of villages and other property, whose annual income exceeded 70,000 Mithqals in gold. A list of the names of these hamlets is available in Zahabi.

Court's Patronage

Sometimes the ruling class made endowments for the benefit of some renowned college outside the kingdom and Al-Azhar has been the beneficiary of such an endowment by a Tunisian ruler.

There were also other heads of public revenue which were earmarked for educational purposes. Jahangir, the Mughal ruler of India decreed that all the property left by a trader, who had died in the kingdom of the Great Mughal and which lapsed to the Public Treasury in absence of any legal claimant was henceforth to be utilised for the foundation, maintenance and rehabilitation of educational institutions and other works of public welfare. In the words of the author of Naasir-i-Jahangiri, the Farman had a profound influence in tenanting once again those colleges and schools which had turned into a wilderness in the past.

But even more important than the endowments and benefactions of the ruling class and the aristocracy was the active support and help of the people and the spirit of reverence and love for learning which inspired them ; therein lay the chief strength of the Islamic educational system.

One of the earliest colleges was established through private donations when the people of Nishapur invited the great divine Abu Bakr Foruk to their town and subscribed generously for the building of a college for the savant. The accounts of important towns of the Islamic world glow with a rich and varied description of the colleges raised through the benefactions of private individuals.

It appears that in certain cases, trade guilds and other social groups were responsible for establishing educational institutions of the higher grade. A number of colleges were associated with the names of trade guilds and although in the case of the college of Warraqin in Misr we know definitely that it received its name because it was located in the street of Warraqin, the same may not apply to the case of the two colleges founded in the town of Allepo, a great industrial centre where such guilds must have been rich and influential. These two institutions were called the college of the glass makers and the college of the ironsmiths respectively.

According to Ibn Khaldun, the usage of making endowments for educational purposes was popular in Egypt among the aristocracy. The chief motive in his opinion was the preservation of the property in the interest of the eldest son who was to manage the trust on behalf of the institution for which it had been made. But he adds that all were not actuated by this motive and the tradition of making charitable donations for education was getting strong in the country. These benefactions took various forms and included arable land, gardens, inns, street shops, Turkish baths and even flour mills. Sometimes savants and scholars of means made a personal adventure in this field and laid foundation of the colleges which were erected and maintained by themselves. Ibn Batuta mentions a family of learned scholars who maintained a College in their home town and the family members formed the teaching staff of the institution.

As a general rule there were no restrictions on the persons who could avail of the financial assistance given out of the income of an endowment, but in case the benefactors had stated clearly the conditions which were to be fulfilled before an allowance was granted, they were adhered to by the Nazir

(Manager) of the Waqf. For instance certain donors made endowments in favour of a particular sect while in one case at least the benefactors had clearly stated that it was exclusively meant for the Arabs. But such individual distinctions were not a common feature of the endowment system. Sometimes the donor indicated in the deed a clear preference for people coming from a particular area and it was not necessary that they should be his compatriots. Sultan Nuruddin Zangi for instance made an endowment in Damascus for the people of Maghrib.

The management of these trusts and endowments rested entirely in the hands of the teachers of the college and in the accounts of these colleges one invariably comes across the phrase, "endowed in favour of the savants of the Hanafite, Shafiite or Malikite faith." The endowment was managed by the teachers in most cases through a Nazir. According to Ibn Zubayr there were thirty colleges in Baghdad whose endowments were managed by the teachers themselves. In the case of the Nizamiyya, the first manager of the trust was the son of the founder, Khawaja Abu Nasr bin Nizam-ul Mulk, who managed the property with the help of the teachers.

Even in the presence of a department of public endowments in the country, some part of its management remained in the hands of the teachers. For instance in the Al-Azhar, the heads of the various Rawaqs or hostels have been performing the function of the manager for the trusts partially while the major portion of the trust was under the supervision of the State department. But this department is a recent addition to the system of administration and in all probability, the teachers held undivided responsibility for the management of the endowments in the past.

Sometimes the State held judicial enquiries into the terms of the Waqf deed in order to see that the income is being utilised for the specific purposes indicated by the benefactor. There is the case of Nuruddin Zangi how he made a public enquiry into the Waqf deed of the great Mosque of Damascus in the presence of all the savants and chief personages of the town and how the finest and most subtle distinctions of law were thrashed in the presence of the august assembly.

Love for Learning

As a general rule the Waqf deeds were honoured by the kings and the courts and they were respected by the public opinion. But there were exceptions and endowments were sometime misappropriated by unscrupulous persons although the irresistible pressure of public opinion got the wrong redressed in most cases. The history of the college of Amir Jamaluddin Astadar in Cairo indicates the vicissitudes through which a Waqf deed might pass.

The founder of this college had established six chairs for various branches of learning and had endowed them in a magnificient manner. Every pupil pursuing a course of study in the college was to receive three Ratl of bread daily and thirty dirhams per mensem as stipend while the teachers received a salary of three hundred dirhams a month and the surplus of the proceeds of the trust was to go to his progeny. The founder did not own the site personally but obtained it in exchange for a tract owned by the State.

Upon his death doubts were raised about the legitimacy of the exchange and the conditions of the Waqf deed and when the judges decreed the deed null and void, the king Malik Nasir purchased the site for 12000 dinars from the descendents of the founder and ordered the cancellation of the waqf deed. A new Waqf deed was drawn up whereby the clause which made the descendants of the founder, the beneficiaries of the surplus was abrogated. A portion of the property left by the founder which could suffice for meeting the conditions of the trust was retained for the college while the rest was partly constituted into a trust in the interest of his progeny and partly made into an endowment for the tomb of the founder. When Malik Nasir died, the inheritors who were highly influential people got it annulled in their interest and the endowment reverted to them as trustees. This incurred the indignation of some mystics who belonged to the college and they proved in the court, that the original founder had appointed katib-al-sir a state functionary as the trustee and the inheritors had no claim to the property. The matter came to a close when the management of the trust finally reverted to the State functionary, who had been entrusted with this duty according to the original deed.

Miqrizi, from whose book the account has been taken gives a detailed account of the proceedings of the case at its various stages. The whole episode throws light on the scrupulous care taken in preserving the form if not the, spirit of the educational and religious trusts and a genuine desire of the people to utilise the proceeds of a Waqf for the specific purposes for which it bad been made.

11

Methods of Education

Competent authorities on Educational Method like Zarnuji quote a well known Tradition in support of maintaining a harmonious balance between work and play and keeping a healthy control on over-work and strenuous efforts which may cause a heavy strain for the pupil. The Tradition runs, "Verily you should act with kindness and restraint in matters of religion and don't be too hard on your Nafs (Baser Self) in the course of devotion and prayer. It is your beast of burden and if you ride it to death in the course of the journey, it will not arrive at the journey's end."

A recognition of the principles of attention and the need of a variety of occupations after continuous application to a specialised form of intellectual activity is borne out by a Tradition in Bukhari, "Read out the Quran as long as your hearts are in it; when tired of recitation, you should stop reading and postpone it for some other occasion."

A change over to other subjects of study and a variety of intellectual occupations was an accepted usage of the companions. Ibn Aqbas would send for poetical works when he got tired of Kalam (Scholastic Philosophy).

The principle was not only observed by the Prophet for the reading of the Quran but he always kept it in view when preparing the programme of his addresses and preaching. According to Abdullah bin Masud, he was not a solemn-looking, awe-inspring figure on the pulpit; he would often indulge in pleasantries in the middle of an edifying discourse and would make attempt to tickle the human side of their nature, so that they may not feel tired and lose interest in the subject.

Frequent Lessons

For this purpose, he appointed particular days in the week for addressing the assembly and Ibn Masud also followed his example in giving only weekly discourses to his audience. When a member of the audience insisted that he should hold a discourse every day, Ibn Masud protested that he did not hold it desirable to make his lectures burdensome and that he made an allowance for his listeners just as the Prophet did.

According to Ibn Masud, the Prophet took into consideration the problem of time and always held the disaffection of the audience as undesirable.

Sowing in Rich Soil : And he always took the greatest care that the seed of truth which he was sowing broadcast should fall into the rich soil where it should blossom forth in full bloom. He enjoins that the teacher should discover the capacity of his pupil and find out how far he is spectible to moral and intellectual influences.

But once he is convinced of the genuine enthusiasm of the pupil for knowledge and moral progress, he is prepared to provide all kinds of facilities for him. The copying out of Traditions was banned in the earliest stage in order to safeguard the authenticity of the Quranic Text which might not be confused with the Traditions, but considerable concession was made in this respect later on and on the representation of a visitor who complained of bad memory, the Prophet advised him to avail of his right hand and made a sign implying the art of writing.

A number of Traditions deal with one of the most fundamental problem of class instruction, viz the adaptation of the teaching material to the intellectual capacity of the pupil.

According to a Tradition, "I belong to the group of Prophets and I have been commanded by the Lord to treat people according to their ranks and talk to them according to their intellectual capacity." It is further confirmed by the verse of the Quran, "Don't give away your property to the fools. A tradition of the Prophet is strongly reminiscent of the parable of Bible on casting pearls before the swine and seems to be a further amplification of the same." "Don't put a diamond necklace on the swine because wisdom is better than diamonds and the person who thinks low of wisdom is worse than the swine."

Another Tradition that lays strictures on imparting knowledge to the undeserving has a rather poignant significance for the great tragedy of Jesus Christ.

> "Whenever a person says something to a people which is beyond their understanding, it results in Fitnah or a period of trial and travail for a part of these people."

It is interesting to discover that while Jesus has emphasised upon knowledge and its benefit for the individual, Muhammad (PBUH) has referred pointedly to the social purpose for which knowledge is to be utilized and it influences on men in general.

Bridle-bit of Hell-fire : The above Tradition which emphasizes the imparting of knowledge to the deserving seems to be apparently in contradiction with another where he condemned a scholar with the bridle-bit of hell-fire if he kept his knowledge a secret.

This seeming contradiction is resolved by the remarks of a scholar who was approached for enlightenment by a person of some intellectual limitations. When the savant kept silent on his query, his interlocutor reminded him of the Tradition about the bridle-bit. The savant retorted that he should move off with his bridle of fire because this function of briding him up would be performed more properly by a person who had the capacity to understand and had approached a scholar for the receiving of knowledge.

The Prophet was always keenly conscious of the limitations of his audience and he would always adapt his style of address and even its vocabulary and idiomatic phraseology to the capacity and the cultural background of the person whom he addressed.

Knowledge of Dialects : It is interesting to learn that he had a knowledge of the finer shades of differences in grammatical usage and vocabulary as regards different dialects spoken by various tribes in the Peninsula and would address them accordingly.

For instance, in the Tradition of Amiri he said, "Sal Anka," while in accordance with the correct grammatical usage he should have said Sal Anma Shita. In this case, he used the dialectal usage of the tribe of Banu Amir.

According to Atbah bin Saad, he used and in place of – and introduced the nunnation of 'ayn' according to the usage of his tribe. He seemed to have some knowledge of the Abysinian language. During the Meccan period, two groups of Muslims migrated to Abysinian on two occasions and there was a fair sprinkling of Abysinian slaves in Hijaz.

As a downtrodden section of the community, they had a special claim on the Prophet and there is evidence to show that he knew a few words of their language. In one case he used the word (beautiful in Abysinian), when he was showing an embroidered sheet of Yeman to Amamah, an infant granddaughter who had seen the light of the day in Abyssinia.

In another case he used the term for 'murder' a word which is of Abysinian origin. According to Abu Hurayrah he is said to have used a Persian phrase also.

Style of Epistles : When dictating his epistles to his correspondence secretaries, the language and style were adapted to the cultural and literary background of the addressee. According to Qadi Ayaz there is a remarkable difference between the style of epistles addressed to the higher classes and to the masses.

Qadi Ayaz gives extracts from his letters to Zi-al-Shaar al-Hamadani, Wail bin Hajr-al-Kindi and others, the rulers of Hadrmut and Yemen and they are a fine specimen of literary expression in rhythmic prose.

The style of these letters is in a sharp contrast with the document which he ordered to be drawn up on the subject of Sadaqa (charity).

Art of Adaptability : The main aim was not to parade his knowledge of these linguisitic curiosities but to bring home to the people he addressed, the great message and spoke to them in a language which would open windows into their hearts. On certain occasions the Companions would ask him to explain the unfamiliar phrases and expressions which he used in his interviews on such occasions.

He had acquired this wonderful adaptability on account of his early training both in the language and idiom of the town and the countryside. When the companions expressed their admiration of his style he told with legitimate pride that he belonged to the Quraish (who were townspeople) and was brought up among the Bani Saad a tribe living in the countryside.

Speaking Power

The addresses which the Prophet delivered on various occasions from the pulpit or outside are couched in a simple, direct and forceful language. They are a pleasant combination of high idealism, universal truths and hard realities of concrete situations. There are no flourishes of oratory, none of its frills and furbelows, they throb all along with suppressed spiritual fervour and restraint.

As for effect and inspiration, none could wield this powerful weapon to greater advantage. He personally claimed to be the most eloquent of all the Arabs, one who was sent with the most comprehensive of Word, and his claim had abundant justification. He was a scion of the Quraish and had received his early training among Banu Saad, the two people famous for their mastery of the language throughout the country.

Address Techniques : The style and the technique of his addresses require a careful study not only because they are literary masterpieces but because they functioned as potent force in moulding the style of whole generations of teachers and preachers. One of the most important problem for the teacher and orator is to attract the attention of the audience and the Prophet would arouse them by a word of exclamation or by positing a question. He initiated his soul stirring address on the Mountain of Safa with the call "Ya Sabahah", an exclamation used when a tribe is unexpectedly raided early in the morning. And in fact the whole of the Peninsula was being stormed at that period by the forces of evil and ignorance, an affliction which was certainly more disastrous than the raid of a neighbouring tribe. Their curiosity aroused, the Prophet asked whether he should inform them of an enemy which assailed them every morning and evening.

Motives and Purposes

These addresses were extremely powerful and dynamic weapons for the moulding of public opinion, and proved useful during that critical stage of society when great changes spiritual, social and cultural were on the horizon.

While the ancient addresses of Jahiliyyah were mainly directed for inciting people to war, the Prophet utilised this dynamic weapon for a variety of purposes. They were used for spiritual counselling, warnings and blessings proclamations and announcements. Through these orations he called people to religion, self-surrender and self-sacrifice. The address of Hajjat ul- Wida is a supreme example of an inspired oration on individual rights, that of the Mount of Safa on spiritual bearings delivered in the language and the style of a harbinger of fateful news.

A Challenging Question : Sometimes his address opened with a challenging question and his address on the battlefield of Hunayn is strongly reminiscent of the beautiful triology of questions posited in the Sura Wadhdhuha. "O People of the Ansar," he began, "Didn't I find you stragglers from the Path and God blessed you through me." And the audience replied, "Verily the Prophet of God is the custodian of truth." He continued positing a chain of questions in the same vein and every time the audience hailed him with an 'aye'. But after the climax came the anti-climax, the positive interrogation was followed by the negative. In an outburst of enthusiasm for their dignified acquiescence he declaimed passionately, "But why do not you say that you came to us as a fugitive from home and we gave you shelter; you were in want and we lavished our sympathy on you; you were friendless and we befriended you."

Then came the summing up of this grand oration with an appeal to those members of the audience who were dissatisfied with the division of the spoils. Once more he put them a concluding question which clinched the whole issue. "Won't you prefer," he says," that others' share should be camels and goats while yours the Prophet of God himself."

Rhythm of Repetition : A formidable weapon in the hands of a speaker is the judicious repetition of certain words or phrases and the Prophet could use this device with tremendous effect. His address on the occasion of the last pilgrimage is a supreme example of this technique as harmonised with the device of interrogation.

They are not the frills and flounces of forced rhetorics but the blossoming up of an inner urge for rhythm of thought and expression. It synchronises with the tone of the audience which pulsates with that of the speaker. This progressive repetition and questioning raises the whole process to the level of a shared experience between the speaker and the audience. The well-timed question, with its reply echoed back from the audience weaves constantly a meshwork of emotional and spiritual ties which helps in the growth of an atmosphere of sympathy and understanding.

Some of his remarks are unrivalled in sustained emotion and simple and dignified beauty of expression. One would have expected a funeral address on the death of his son Ibrahim but it was too great a sorrow for an address. When a Companion made some remark on his bursting into tears, he said, "The eye sheds tears and the heart is full of sorrow and we don't say anything except that we have surrendered ourselves to the Will of the Lord and O Ibrahim, we are certainly heart-striken by thy bereavement."

***Rhythm of the Entire Personality*:** In his method of delivery he appears to have expressed himself not merely by his word of mouth but by his entire personality. According to 'Abdullah biṅ Umar,' he was discoursing on how God would hold heaven and earth in his mighty grip. He closed his fist and then unclosed it while his whole body swayed from one side to another and the pulpit shook under him. Sometimes he was so moved by the rising upsurge of spiritual fervour that he would repeat a phrase more than once and then make an eloquent pause in his speech. It was no mere oratorial gesture, rather it was an expression of the rhythm which regulated his inner life.

Dramatic Air : One of his early addresses which he gave on the Mount of Safa has a dramatic air of extreme realism. He has used in this oration the technique of a vitalised dialogue between the speaker and the audience with great effect. The great queries and the rejoinder echoed from a thousand lips covers up the gulf between the two and merges the divergent tendencies of thought into one big unified current.

When the verse "*Wa anzar Ashiratika al aqrabin*" (Warn thy relations the nearest ones) was revealed to him, he got up the Mount of Safa and spoke out, "O people of the Quraish' and the Quraish who were obviously surprised to hear his ringing tones from the top of a hill said, "Come along, Muhammad is calling you from the heights of the hill." Then they collected round him and said, "What is the matter with you." Thereupon he said, "Would you believe me if I warn you that there is an army under the foot of this hill." They said, "Yes, you have never been charged with falsehood and we have never experienced anything untrue from thee". Thereupon he said, "I am going to forewarn you about a terrible punishment;" and then he called out the various branches of Quraish one by one by name and said, "God has ordained that I should warn my kith and kin and I have no authority to benefit you in this world or the next except that you say the formula "There is no God but Allah."

Pauses as Pointers : The principle of carefully planned pauses and the introduction of small intervals for cogitation and the searching of hearts, the principle of gradation rising by degrees to a certain climax of words and moral fervour, the principle of recurrence and repetition, all are evidenced in his well known address on Hajjat-al-Wida.

He delivered this address while seated on a red-coloured camel, and the mastication suds flowed down on the spectators below; a boy among the audience could picture clearly the impressive spectacle when he listened to the address while standing on the shoulders of his father who was seated on a camel.

The address opened with a pathetic note in which he declared, "O men, listen to my words because I don't know whether I would ever meet you again after this year, at this place."

These fateful words must have quickened the whole gathering into an attitude of great expectancy. The last words of a Prophet must be worth listening and remembering.

Then he posited a query and said, "What day is this," and the audience replied, "God and his Prophet know better." Thereupon came an extremely eloquent pause. He paused so long that the audience thought that perhaps he was going to rename the day. Then he spoke out: "Is it not the day of sacrifice!. And they replied, "It is so."

Then he asked, "And what month is it?" And again came the same reply followed by a long pause and the people began to think that he was about to give it another name. Then he asked, "Is not it the month of Zil Hijj?

Then he asked, "What town is this?"

This series of questions following by three intervals, crowded with furious thinking and expectancy on the part of the audience was the most appropriate introduction for what was to follow.

According to another version he had asked, "What day was the most auspicious?" And the people said, 'This day, "and what month, and what town," were the next two questions.

After this came the climax when he declared.

> "Your blood and your properties are as sacred as trust as the sanctity of this day of yours, in this month of yours, in this town of yours."

Then he gave them his parting words of counsel with the tragic air created by the spell of his opening words about the approaching end.

> "Beware! don't be led astray from the path and kill each other. Beware, have I brought home to you the Truth?"

> "Beware, one who is present may carry my words to him who is not present because some of those who are absent may preserve my words more faithfully than those who are present. Beware haven't I propagated the Truth," and according to a version, at the end of this grand oration he turned towards Heaven and said, "O God I have brought Thy words home, O God be these my witness."

When the Prophet addressed people his eyes became red, his voice would grow high and his emotions were aroused. He looked very much like one who delivered the warning about the impending attack of the enemy who would come down in the morning or evening.

On such occasions he would say, "I and the Day of judgement have been sent like this," and with this he would join the forefingers and the middle one together."

***Address on a Battlefield*:** The address given after the Battle of Hunayn was delivered in an extremely delicate situation. The spoils of war obtained during the campaign seemed to have surpassed all expectations and some ill-feeling was created in the course of distribution, the disaffected parties being the Ansar of Medina and Arabs of the desert.

The address is a noble attempt to resolve the situation by a heart moving appeal to the Ansars. The Prophet recounts in his deeply emotional style the spiritual blessings which he had brought to the Ansars and when the climax had been reached, he unfolds the anticlimax by describing the support and help which the Ansars brought to him and after a survey of the credit and the debit sides of this grand human change, he makes them realise the great union of the soul with which they are wedded together. He sums up with the convincing note "Let others take worldly wealth, because for you is the Prophet."

His dramatic entry into Mecca and his short cryptic speech in the serene setting of the Holy sanctuary of Mecca had all the impressive grandeur of a Greek play.

He entered Mecca on a dromedary and made seven circumambulations of the Holy sanctuary. Then he took the keys of the Kaaba from Uthman bin Talhah, its keeper and stood in silent dignity at the gate of the Kaaba. He broke the solemn spell of silence with these words.

> "There is no God but Allah. He is without compeer. Honoured is His promise (Waadu-hu), supported was His Believer (Abdu-hu), routed were the rival groups by the One (Wahdu-hu). Beware that all matters of pride, whether blood money or wealth, are under these feet of mine except the service of the Holy sanctuary or provision of water to the pilgrims."

Then he called out, "O tribe of the Quraish, verily God has taken away from you, the arrogance of Jahiliyyah and the pride of lineage."

> "Man derives their origin from Adam and Adam was created out of clay."

Then he said, "O tribe of the Quraish, what do you think I am going to do with you!" They said, "Beneficence – thou art a beneficent brother and the son of a beneficent brother" and he declared, "Well go off, you are all free."

Spiritual Counselling : The above oration had a dominantly political air about it but most of his addresses were devoted to spiritual counselling, the vanity of man and his ambitions and its baneful influence on his sense of social responsibilities.

In one of his addresses he has made a scathing criticism of the self-complacency and the egoistic nonchalance of man and how blindly he persists in his course of evil. "O men, it seems to us as if death has been ordained to all except ourselves and the duties are imposed on all except on us, and we accompany the dead on their funerals with the knowledge that we are sending them on a journey whence few return to us. We put them in the graves and enjoy their inheritance as if we will continue for ever after them.

> "We have been oblivious of all counsel and we feel secure from all calamities. Blessed is one whose sins have occupied him from sinning against others and who gives in charity from what he has earned in an honest way."

The note of warning which he often struck in his speeches gave him the air of the guardian angel or the watchman of the tribe.

In one of his addresses he compares himself to a Raid or the person who is sent by the tribe to search for a water hole or pasture ground in the desert.

He says, "I am unto you as a Raid is for his tribe and a Raid never tells lies to his people."

> "And By God you will die (as surely) as you sleep, you will be resuscitated as surely as you awake. You will have to render account for all what you have done. You will be rewarded for your good with good and you will be repaid for your evil with evil and verily heaven is eternal and hell is also eternal and those of you who have been warned first are nearest to the Judgement Day."

Historic Orations: His addresses were both long and short and their length was intuitively adapted to the needs of the situation. Generally, the Prophet did not like to deliver lengthy addresses and he approved of a person who shortened his address and lengthened his prayer on Fridays. According to Ibn Masud, "he would cut short his address in order to save us from inconvenience."

But when needed, he would give long orations. The text of one of his addresses which he delivered in the course of an afternoon was "Verily the world is a verdant fruit. Beware and God hath made you his vicegerent in it in order to test how you perform your duties."'

He opened his address after the afternoon prayer and continued with it till there was left nothing of the sunlight except its rosy reflection on the fringes of the palm boughs.

But sometimes these addresses were gems of artistic brevity and his successors often followed his example in this respect. For instance, the first address which Umar Ibn Khattab delivered after his election as the Caliph comprised one single cryptic announcement on the duties of the ruler and the rights of the ruled.

He said, "O men, verily by God the weakest is the strongest with me until I acquire his right for him and the strongest is the weakest with me until I wrest the rights of others from him." And after this brief and cryptic statement he descended from the pulpit. The simple and direct way in which he summed up the political rights and obligations of the ruler and ruled on the day of his election was as neat and perfect as a crystal. He said on another occasion:

> "Verily people are like a docile camel which follows its guide, and it is for the guide to see where he leads it to and by the God of Kaaba I will certainly guide you along the right path."

Literary Flavour : The Companions who had passed their whole lives in the closest association with the Prophet would sometimes marvel at this unexpected manifestation of literary florescence.

Abu Bakr had a fine taste for poetry and had the opportunity of listening to some of the greatest orators. He had a knowledge of the literary styles of various tribes. Once he was so much impressed by the expressive language of the Prophet that he could not help asking him, "Who taught thee?" and the answer was, "My God, and what an excellent training He has imparted to me."

His closest Companions would often marvel when he conversed freely in the dialect of the tribal groups who visited him from all parts of Arabia. When Ali saw him talking with the deputation from Banu Nahd he said, "O Prophet of God, we are the descendants of the same ancestor but we observe you talking to the Arab deputations in a language which we don't understand."

An eloquent example of the Prophet's knowledge of different dialects spoken or written in Arabia is his letter which he had dictated to Wail bin Hajr al-Kindi, one of the princes of Hadrmut.

The letter is notable for the choice of vocabulary and the selection of words and phrases which has been carefully chosen to impress a grandiloquent prince of a high lineage. The words have a phonic, rhythmic and picturesque value of their own which accords with the intellectual and social background of the person to whom the letter had been addressed.

For instance, the words ' Ya taraffla' meaning, Wail bin Hajr 'trails his skirts' over the rest of the princes, brings forcefully to the mind a picturesque image which cannot be so graphically represented by the words 'Yatrasa'.

Other words which describe punishments laid down for

various crimes echo the sense by their harsh, crisp and impressive notes.

Tete-a-Tete Discussions : But his method of tete-a-tete discussion and everyday conversation with persons whom he buttonholed on the wayside or in the mosque has a far more educative value for the teacher than his ceremonial orations. He was most epigrammatic in his sayings and had an unparalleled mastery over a happy and graceful turn of word and phrase. The rhyming of words and phrases, the rhythm of thought and idea, the use of contrasts and comparisons were some of the devices which made his words stay in memory like a haunting music, and his way of expressing them left a lasting impression on the mind. Years after, the Companions could visualise the exact pose and manner in which the Prophet had related a particular Tradition.

Eloquent Fingers : Once he was relating a story out of the history of Israelites and described a mother suckling her babe. While narrating the Tradition later on, Abu Hurayrah added that he could even now picture before his mind the Prophet sucking his finger to show the movements of the child. He had an intuitive knowledge of teaching technique and would explain the abstract through the concrete, the complex by means of the simple. He would often use his hands and fingers in impressing an idea on his audience, the latter playing a specially expressive role in the process. He would indicate close proximity by referring to the closeness of the middle finger with the finger next to the thumb.

Once he compared the Muslims to the foundation stones of an edifice which re-inforce one another and he illustrated it by placing the fingers of one hand in between the fingers of the other.

Most of the Traditions which involved an action which could be demonstrated with the help of the movement of the fingers of the hand describe also the actual movement made by the Prophet on that occasion.

He has described the miser and the generous in an extremely apt simile. They are both like those persons who have coats of mails on them. They are so close fitting that their arms appear to have stuck fast to their chests and their necks and when the generous person desires to give away, his coat of mail becomes wider and longer till it is so ample that it reaches his finger tips and trails over his footsteps and obliterates the foot-prints. As for the miser, his coat of mail shrinks up and every link of it refuses to be flexible and refuses to yield.

The Tradition has been narrated by Abu Hurayrah who tells that when the Prophet described the shrunken coat of mail, he pointed with his fingers towards his neck and made as if he desired to stretch it further but was not able to do so.

He would avail of every day situations for the purpose of moralising. The simple and direct reasoning associated with concrete situation went home and had the desired effect. Once when he was passing by the corpse of a kid he asked whether anyone would buy it for any price. On receiving a reply in the negative he told that the worldly riches were more contemptible in the eyes of the Lord than the dead body of this kid.

On another occasion a captive woman was brought into the presence of the Prophet and her breast was laden with milk. From time to time she would catch hold of any babe in the assembly, clap him to her breast and give him a suck. The Prophet was moved and asked the Companions whether that woman would consign her child to the flames, "Never", came the reply. "Verily", said the Prophet, "God is more compassionate on his Creation than this mother on the child."

Historic Doctrine : Sometimes he would impress a lesson by what may be described as a practical demonstration of the Doctrine of Natural Consequences. The Prophet had emphasized more than once the putting out of light or fire before retiring for the night. Once he was sitting on a mattress, when a rat crept along and carried away the wick of the earthen lamp burning in the room. The servant maid raised hue and cry but he asked her to keep quiet and observe the consequences. The rat left the wick on the mattress on which he was seated and a part of it was burnt. It was after this practical demonstration that he advised that lamps should be put out before retiring.

Method of Demonstration : Once Janadah brought some camels to the Prophet One of the animals had been branded on the nose. He said, "O Janadah could not you find any other place to brand the animal. You shall have to compensate for it."

Thereupon he pointed out the proper place on which the animal should be branded and made him brand the animal in his presence.

At first Janadah kept the branding instrument against the neck but the Prophet asked him to move on to the rear. He went on repeating the instruction till the instrument was against the thigh of the animal. Then he said, "Now, with the blessing of the God" implying that it was the most proper place for branding.

Teaching Technique

An interesting feature of his education in morals was that it was extremely concrete and realistic. It was colourfully illustrated by similes and metaphors which were culled from everyday experience and which brought the light of his concrete objective realism to play about the point. The study of his verbal illustrations of moral precepts would prove a subject of immense interest for the teacher of method.

Sometimes he would proceed beyond the limits of verbal illustrations and present for his moral teachings illustrative material in concrete.

According to a Tradition by Abdullah bin Masud one day the Prophet drew a straight line in his presence and told that it represented the Path of the Lord. Later on he drew a number of lines to its left and right and added that they were other paths (besides the True one) and they were all guarded by a Satan who calls (people) to himself. Then he recited the Quranic verse, "Verily my Path is the straight one, so follow it."

Once he drew a figure illustrating concretely the destiny of man on earth.

He drew a square and inscribed a line in the middle of the square. He drew another line which went outside the square. After that he drew a number of short lines which projected outward from the four sides of the square towards the line which he had drawn in the centre. Then he explained that the line drawn in the centre of the square represented man and that the square symbolised his destiny. He was hemmed in from all direction by it, and the solitary line going out of the square is the line of hope while the shorter lines are the calamities. If he escapes one, he will be destroyed by another.

> "The true Path is the straightest path. It had no deviations or dangerous turnings. It was bright as the day and it could be traversed easily by the Arab of the desert or the children at school alike. But nevertheless it has its 'catches' and its 'danger points'."

The point has been brought out through a variety of expressive similes. According to another Tradition, the True path leads between the walls which are broken in by a number of doors closely draped with curtains and there is a 'Caller' who stands on the head of the path (nearer end) and another who stands above (the farther end) while God calls man towards the Dar-ul-Islam (House of Peace) and leads all whom he desires on the Straight Path. Now the doors opening on both the sides are Hudud Allah (punishments prescribed for sins) and none lapses into them unless the curtain is raised and one who calls from above is the preacher of God.

According to Ibn Masud, the (Sirat) on the straight Path represents Islam, the doors are the Muharim (prohibitive commandments) and the curtains are the Hudud (punishments). The caller who stands at the head of the Path is the Quran and one above him is the Preacher of God who has a place in the heart of every Believer.

The entire simile represents in a colourful and realistic manner the progress of the Faithful towards the Kingdom of the Blessed. The great call which is ringing into his ears from the Olympian heights towering above and the immediate dangers which beset his path at every footstep lend the entire scene the charm of a romantic adventure on the path of Allah.

Teaching by means of parables has proved a highly effective instrument of moral instruction in the hands of great masters and the method has been equally effective both in the case of children and unsophisticated adults. The children are attracted by the story element and the adults by the moral tone of the parable. This kind of literature provides a simple and naive form of illustrating some moral principle. While a simile or a metaphor stands for an isolated idea and is used for embellishment or clarity, the parable illustrates a principle of moral life in a more developed form and has the additional quality of clothing the idea with substance and reality. It is simple and direct and has a greater appeal for the uninitiated humanity.

The parables occurring in the Traditions are longer and fuller as compared with those in the Bible and add something immediately human to the moral fibre of the story. There is the well known parable of the blind, the bald and the leper; Two of whom were cured of their physical ailment through the mercy of God and were blessed with plenty and pelf but they could not recover from their moral afflictions.

The blind man in the Tradition symbolises one who had his inner sight restored. Another beautifully simple parable describes the three religions as three groups of farm labourers. While the first two groups left the task unfinished and retired unremunerated, the third group which represents Islam and had joined late in the afternoon, received the fullest reward for the day's labour because it had fulfilled the Will of the Master. Another parable is that of the three travellers who were entrapped in a cave by a falling boulder.

This parable originates like a few others from the Old and New Testament. In this parable the three groups were employed by the same master. The Jews worked from morning till noon and received one Karat each; the Christians from noon till the time for the afternoon prayers and they also received the same wages. The Muslims who worked from the afternoon to the evening prayer received double the wages and when the first two groups objected that they had worked more and received less, the Lord said "Have I been unfair to you. Verily this is my beneficence and I grant to whom I please."

The simile of casting pearls before swine was further amplified by the Prophet who described the person who brings knowledge to the undeserving as one who adorns the neck of the swine with a necklace made of jewels, pearls and gold.

Figures of Speech : The similes and other figures of speech which he used did not belong to the domain of rhetorics; they were an essential device for making his meaning clear and were accordingly adapted to the intellectual level of the audience. While the poet uses them for their wealth of imagery and emotional associations, they are used in the Traditions for emphasizing the qualitative and sometimes the quantitative value of an abstract quality.

For instance he claimed to be the Last of the Hierarchy of Prophets and he compared himself to the capping stone of a noble edifice without which the whole plan could not be brought to completion; on another occasion he compared four classes of people to four kinds of fruit. There was the Believer who read the Quran and acted upon it, he was to be likened to the orange, fragrant to smell and delightful in taste. The Believer who acted upon the word of the Holy Book but did not read it was like the date which though delicious in taste had no smell; the hypocrite who read the Quran but did not act upon it was like the fruit of the sweet balsam, sweet in smell but bitter in taste while the hypocrite who did not recite the Holy Book nor did he act upon it was the colocynth, bitter in taste and foul of smell.

Sources of Illustrations : One of the most frequent sources from which quite a repertory of illustrative material has been derived is the phenomena of nature and the Quran provides a number of elaborate similes from the world of physical nature with which the desert Arab was familiar.

The date-palm, the pasture grounds, the arable lands in the oasis, the heavens above and the earth below all appear to provide him with a rich source of material for illustrative purposes.

He compares the Believer with the date-palm, an evergreen plant which always bears fruit and foliage. Elsewhere he is compared to a tender plant that is bent by the gust of the wind and another time is straightened up, showing that he has the flexibility to bend himself to the Lord of the storms, while the Munafiq (doubter) is akin to the cypress which never bends but is uprooted all of a sudden. The Quran also compares faith to a growing sapling that brings happiness unto the heart of the grower.

Three Tracts of Land : He compares his influence to the abundant rains from above that fall on land and compares people to three kinds of soil. The first kind imbibes the genial influence of the kindly rains and is covered with a luxuriant growth of green grass and verdure. The second tract with a rocky bed withheld the moisture and provided water for drinking and agricultural purposes. The third kind did not absorb moisture or store it because it was a flat and barren waste.

Figures of Speech from the Sea : The Quran and the Traditions reveal a fairly intimate knowledge of the sea. The Quran speaks of the storms and the silent seas, the boats, the pearls and the corals. In the Traditions the sea is used as a symbol for vastness. "The riches of this world are nothing as compared with those of the next world (eternity). One who loves lucre is like one who dips his finger into the sea and awaits what it brings back to him."

It appears that he was familiar with the double deck boats that plied on the sea and carried passengers. There is the highly instructive parable of the person who neglects Hududullah or prohibitive commandments. He is likened to a person travelling on the lower deck of a boat and how he tries to bore a hole into the bottom for obtaining water. His action means destruction for all of them.

The spirit of the Hudud was not the protection of the rights of a particular class or individual but that of the society as a whole.

In the well-known Tradition related by um-Haram he described how man sat in the boats as kings on their thrones.

Animal Kingdom : The animal kingdom provided him with some extremely instructive analogies. Once he compared men to the moth who would rush upon fire in an insane urge for self-destruction. The Prophet likened himself to the man who tried to extract them from fire (of hell) but they seemed to overwhelm the fire. Again he compared the unbeliever to a goat that stood indecisively between two flocks, sometimes tending towards one and then towards the other.

For him faith is like a powerful binding chain or the peg which provides the Believer with some principles that give moral stability in spite of slight aberrations or moral defalcations he may be prone to. He compared the Believer to a horse tied to a peg who moves round the peg but ultimately reverts to it. Likewise the Believer commits a fault (sahw) but ultimately returns to the fold of faith.

The Prophet had himself looked after the grazing animals when in Mecca and some of the most striking similes come out of his experiences. He has compared himself to a shepherd and the Satan to a wolf for humanity who pounces on the goat that strays away in stubborness or saunters away in search of grass and is lost. He warns them of the vales (and their attractions) and exhorts them to be one with the Jamaat and the common people.

According to him every tribe or important person had his Hima or the reserves for grazing purposes. Every ruler had his Hima and God's preserve were his Muharim (forbidden things).

Somewhere else he speaks of a person who reports only the wicked things out of what he hears from a friend. He is like unto a person who has been allowed as a shepherd to make his choice of the whole flock to slaughter an animal for himself and he finally catches hold of the shepherd's dog by the ear.

The Camel : In most cases the Prophet would carry an edifying discourse on the back of a camel and the animal came extremely handy by way of illustration. When a desert Arab put him an irrelevant question while seated on his camel he said, "I don't know who's more lost, the rider or the ride." Once while proceeding for Hajj, his followers recited the holy formula (Tahiti) and raised their voices to an inordinate pitch, he said, "God is not devoid of the power of hearing. He is nearer to you than the neck of the camel (you are riding.)"

In his well-known Tradition that every child is born according to nature and it is his parents that make a Christian or a Jew of him, he refers to the inner Good that lay in man. The statement was further amplified by a reference to the calves born of an animal. There is none born with a split ear. According to him all these deformations arise out of post-natal causes and not out of innate nature.

Smaller Fry : The Quran refers occasionally to the most insignificant of living beings by way of metaphor and the bee, the mosquito and the fly are included in the list. Quran mentions specifically that God is not ashamed of quoting the simile of a mosquito. The Traditional literature uses "the wing of a mosquito" for indicating something extremely insignificant. "If the worldly riches had been worth a mosquito's wing in the eyes of the Lord, he would not have granted to the unbeliever even a drink of water out of it."

Again one who takes back what has been given as a gift is likened to the dog that licks up its own vomiting.

Naked Runner : The tribal life and its Traditions of eternal warfare provided a fruitful source of illustrations. He would compare himself to a Raid or the Guide who is sent in advance in search of new pastures. His people repose an implicit confidence in his integrity and he asked with vehemence how could such a trusted person tell them anything but the truth. Elsewhere he compares himself to the 'naked' runner, a usage of the Jahiliyah when an unclad messenger would go from tent to tent warning them of the impending attack by a hostile tribe. In a rather elaborate Tradition he describes the parable of a guide who came upon a caravan stranded in the desert and how he leads them to an oasis with running rivulets and green orchards and when he proposes to lead them on to yet more green fields and pastures now they are adamant in their refusal to move onwards.

Significant Allegories : There is another class of Traditions which have an impressive fascination of their own and are awe-inspiring in nature. They have been the precursor of a new class of literature in Arabic and other languages and have inspired the imagination of generations of poets and writers, finally culminating in that graceful specimen of this class of literature, the Javed Nama of Dr. Iqbal. According to Asin, the Comedia Divina of Dante was directly inspired by this class of Traditions.

These Traditions have a fiery grandeur of their own and must have proved a powerful check on the antisocial propensities of the wild Arab whose passions often blazed like the simoom which sweeps across the vast barrenness of the desert. These Traditions have an air of classical restraint and have a deep undercurrent of suppressed sympathy for the condemned. But nevertheless they reveal a fine sense of justice and the closest correlation between sin and punishment. Among a people who had cherished for so long the rule of "an eye for an eye and a tooth for a tooth", these Traditions must have exercised a considerable moral influence. They are fine examples of the Doctrine of Moral consequences.

In the course of the morning assembly he would describe his experiences in a dream and invite others to narrate theirs. Once he told how he saw the liar being tormented by having his mouth ripped open; how the scholar who taught the Quran to others but neglected it himself was punished by having his head crushed.

In one of his allegorical dreams, the Prophet saw a man swimming in a river of blood while another stood on the bank with a stone in his hand. When the first person tried to approach the bank, the person standing on the bank struck him with the stone; his mouth opened and the stone made its way down his throat. He collapsed once again into the current and the same tragedy was repeated again. According to the Prophet the man swimming in the river of blood was an usurer.

The Traditions on the Ascension or the Miraj contain some hair raising details of the punishments meted out to the sinners who were condemned to hell and in all cases, a principle of poetic justice appears to determine the nature and the intensity of punishment. A scholar who did not accost a seeker after knowledge with a reply will have a bridle-bit made of hell fire in his mouth and the man who learning and did not benefit others by his scholarship will burst his belly and carry his entrails like the mule which drives the flour mill.

According to a Tradition the hoard guarded by a person in the world would change into a python on the day of Judgment and would chase the hoarder. And he would munch his head with his jaws like a camel. The interpretation of dreams has transformed itself into a respectable science in the hands of psychologists like Freud who has made a remarkable study of the dreams of the Leonardo da Vinci. But the Freudian School works within very great limitations and it is hoped that the psychologist of the future will present a deeper and more meaningful analysis of the subject in the light of a broader and higher conception of the main springs of human action and thought.

Historic Style : The Prophet's style of speech and manner of addressing others profoundly affected the method of work in the schools of the Islamic world. Qadi Abu Jamaa recommends the repetition of a sentence three times after the manner of the Prophet who used to repeat his sentences thrice. He never burried, but expressed himself always with great deliberation and case. We have it from Aishah how once she was visited by Abu Hurayrah when she was offering the night prayers.

Abu Hurayrah seated himself on one side of the room, related to her hurriedly a Tradition and she had hardly finished her prayers before he departed. Upon this Aishah told that if she could catch hold of Abu Hurayrah she would have informed him that the Prophet was never so hurried and indistinct in speech as Abu Hurayrah.

Tartil, not Tarsil **:** According to Bukhari, the Prophet spoke word by word so that one could count them if he desired. Tartil instead of Tarsil was the running note of his speech. He did not approve of any interruption in the course of his speech and they were not infrequent in a society which was composed of a large section of members living an individual life of their own in the desert. But such strangers to the ways and life of an organized group life very seldom put him out of temper and he would reply to such intruders after he had finished with the topic on which he was discoursing at that time. Irrelevant queries were positively discouraged by him.

Principles for Audience **:** In a chapter on the manner of listening to a Tradition, Tirmidhi gives that the Prophet had enjoined that it should not be listened to in a posture when one is reposing or reclining against a support, implying thereby that the listening posture requires alertness, physical as well mental. The teacher, of course, had the right to recline against a column or to sit on a raised seat after the usage of the Prophet.

The Prophet always had a word of warm welcome for every visitor, and advised his people to extend such cordiality to all. He prophesied a future for his followers when people would flock to them from far and near and he advised them to welcome these seekers after knowledge with a Marhaba (welcome). "When people flock to you from the four quarters of the globe, advise them well and receive them with soft and loving words."

The time appointed for addressing the people was usually after the morning and the afternoon prayers.

After every prayer in general and the morning prayer in particular, there was always a gathering which had been already motivated for such knowledge. These addresses which were declaimed with moral earnestness moved the hearts to their very foundations and some of the audience would burst into tears on such occasions.

He had appointed a special day in the week for addressing women and this arrangement had been made on the express desire of women.

Recitation and Inscription : Among ancient peoples and old societies, power of forceful expression and declamation was highly prized and among the old Greeks and Romans, oratory formed a prominent feature of the school curriculum. Among the Arabs, political addresses or literary declarations have played an unprecedented role in history and have directed and sometimes diverted the course of historical events.

In the Name of Almighty

The Divine Education of the Prophet originates with the revelation of the Sura Iqra, "Read in the name of the Lord who has created Man from congealed blood. Read, Great and High is thy Lord in His Beneficence." Reading is to be interpreted here not in the sense of the reading aloud lesson in the classroom but as a piece of inspired recitation expressing the glowing enthusiasm of an entire personality, emotionally and intellectually.

Again and again, the Prophet has enjoined on his people the reading of the Holy Book. "The highest form of prayer for my people is the reading of the Holy Book." Again, "The most virtuous amongst you are those who learn the Quran and teach it and the entire group which comes together for reciting the Holy Book and learning it are blessed with peace and tranquillity." According to a savant, "Every verse of the Quran is a stage of paradise and an illuminant for your houses."

How to Read?

As the recitation of the Quran played such an all pervading part in the social and cultural life of the period, it gave rise to a class of readers (Qura) who later on developed into several specialist schools of reading. It appears that the reading of the Quran formed the main item of education in those days and the Companions often indulged inordinately in their enthusiasm for its recitation.

The Prophet had to issue instructions that the reading of the Holy Book may be stopped for a while when one gets tired of it. The style of expression and pronouncing words was deeply influenced by the Traditions of the Prophet, whose reading is described as Tartil (distinct and deliberate), pronouncing each word clearly and with the proper accent. When a child learnt for the first time to stumble into speech, the Prophet advised that he should be made to repeat *'La Ilaha Illallah'*, a combination of sound, rhythmic in cadence and facile to pronounce.

Ornamenting the Quran : The Prophet had a keen ear for rhythm and several Traditions reveal the emphasis which he placed on sweet and rhythmic recitation of the Holy Book. According to a Tradition, "God has never enjoined anything so much on the Prophet as the rhythmic recitation of the Quran." "One who does not read the Quran melodiously does not belong to us." "Ornament the Quran by your voices." Again, "Verily God listens to the Reciter of the Quran better than the master of a singing girl listens to her music." According to Abu Hurayrah, "God has not given any command to the Prophet similar to that which appertains to the melodious voice for reciting the Quran."

The Companions were vividly alive to the aesthetic aspect of Quranic recitation and when the Prophet recited a verse to them, one of them told that it was as refreshing as the rain from within and fruitful from without."

Gift of David : The taste for rhythmic recitation was widespread and when once the Prophet overheard a slave reading in a melodious tone, he thanked God who had blessed his people with such a good person.

Abu Musa al-Ashaari was noted for his good voice and the Prophet was often so enchanted by his recitation that he would forget everything else and when the company called out that it was high time for prayers, he would remark, "Are we not already in the midst of our devotions?" He often told that Abu Musa had the gift of David's music.

How to Recite?

The remarks of the Prophet on the subject of recitation (Qirat) were made with reference to the Quran and he has emphasized its recitation for the blessings which it brings to the individual and to the society. But in all his behests in matters of religion and education he is always inspired more by its social significance than the benefit which it brings to a particular individual. This viewpoint has been brought home by a number of beautiful and expressive similes with specific reference to recitation.

"One who learns the Quran and does not recite it is like a person who has preserved musk in a bag and holds its mouth tightly closed. While the other who recites it has loosened the strings of his bag and its fragrance is wafted all around. In this case, his learning has a social utility, beneficial for himself and for others.

Orange and the Aloe : There is another Tradition which has been narrated by Abu Musa al-Ashaari, that melodious reader of the Quran is he whose recitation was so much appreciated by the Prophet. According to Abu Musa, the Prophet had said, "The Believer who recites the Quran is like the orange that has a good taste and a delightful flavour. And the Believer who does not recite is like the date which is delicious in taste but has no flavour. The Munafiq who recites the Quran is like the Rayhan which has a good fragrance but is bitter in taste and the Munafiq who does not recite it is like the aloe which is bitter in taste as well in flavour." Hence faith in the holy word and its propagation both have equal importance.

The above simile throws light on the social and the individual benefit which accrues from the recitation of the Holy Book and it can be generalised and applied to the educative process as a whole.

The social aspect of the process being so important, the Prophet preferred to hear the recitation in company and would often request one of the company to recite.

Good reciters of the Quran were very much prized in the early days and an emancipated slave (Mawla) was made the head of his tribe among the people of the valley during the period of Umar Ibn Khattab, because he was a Qari (Reciter).

Style of the Prophet : The Prophet's style of recitation was that of Tartil. It was neither quick nor hasty. Rather he would pronounce one letter after another separately and distinctly and would introduce pauses after every verse (Ayat). He would enunciate lucidly the long accented sound (Mad) in al-Rahman and al-Rahim)

He would recite the Quran both in a loud (Jahr) or low (Khafi) voice. But the distinguishing feature of his recitation was not so much its pitch, speed or volume; it was lucidity and clear intonation. According to Ibn Abbas when he recited in the courtyard a person sitting in-doors could clearly hear his recitation. According to Um Hani she used to hear his recitation clearly when she (had retired for the night and) was on the roof.

Musical Rhythm : There is evidence to prove that the Prophet himself recited the Quran with musical rhythm specially in moments when he was emotionally aroused. When on the day of the Victory (Yawm-ul-Fath) he entered Mecca on a camel, he was reciting according to Abdullah bin Maghfal, the verse, "*Inna Fataluna laka Fathan Mubina*," and he repeated the letter alif three times. According to Ibn al-Qayyam Ibn Jawzi, this Tarje or repetition did not arise out of the movements of the dromedary on which he was seated but it was a voluntary expression. Abdullah continues that had he not feared that the people would gather round to listen (to him, disturbing thereby the order of the victorious march) he would have followed the example of the Prophet.

It has been remarked elsewhere that the Prophet liked immensely the recitation of Abu Musa al-Ashaari and once the Prophet heard him reading the Quran, and when Abu Musa was informed of it he told that he would have made the Quran more beautiful and would have embellished it with his voice had he known it.

***Melancholic and the Ecstatic Note*:** Umar Ibn Khattab who was a man of extremely puritanic temperament liked immensely the recitation of the Quran by Abu Musa al-Ashaari and would often exhort him to recite by saying "*Zakkarna Rabbana*" (Make us remember God).

Then Abu Musa would make a recitation and read it with melody (Lahn). Thereupon Umar could say, "One who desires to introduce music (Ghina) in the Quran should do it in the style of Abu Musa al-Ashaari." The chief note of Abu Musa Ashaari's recitation was melancholic (Huzn) and not ecstatic (Tarab). When Aqbah bin Amir who had a beautiful voice was requested by Umar Ibn Khattab to recite, he read a verse with such effect that Umar Ibn Khattab wept profusely and said, "I could never conceive that this verse was of the revealed ones."

It is interesting to note that an authority like Ibn Qayyim Jawzi who was a very close disciple of Ibn Ṭaymiyyah and who is the main exponent of the orthodox school sums up the discussion by saying that although recitation with musical notes is not permissible but it can be done in the style of the ancients who embellished their voices while reading the Quran and read it with the fullest emotional expression, melancholic or ecstatic.

Symbols of Vocalisation : The genius of the Arabic language and the great solicitude which the Muslims showed in the preservation of the Word of the Holy Writ and the Traditions gave rise to the need of formulating rules of Grammar and vocalisation. By the time of 'Umar the Muslim armies had crossed the confines of the Arabian Peninsula and had annexed many a non-Arab countries to the Islamic State.

The process of political domination went along with that of moral and religious conquest and the need for presenting the sources of Islamic inspiration in a correct form to these people became insistent in the days of the early Caliphs. Even the Beduin who lived a life of his own in the heart of the desert found difficulties in vocalising the text but for the non-Arabs it presented a more formidable problem.

It is related on the authority of Abi-al Aswad-ud Dawali that one day he visited Ali. He looked disconsolate and out of spirits. Ali was feeling very much perturbed because he had heard some one reciting the Quran with wrong vocalisation. He told Abi- al Aswad that he had decided to compose a book on the principles of Arabic grammar.

Abi-al Aswad welcomed the idea and told that he would give a fresh lease of life to the language and preserve its vocabulary through this action. When he visited him again after three days, Ali showed him a book wherein he had defined Ism, Fel and Harf (noun, verb and preposition). He instructed Abi-al Aswad to proceed with the work who added Huruf an-Nasb to it. According to another source, Ali was the first scholar to devise the symbols for vocalisation.

Moderation in Recitation : The Quran enjoins upon the Prophet to be moderate in the reading of the Quran. The injunction laid down that the self-imposed rigorous discipline should in no way tax the energies of the Prophet and the Faithful. Whenever he heard of cases where a person kept longsome nightly vigils for recitation, he prohibited him from doing so. A prominent case was that of the young enthusiast, Abdullah bin Amr bin al-Ath.

The Prophet followed the spirit of the Quran by permitting such individual variations in reading which did not interfere with the meaning of the Holy Writ. Once Umar Ibn Khattab heard Hisham bin Hakim bin Hizam reciting the Quran which in his opinion was not after the style of the Prophet. He was so much aroused that he was about to pounce upon him for this sacrilege when Hisham finished his prayers, Umar caught hold of his sheet and took him straight to the Prophet. The Prophet heard both of them reciting the same verse and approved both the recitations. He concluded his remarks with the words "Verily Quran was revealed in seven letters. Read out of it which is more feasible for you."

Place in the Syllabus : The Problem of the placement of reading in the syllabus received a good deal of attention on the part of Muslim educators and Ibn Khaldun devoted a chapter to the critical study of the problem in his Prolegomena. His illuminating analysis of the contemporary methods of teaching reading in different countries reveals a thorough grasp of educational principles and the capacity to study problems from a scientific and detached viewpoint; under such genial influences the Islamic institutions developed a noble tradition of the art of oral expression.

Unfortunately, the present schools of the community, whether indigenous or imparting Western education, have lost the art and it is high time to recover once more the spontaneous and joyful expression of personality through the spoken world which will always maintain a social and political significance peculiarly its own in any democratic society and opens out a channel for the building up of a well integrated personality.

Implications for the Present Day System : The Prophet and his Companions have endowed their people with a rich legacy in the form of the Quran, the Traditions and their addresses. They vibrate with an inspired style, simple and direct, illumined with moral fervour and emotional restraint; the present-day textbook writer will discover therein a rich field of literature which is nearer to the elemental make-up of the child than the sophisticated literature of the later times.

For centuries, the Muslim child has opened his school career with a chapter of the Quran but often the veneration in which the Holy Text was held by the Muslims worked adversely against a harmonious education of the child when the Holy Book and specially its last chapter which is a miracle of elegance, brevity and pointedness was chosen as the chief content of education for the earlier years. Educators like Qadi Abu Bakr Ibn al-Arabi boldly criticised the practice on pedagogic grounds and recommended priority to subjects which claimed a direct and closer appeal to the innate interests of the child and which may have a higher utility value for him. The Quran was removed by him to the third stage of Education, the two preliminary stages being devoted mainly to mother tongue and arithmetic.

Difficulties Ahead

It would be interesting to make a comparative study of our efforts for a more efficient teaching of the Arabic language as compared with the solicitude of the Muslims in the first century of the Islamic era. The problem is beset with peculiar difficulties in this country and is all the more complicated by the variety of cultural and linguistic groups who take to the learning of the Arabic language. When one comes across the pathetic spectacle of the Manipuri or the Bengali Muslims struggling with the Arabic syntax in the Persian-cum-Urdu medium of instruction, he feels that the scholarly class of this country has yet to perform the impossible and write a suitable Grammar of the Arabic language in Urdu and other Provincial languages of the country for the benefit of the learner of the language.

We may be legitimately proud of the contributions of our scholarly class to the study of Islamic law, dialectics and literature but we must see whether we have been successful in making it a spiritual heritage of the masses or how far we have helped the average learner in surmounting the preliminary, yet impregnable difficulties in mastering the language, thereby transforming him into a genuine and effective missionary of its spiritual heritage.

How to Write?

The art of writing and penmanship has a glorious record in the history of Islamic education. The word 'pen' has a strange fascination for the historian and beautiful legends are related about its origin and the priority of its creation. According to a Tradition, the Pen was one of the earliest of creation; and in the Quran, there occurs a verse which runs as follows: "Read in the name of the Lord who created Man from a drop of congealed blood. Read and thy Lord is highly Benevolent; verily He is thy Lord who taught thee with the Pen and taught man what he did not know." Implying the sanction and approval of the art of writing by the Divine Power and commending its use for Men.

Pen, a Hallowed Name : Qalam is a hallowed name in Muslim doxology because it occurs as an oath in the Holy Book and one of the most glorious rhapsodies in the praise of God states that if all the vegetation on the earth's surface provides the quills and water of all the oceans, the ink, they would dry up before the Praise of thy Lord comes to an end. In another place, we come across a verse "By the ink-hom and by all that you write."

The Islamic Tradition traces the significance of the art from primitive times and there is the legend of an Evil Spirit enquiring from Solomon about the nature of speech. He replied that it was like the breath of the wind and when asked how it could be preserved, the reply was, "Through writing."

In the beginning it was considered advisable to preserve only the Quranic text in the form of writing partly on account of the scarcity of parchment and partly from fear that other kind of literature like the Traditions might not be confused with the text of the Quran. But when experience proved all such fears to be baseless, the writing of the Traditions also received the approval of the Prophet. When he delivered his address of victory after the fall of Mecca, he allowed the preparation of a written text for the benefit of a person called Abu Shah, apparently of non-Arab extraction, who hailed from Yemen. The Prophet established the Tradition of teaching the art and encouraged it by all possible means.

A Tribe with a Single Literate : Very few persons knew how to read and write in the days of Jahiliyah. The skill of writing was rarer than that of reading and Ibn Saad the author of Tabaqat makes a specific mention in case of those who knew the art of writing as a noteworthy qualification that was conspicuous by its rarity. It was more or less the same case with the skill of reading.

When the Prophet sent his epistle to Bakr bin Wail after a deputation from the tribe had visited Medina, it was a problem for them to discover a person who could read it as there was only one man, in the whole of Yamamah who knew the art of reading. The progeny of this man was known henceforth as Banu Qari (the progeny of the Reader) because he had read out the epistle of the Prophet.

Captives, Turned Teachers : Medina was a settlement of an agricultural community who were more backward in three R's than the Meccans who were businessmen and had their trade relations with Yemen and Syria. There was a scarcity of persons who knew the art of writing.

Hence the Prophet did not like to lose any opportunity for the propagation of this art and when seventy Meccans were made captives in the Battle of Badar they were asked to teach the skill to ten children or adults as a compensation for their ransom money which was forty Awqiyah for each captive. Those who had no ransom money to pay readily agreed to the arrangement and took to the work in right earnest. Zayd bin Thabit was one of those who learnt the art from these captives.

The Prophet was keenly interested in the propagation of the skill of writing among his people. He had once requested Shifa bint Abdullah, a scholarly lady of the period, to teach writing to Hafdhah, the wife of the Prophet who was the daughter of Umer.

When the Prophet Wrote : The Prophet had no knowledge of reading or writing and this fact has been advanced in the Quran as a forceful argument in favour of the claim that Quran is a revealed book. "Before this we never made you learn how to read or write," says a verse of the Quran.

The words "The Prophet wrote" which occurs in some Traditions are advanced by some as a proof of the Prophet's knowledge of the art of writing but obviously it does not-imply actual writing by the Prophet but only dictation. It appears that once he wrote his name. According to the Tradition of Al-Qaziyyah, the Prophet took the paper and as he could not write well so he wrote in place of Rasul-Lillah' the word 'Muhammad. It is narrated that he wrote Muhammad in his own hand on the Day of Hudaybiah.

Although the Prophet did not write himself he seems to be acquainted with the form of letters and art of calligraphy. There is a Tradition which according to Muawiyah, throws light on his taste for artistic expression: Something was being written in the presence of the Prophet when he said, "Take care of your ink-pot, mend your pen in a slanting direction, straighten up the' Ya,' indicate clearly the points of 'Sin,' don't make the 'Mim' blind, write the word 'Allah' well, place a 'mad' on Rahman and write the word 'Rahim' well.

***Correspondence Secretaries*:** Literacy was not very common among the Quraish and it is said that no more than seventeen persons knew the art of writing among the Meccans. Some of the more distinguished Companions, knew the art and the Prophet did not find much difficulty for correspondence work.

According to Zad al-Maad, the following Companions functioned as correspondence secretaries (Katib) of the Prophet. They were Abu Bakr, Umar, Uthman, Ali and Zubayr.

But finally this office was entrusted to Zayd bin Thabit who received further training during his stay with the Prophet. Zayd bin Thabit did not know Syriac and the Prophet had to depend mostly in this connection on the Jews. But the Jewish scribes could not be relied on. So he asked Zayd to learn Syriac which he did within a short period of fifteen days. After that the entire correspondence in the language was carried on by Zayd.

***Zayd bin Thabit* :** Zayd bin Thabit did a great service in compiling the Quran under Abu Bakr and Uthman. He was highly respected for his skill and learning. Once Ibn Abbas took hold of his stirrup as a mark of honouring the scholar and when Zayd protested and said "Oh Cousin of the Prophet, leave it off," Ibn Abbas replied, "We have been asked to honour our scholars in this way." Thereupon Zayd kissed his hand and replied, "And we have been asked to respect the family of the Prophet like this."

Zayd bin Thabit was entrusted with the duty of compiling the Quran by Abu Bakr when a large number of readers had been killed in the battle of Yamamah. He compiled it from fragments, leaves of date palm, soft stone and from those who knew it by heart. Zayd was selected by Abu Bakr because he used to copy out the Wahi — the words of God as revealed to the Prophet. The copy prepared by Zayd remained with Abu Bakr and then passed through Umar and Hafdah, his daughter, to Uthman who ordered another copy of it to be made for a fresh compilation. He appointed a committee of three including Zayd bin Thabit for preparing the new compilation.

Growth of Kitabat : The Muslim Law provides facilities for the slaves to work for their liberty by earning the ransom money for their masters. The profession of the Scribe was popular with the slaves who desired to work for liberty and we come across the name of a freedman of Aishah who copied the Quran for her mistress.

With the growth of contacts with countries outside Arabia, the drawing up of business deeds became an essential feature of the economic life of the period and all books on Fiqh contain invariably a Chapter on Kitabat. The Deeds of Will were a part of the normal business and we have reliable evidence to prove that the Prophet sent for writing material on his death-bed so that he might leave behind a will in writing for his people. The text of his epistles to some of the contemporary kings and others are extant in the collections of Traditions and treatises on Islamic History.

Savant's Ink and the Martyr's Blood : Zarnuji quotes a tradition on the authority of Hilal bin Yasar who once saw the Prophet discoursing on knowledge and wisdom in the presence of his Companions. He approached him with all promptitude and requested that he might also receive the benefit of his wise words. The Prophet asked whether he had pen and ink and receiving a reply in the negative, he advised him not to discard the inkpot because the inkpot comprised all the good which might be done till the Day of Judgment.

Elsewhere we have made a reference to the comparison which is frequently made in the Traditions between a teacher and a martyr, and according to one of them the ink of the savant will be weighed against the Martyr's blood on Doomsday while, according to Hassan Basari, when these two will be weighed together, the ink will outweigh the blood.

Gaining Education

The Age of the Prophet was the age of human contacts, the age when the oral word dominated the written; when knowledge originated and was published orally; when word divorced from personal associations of a heated declamation or verbal flourishes lost much of its charm. It is surprising that a tradition of the cult of writing sprang so abundantly after the advent of Islam in spite of the great paucity of parchment, persons living in much later periods like that of Imam Shafii and Abu Yusuf using bones and potshreds for writing purposes.

This got certainly some impetus from the Tradition enjoining the Faithful to captivate knowledge through writing, and some of the Companions did captivate it in an admirable manner. We learn from the frank avowal of Abu Hurrayrah that 'Abdullah bin Umar who preserved the Traditions in writing had a richer knowledge of them than himself who retained them by memory.

The Prophet allowed a Companion to take down everything on which he discoursed, a duty more or less similar to a stenographer and he waived off all objections raised by others in this connection. According to a savant one who does not preserve knowledge in writing should not be counted among scholars. Again according to Khalil bin Ahmad, he never heard anything but he put it in black and white; and never wrote anything but he memorised it and he never memorised anything but he got some benefit out of it.

Hisham bin 'Urwah's manuscripts were destroyed on the Day of Conflagration and when he was apprised of the tragedy, he exclaimed, "I wish I had perished with them along with my progeny and property." By the time of 'Umar bin Abdul 'Aziz, the art had become so popular and the material preserved in writing so abundant that whole volumes of religious lore were copied out and manuscripts despatched to the various parts of the Dominions.

There are good many injunctions emphasizing the importance of a clear, bold and graceful style in writing. Ali summarises it in one of his most illuminating aphorisms, "Illumine the pen as it was illumined by God." On another occasion he had told that writing represents symbols and hence the more expressive it is, the more appropriate it would be. He prized grace and beauty in writing because it contributed something additional to its inherent function of expression.

The instructions laid down by Ali on the art of writing not merely reveal his great love for learning but also his passionate desire to propagate the art in a correct and beautiful form. The minutest details which he adds to his instructions would do credit to any modern educationist and would prove as useful to the novice today as thirteen centuries ago. He would like the cut of the pen to be elongated and broadened with its angle inclining towards the right. His instructions on the writing of the alphabet are a delightful combination of the harmony of form, sound and movement. For instance, it was a delight for him to hear the vibrating note of the pen when the pen completed the finishing stroke of the letter 'Nun', the slower movement in rounding up the 'lam', the firm and steadier hand in writing 'Ba', 'ta' 'tha', and so on.

In the opinion of a savant, writing is that characteristic function of a man by dint of which his innate capacities find channel of expression through activity. This symbolic instrument for business transactions and social life became a medium of expression for that love of beauty and rhythm in form which has contributed to the artistic heritage of humanity, those glorious masterpieces of calligraphy which harmonise so delightfully the utilitarian and the aesthetic aspect of Art. The Kufic script of the Prophet's time with its straight lines and rigid curves did not provide ample scope for artistic expression but the later masters founded those Great Schools of Calligraphy which supplied a new and comparatively easy outlet of expression for the school child and which later on developed into a preliminary stage for artistic expression in other media.

12

Education for Women

Role of Faith

In dealing with women's education from the Islamic perspective, it is recognised that wider issues pertaining to a modern Islamic curriculum have not been addressed. The latter is, indeed, a crucial issue, but our concern here has been one of the key questions of principle that should surely guide current attempts to formulate an authentically Islamic education system, namely the approach to women's education in such a system.

Long as the education system is governed by the spirit of Islam throughout, there will be a harmony between, these two modes of social activity, permitting women to express themselves in accordance with their natural dispositions, and to be given the respect and honour which is so central to the real social message of Islam.

Knowledge and education are, highly emphasised in Islam. Both are integral parts of the Islamic religion. Islam encourages its followers to enlighten themselves with the knowledge of their religion as well as other branches of knowledge. It holds the person who seeks knowledge in high esteem and has exalted his position). In reality, the entire aim of the Divine revelation and the sending of Prophets to humankind has been stressed in the Quran as the communication of knowledge. The Book says: 'The Prophet recites unto people God's revelation; causes them to grow and imparts to them knowledge, and wisdom'. The Divine desires every believer to be well educated in religion, to possess wisdom and broad intellectual knowledge.

The purpose of raising a Prophet in a nation is to teach and to impart knowledge.. The Quran is full of verses which praise learned people, encourage original thinking and personal investigation and denounce unimaginative imitation. It also emphasises the importance of the study of nature and its laws. According to the Quran, learning is an unending process and the entire universe is made subservient, to man, the agent of God, who has to abide by the truth and not by narrow notions of hereditary customs and beliefs. The verses in the Quran which enjoin people to learn and observe nature outnumber all those related to prayer, fasting, and pilgrimage put together.

In the Hadith literature, knowledge is highly appreciated and encouraged also. The Prophet Muhammad always emphasised the importance of knowledge to his followers and encouraged them to seek it. Learned people are regarded as the inheritors of the Prophetic wisdom. In this connection, the following Hadiths can be quoted: 'The Prophets leave knowledge as their inheritance. The learned ones inherit this great fortune. 'Search for knowledge though it be in China'.

Studies were conducted in the Mosques, circles of discussion (*halaqat*) were set up; and teachers were simultaneously students learning from their superiors and, in their turn, teaching their own students. Education was considered a matter of religious duty-a manifestation of the Muslim's submission to the will of Allah and an act of piety which could lead to a deeper knowledge of the Creator—the One. Hence we find that all members of society participated in that process. Since education was free of charge, opportunities were available to everybody, rich or poor alike. The Prophet said 'Treat equally poor and rich students who sit before you for the acquisition of knowledge'. Gifted students were helped and highly encouraged to continue their education, so that they would be able to fulfil their aspirations.

Moreover, the seeking of knowledge was not circumscribed by age limitations; the Prophet said 'Seek knowledge from the cradle to the grave'. Therefore, we find that the companions of the Prophet sought knowledge even when they were at an advanced age. Also, there was considerable academic freedom; in the classes, the students were entitled to ask questions and to discuss themes with the teacher-indeed, their reputation depended heavily on their success in such sessions of debate and discussion.

Initially, the learning process of the Muslims started with the Prophet who himself used to teach his companions the principles of Islam. When he migrated to Medina, he immediately started the process of eradicating illiteracy. His mosque also served as a centre for Muslim learning. He was so interested in this matter that, soon after the victory of Badr, he instructed each of the Meccan captives, who were literate, to teach ten Muslims how to read and write as a condition for their release. He also sent teachers and missionaries to different parts of Arabia so that they could teach the newly converted Muslims the principles of Islam. He also set up circles of learned men to study and teach the Quran. Later, mosques were set up in every locality and since then have remained as the essential location for educational activities among the Muslims.

The Prophet's example as a teacher constituted a sacred precedent for his followers. Hence they considered it their duty to set up mosques and schools in their domain. In the course of time, the simple pattern of the Prophet's school developed into a comprehensive and coherent educational system, fully integrated into the social and economic way of life. This educational system was based on moral and spiritual qualities. It recognised no separation between sacred and secular. Indeed it 'breathed in a universe of sacred presence'.

Whatever was known contained a profoundly religious feature, not only because the object of every type of knowledge is created by God, but also because the intelligence by which man knows is in itself a Divine gift. The education system therefore dealt with the whole being of the person whom it sought to educate. Its aim was not only the training of the mind but also the entire personality of the student. The teacher in this system was the transmitter of knowledge as well as the trainer of souls. Even the term 'teacher' in itself gained the meaning of trainer. It was embodied with ethical connotations which in the modern world have almost disappeared from the process of teaching and the transmission of knowledge, especially at the higher levels of education.

The Islamic educational system neither separated the training of the mind from that of the soul, nor regarded the transmission of knowledge or its possession to be legitimate without the possession of proper moral and spiritual principles. Indeed, the acquisition of knowledge without these principles was regarded as very dangerous both to individuals and society.

However, despite the fact that the Islamic educational system encompassed the whole life of traditional Muslims, certain distinct phases can be discerned. The first stage started at home where both parents acted as teachers in matters such as religion, language, culture and social customs. This period was followed by the Quranic schools (al-Kuttab) corresponding to elementary school. The aims of these schools were to enable the child to read and write the Quran, and to master the language as well as learn other subjects such as proverbs, poetry and, later, arithmetic. These schools formed the preparatory stage for higher studies where the students could then attend the *Madrasa*.

The *Madrasa* often incorporated the Jamiah which can be said to correspond at one and the same time, to secondary school as well as to college and university education. The activities of these *Madrasas* were divided into two parts. The religious or the transmitted sciences, and the intellectual sciences. The religious sciences included the study of the Quran, the Hadith, linguistics and theology and they dominated the educational activity of most *Madrasas*. The intellectual sciences included the study of logic, mathematics, and the natural sciences, as well as philosophy.

These divisions of the sciences were reflected in the curriculum of the *Madrasas* and were taught alongside each other. These *Madrasas* enjoyed a high position in society and, in the course of time, they developed into fully fledged educational institutions performing an important role throughout the Muslim world, such as the Qayrawan in Morocco and Al-Azhar in Egypt. Later on, we find the development of a university system with several campuses such as al Nizamiyyah and Al-Mustansiriyah in Baghdad and Al-Nuriyyah in Damascus.

In addition to the *Madrasas* where theoretical learning was conducted, there were a number of observatories and hospitals. Some of them acted independently as institutions of scientific learning and experimentation, others were appended to the colleges. Al-Mamun's famous Shamsiyyah observatory was a most remarkable example. It was followed in many other cities. Moreover, these higher institutions continually provided society with its intellectual elite, and socio-political thinkers.

New Trends

There is no priority for men over women in relation to the right to education. Both are equally encouraged to acquire education, as already shown, 'from the cradle to the grave'. Indeed all the Quranic verses which relate to education and which advocate the acquisition of knowledge were directed to both men and women alike. In accordance with the all-embracing concept of Tawhid- Oneness-when Islam elevated women physically by abolishing female infanticide, it could not overlook the need for their mental and spiritual elevation. By contrast, Islam would view the neglect of these dimensions as virtually tantamount to murdering their personality. The Quran says: 'They are losers who besottedly have slain their children by keeping them in ignorance'. Neither the Quran nor the sayings of the Prophet prohibit or prevent women from seeking knowledge and having an education.

Prophet was the forerunner in this regard, in declaring that seeking knowledge is obligatory upon every Muslim man and woman. By making such a statement, the Prophet opened all the avenues of knowledge for men and women alike. So, like her male counterpart, each woman is under a moral and religious obligation to seek knowledge, develop her intellect, broaden her outlook, cultivate her talents and then utilise her potential to the benefit of her soul and of her society. The interest of the Prophet in female education was manifest in the fact that he himself used to teach the women along with the men; he also instructed his followers to educate not only their women but their slave girls as well. The following Hadith puts it thus: a man who educates his slave girl, frees her and then marries her, this man will have a double reward. The wives of the Prophet, especially Aishah, not only taught women, they taught men also and many of the Prophet's companions and followers learned the Quran, Hadith and Islamic jurisprudence from Aishah.

There was no limitation placed on women's education. Women were allowed to learn all the branches of science. She was free to choose any field of knowledge which interested her.

Nonetheless, it is important to stress that, because Islam recognised that women are in principle wives and mothers, they should also place special emphasis on seeking knowledge in those branches which could help them in those particular spheres. In accordance with the dictates of the Quran and the Hadith encouraging women to develop all aspects of their personality, it was believed that an educated Muslim woman should not only radiate her moral qualities in the environment of her home, but she should: also have an active role in the broad fields of social, economic and political development.

The Quran, in particular, commands men and women to perform their prayers, pay their poor-tax and enjoin good and forbid evil in all forms: social, economic and political. This means that both have an equal duty to accomplish these tasks. In order to do so, they must have equal access to educational opportunities. For how can a woman uphold good social and economic policies or disapprove them if she is intellectually not equipped for the task? Following the injunctions of the Quran and the Sunnah concerning female education, early Muslim women seized this opportunity and laboured to equip themselves in all branches of the knowledge of their time. They attended classes with men, they participated in all cultural activities side by side with them and managed to win their encouragement and respect. Early Islamic history is replete with examples of Muslim women who showed a remarkable ability to compete, with men and excelled them on many occasions.

Religious studies was the favourite subject for women in early Islam, and a considerable number of Muslim women managed to become notable figures among traditionists and jurists. On top of the list was Aishah, the wife of the Prophet. She was a renowned scholar of her time. Her foresight and advice in the affairs of the Islamic community were regarded as highly important by the early Islamic rulers. She was credited with thousands of traditions received directly from the Prophet and is to the present day considered a great authority on Islamic Jurisprudence. Another famous name in this subject was Nafisah, a descendant of Ali who was a prominent jurist and theologian. It is mentioned that Al-Shafii, the founder of one of the schools of Fiqh used to attend her lessons and public lectures. Shuhda as well was a renowned name in the subject of tradition, especially Hadith, which is a branch of Muslim science which was thought to be exclusively for men.

Muslim women proved their ability to master in Literature and achieved a high reputation among their contemporaries. In the forefront was Al-Khansa, the greatest poetess of her day. Her poetry has survived into the present period. She was admired by the Prophet himself when he said that her poetry was unsurpassed. In addition one could mention Qatilah who composed a famous elegy on the death of her brother which, again, was praised by the Prophet.

The humanitarian duties were performed by women in all the battles fought in Islam. It was a custom that Muslim women accompanied the troops, so that they could bandage the wounded, fetch the water, transport the casualties back to Medina and instil courage in the men whose spirits were sagging. It is said that when the Muslim troops were preparing to conquer Khaiber, Umayyah bint Qays-al-Ghaffariyyah, with a group of women, asked to be allowed to accompany the army. The Prophet granted: them his permission and they performed their duties well.

In addition, Muslim women attained a high status as medical scholars such as Zainab of the Bani Awd tribe who was a prominent physician and an expert oculist. Umm-al-Hassan hint Al-Qadi Abi Jafar-al-Tanjali was a renowned woman of broad knowledge in different subjects, and was especially famous as a doctor.

Muslim women proved to be good warriors and they fought side by side with men. They achieved a considerable degree of success, and on occasion played very important military roles. In this respect mention should be made of Nusaiba, the wife of Zaid Ibn Asim, who took part in the famous battle of 'Uhud'. In that battle she fought vigorously and in the critical time when the Prophet was left alone she fought alongside him and wounded 11 persons with her sword. In the same battle, Nusaiba hint Kab-al-Mazinia headed the Prophet's army against the enemy forces and at a crucial moment managed to minimise the losses of the Muslim army.

In addition, Muslim women also proved their ability to play a constructive role in other activities of the community. For example, they were involved in the political issues of the time and their opinions in political affairs were highly respected. They often took part in the process of choosing the Caliph. They also enjoyed full freedom to express their ideas and were encouraged to participate in the social life of the community. Public life was like a stage where both men and women were actively involved. In the early period of Islam women used to discuss and debate with the Prophet and his companions and even protect their rights if they were breached. It is said that during the time of the second Caliph Umar, a woman expressed her disagreement with him publicly in matters relating to the women's dowry and managed to correct him.

The Quran encourages women to speak their minds and not to be silent; nonetheless we see today some fundamentalists propagating the unfounded slogan that the voice of woman is Awrah (private parts to be covered up) and therefore arguing that it is in her best interest to keep quiet. For how can a woman learn and grow intellectually if she is not allowed to speak and communicate with others? How can she widen her understanding of things around her and speak forcefully and impressively if she is prevented from debating with others publicly?

On the contrary, Islam granted woman the right to hold a job and to involve herself actively in trade and commerce. She is entitled to work outside her home and earn a living. During the early Islamic period women often helped men in their outdoor work and were allowed to move about freely among men. Asma, the daughter of the first Caliph Abu-Bakr, used to help her husband in his field work. The Prophet himself praised women who worked hard and well; he also encouraged women, including his wives and daughters, to engage themselves in gainful work. He used to say 'The most blessed earning is that which a person gains from his own labour'.

Women in early Islam even held formal posts of authority in the community such as Al-Shafa bint Abdullah who was appointed by the second Caliph Umar as superintendent of markets in Medina many times. Hence, women can work as teachers, doctors, lawyers; they can work as employers or senior managers and they can work as Judges. It must be stressed that up until the present time and in most Muslim countries with the exception of Tunisia and Malaysia, the position of Judge is still regarded as a male domain. Women in these countries have traditionally been prevented from assuming this position.

The ban has no legal foundation in either the scripture or the Sunnah. On the contrary, Aishah, the wife of the Prophet, was the forerunner in undertaking the position. She acted as a Judge during the era of the first three Caliphs. Also, Abu Hanifa, the founder of one of the schools of law states that a woman might become a Judge; and consider all matters except the ones that are under the penal code. Jarir-al-Tabari, the famous commentator on the Quran, gives women the right to be appointed as Judge without any conditions. However, despite the fact that the external work of the woman was allowed and respected, a house- wife, unable to work due to domestic responsibilities, did not feel that her contribution was less honourable and less fruitful.

The high status granted to women by the Quranic reforms which prevailed during the early Islamic period did not last long. Firstly, certain pre-Islamic customs reappeared, especially during the Abbasid period; secondly, various social attitudes infiltrated Islamic culture from conquered peoples, and were assimilated as norms and then identified with Islam.

The status of Muslim women started to deteriorate. This was accelerated by catastrophic historical events such as the Mongol and Turkish invasions and the ensuing decline of the Islamic civilisation. The ambience generated by these conditions served to undermine the position of Muslim women who became less and less part of social life in general.

They were neglected and treated as sex objects, assumed heavy veiling and were confined to their small circle of womenfolk with no contact outside their homes; they were prevented from participating in the public life of the community and excluded from public worship in the mosque. But the worst deprivation of all was the denial of their right to receive education. It was believed that basic awareness of the religious rites and memorising part of the Quran was sufficient for women.

While girls were welcome to all religious instruction especially in the lower grades, they were prevented from having further knowledge and education. In fact, the opposition to female education reached its peak when condemnation was voiced against teaching women the art of writing: 'He the teacher must not instruct any woman or female slave in the arts of writing, for thereby would accrue to them only an increase of depravity'. Thus, their role in society centered mainly on preparing them to be good and obedient wives and mothers. Later, when modern education became available, women were denied access to it and only schools for boys were initially developed. Female education was constrained by inherited social customs.

Education for women came to be viewed as being of secondary importance to keeping the home and the family. 'A woman's mission is to be a good wife and a compassionate mother... an ignorant rural woman is better for the nation than one thousand female lawyers or attorney generals'. Female education was viewed as a threat to the traditional customs and the way of life of these societies. Indeed, educated women were feared and mistrusted as they could communicate potentially destructive or innovative ideas. Educated women were considered to be obtrusive and assertive. They did not appeal to men who expected them to serve them obediently. In addition, leaving home to go to school was in contrast with the idea of women segregation. The Islamic ideal of women's education and intellectual development was thus distorted, confused and actively opposed. The result was a disaster.

The illiteracy of Muslim women reached a peak and became a widespread phenomenon in the world of Islam. Consequently, women throughout the Muslim world became ignorant not only of outside affairs, but also of their legal rights in terms of marriage, divorce and inheritance. Very often due to their ignorance of these rights, they were cheated, deceived and misled. This rendered Muslim women unable to claim and defend the rights guaranteed them by Islam. This situation continued up to recent times, until efforts were made to improve female education in different parts of the Muslim world. However, despite these efforts and the rapid progress which has been achieved in the past four to five decades, the opportunities for women's education in the Muslim world, especially in the Middle East, still lag far behind those for men. Nothing substantial has been achieved, despite the fact that all Muslim countries have encouraged the spread of female education, stated that their aim is to try and raise the educational level of women, and proclaimed their intention to attain universal literacy. The accomplishment of these goals seems very far off.

The gap between female and male literacy rates in several places is increasing and the overall level of illiteracy is extremely high. The Islamic world, especially the Arab world, is amongst the areas in the world which has, the highest rate of illiteracy amongst women, the lowest level of schooling for girls and the smallest number of women in paid employment. In 1991, the illiteracy rate among females in Afghanistan was 86 per cent, in Pakistan 78 per cent, in Egypt 66 per cent and in Iran 56 per cent. Although women's literacy varies enormously from country to country and also from area to area in any particular country, women in the Arab world are still a small minority among the student population. In every country the rate of male literacy is much higher than female literacy. Even in those countries which have initiated some reforms, there are still considerable disparities between male and female literacy, as well as major discrepancies between the type of female education offered and the socio-economic needs of the various Arab countries. This has been caused by many factors such as: family attitudes toward female education which still prevail, especially in the rural areas, where the majority of the Muslim population lives; and the high female drop out rate due to the inequality between urban and rural education.

But the most important factor so far has been the historical interpretation of the jurists. This has taken the shape of a clear deviation from genuine Islamic principles by its strong opposition to female education. This factor is still very strong in Muslim society, particularly Arab society, and it influences government policy on education options and opportunities for women. Saudi Arabia presents a clear example where Islam has been used to first deny and then discourage women's education.

In Saudi Arabia, a highly selective and narrow interpretation of Islam have had a restrictive impact upon the lives of women. Traditionally, religion has been used as an excuse to justify the seclusion of women from the educational process. The rigid influence of the conservative theologians has played a critical role in: suffocating female education for several decades through maintaining that girls should be prevented from all state primary and secondary schools.

The extremists argued that education of women would create immorality through corrupting their thinking and diverting their attention away from their essential role as good wives and mothers. They also voiced their fear that the outcome of the conflict of values brought about by such an educational transformation would result in discontent and instability both in the home as well as in society. It was under such pressure that public education for women in the Kingdom did not start until 1960.

Female education was introduced in Saudi Arabia in 1960, when the former King Faisal took the decision to set up schools for girls. Initially, the attempt met with strong opposition from the extremists who demonstrated their disagreement by gathering at the gates of the schools, expressing their displeasure with the new schools and with those who registered their daughters in them. National Guards had to be called to restore order. The opposition continued, unabated, until the government made two essential concessions: first, the government pledged that female education would be in line with Saudi customs, especially that of rigid segregation.

Secondly, it set up a special body called the 'General Presidency for Girls' Education' to be responsible for girls' education. As a gesture of its commitment to preserve Saudi customs, the government placed this body under the control of the Saudi religious authorities who, since then, continue to supervise the education of girls in the Kingdom.

With this compromise, opposition to female education was finally mitigated and schools for girls were eventually established. The idea of schools for girls seems now to be accepted and the number of females enrolled in the educational process is increasing every year. However, despite the fact that female education in Saudi Arabia is becoming popular, and the statistics show that significant gains have been accomplished, equal opportunity between men and women is still far from being reached. This is even more the case in respect of female education in the rural areas, which is an elusive goal yet to be attained. In fact, the policy of female education in Saudi Arabia has been founded on limited bases, aimed more at discouraging than promoting the learning process; this process neither satisfies the needs of Saudi women nor corresponds to the socio-economic requirements of the country. In the elementary schools, for example, girls mostly learn those courses which are assumed to be suitable for them in their traditional role in Saudi society. These courses emphasise mainly the Arabic language, home economics, child caring and religious instruction.

Although the elementary schools have been set up almost everywhere in the Kingdom, the proportion of female drop out after this primary level is still very high, and is a cause of great concern. As the level of education increases, the opportunities for girls to advance or progress become fewer. This is due to the fact that not all levels of knowledge and education available are at the location where the girls happen to be living, and also because in Saudi society women are not allowed to live alone in a residential campus. Hence it is difficult for them to move close to the educational institutions. Secondary schools, for instance, are not available everywhere in the country, neither are colleges.

Vocational education too has been extremely limited except for nursing schools and tailoring centres. As regard university education, the situation is no better. The universities in Saudi Arabia are mainly for males, although some of them have branches in their departments for females. In these branches there is strict segregation of the sexes in classes and all teachers are female. Sometimes, due to the lack of suitable female teachers, the learning process is accomplished through the use of closed-circuit television. This enables male professors to lecture and answer female questions, without coming into contact with them.

In speaking of the remarkable general progress of education in Iraq several years ago one of the officials in the Ministry of Education summed up the great contrast between the present development and that under the Turkish regime. "Very little was done for girls. The Central Girls' School in Baghdad which was established for the daughters of Turkish officials was like a foreign school, and did not benefit the girls of Baghdad. There were practically no foreign governesses, even in the better Baghdad families, such as you would have found in Istanbul or Cairo.

Only a few sent their daughters to the Catholic convent for a smattering of French and embroidery, but education for girls in the real sense did not begin until after the Mandate. At first it developed slowly, but now is going with a rush." What is meant by a rush is evident from the fact that elementary schools are crowded in towns like Baghdad, Mosul and Basra, and each year brings an added demand for more girls' schools. The number of girls, which is at present about one-third of the number of boys, is increasing more rapidly than the number of boys in school. The actual number of girls entering school in 1932 was more than the number of boys entering. The enrolment of girls in primary education has increased 105 per cent. But even though the relative rate of increase of girls is greater than that of boys, there will be for a long time the disparity in the education of girls and boys that is characteristic of the East. The desire that eventually this should not be the case is evident from the new requests each year for more girls' schools.

This urge for girls' education is passing out of the few cities exposed to modern ideas into the smaller towns, where today a girls' school attracts an increasing number. Even from Najaf and Karbala, the two shrine cities of Shiah Islam, requests for girls' schools were sent several years ago to Baghdad, but the reactionary forces in these Shiah strongholds stirred up such an opposition that the requests were withdrawn. More open to new ideas are the semi-nomadic tribes of the desert.

Growth in education may be measured not only in geographical extension and in the larger number of schools and of girls enrolled, but also in the ascending level of girls' education. It has moved steadily up from the little Quran school under the Mulla to the primary school, then to intermediate and secondary schools. The Central Girls' College in Baghdad has extended its course from eight to ten players, and now gives the most complete education for girl's in Iraq. For the small town the new attitude toward girls' education is evident in the numbers in the primary school; in Baghdad the Central College is the index of the Muslim response to education for girls since over eighty per cent of the students are Muslim, and many do not live in Baghdad. The registration in this school each year exceeds the facilities so that a large number must be turned away. In Iraq conservatism has been disarmed by promoting the education for girls within the sanctions of Islamic tradition.

The Baghdad school is a good illustration of the general situation. Purdah conditions in this institution are carefully observed, the school following rather than directly promoting social change. But the atmosphere of the school is steadily becoming less purdah. At the beginning there was no man servant; now a young man janitor moves about the school freely. At first, no men visitors were allowed, not even the English Director of Education; now they are admitted but only with special permits from the Ministry of Education. When they were first admitted, all the girls veiled; now perhaps only one or two out of forty ever cover their faces before visitors.

Although none of the older girls take part in the school exercises, there is a tendency for parents, proud of their daughters, to waive their conservatism and let them appear in public even after they are really past the age of veiling. For example, a well-known family still allows a talented daughter of fourteen to perform in public. She is rather small for her age, and passes without criticism. The consciousness of the veil is still very evident, however, outside the school. Visit the Baghdad School near closing time and you will find a group of old women, perhaps a few men, hovering about waiting to take the girls home. The older as well as the younger girls must have a special guardian, since according to Muslim custom, a veiled woman is helpless outside her own home. These caretakers are often disregarded by the girls; or perhaps "parked" somewhere while the girls manage to shop or go to the dressmaker on the way home.

An extra gift or bakshish smooths the way for this suspicious freedom and then the girl appears at home properly chaperoned. The elderly chaperone is required also to accompany the girls on 'The school excursion, a regular annual event for each class, and a great sign of advancing freedom. These excursions are an interesting illustration of the old and new. The girls go in motor cars, veiled, as far as the outskirts of the city, then up go the veils. Their regular attendants' a nurse or a chauffeur, or some old family retainer, enjoy watching the games and incidentally have a good exposure to modern ideas. "These caretakers," as the Principal of the school remarked,' "are much more aware of the present-day schoolgirl's problems than are the girl's parents."

The slightest innovation in the Baghdad school, as in other schools in Iraq, must be carefully considered in reference to conservative opinion. The need for such care is illustrated by the protest which was made against having a lecture given at the Girls' College by a professor from the Men's Normal School.

One of the students commented on having heard a very interesting lecture. The father, a reactionary Muslim, reported it to the Parliament and the Minister of Education. Since then, the further use of men speakers has not been possible. Indicative of progress, however, is the occasional attendance of a group from the Girls' Normal School at lectures, cinemas or special national celebrations at the Men's Normal School. The girls are, it is true, carefully chaperoned, and sit as a group in the balcony without any individual contact.

The limited social milieu of girls' education in Baghdad is determined not only by public opinion, but also by the attitude of the authorities. King Faisal was very definitely interested in girls' education but believed that it should, be promoted within the social sanctions of Islam. King Ghazi has continued his father's policy. The advance of education, for girls, as for boys, will doubtless continue to receive, the patronage of the Palace, but without any idea of changing social customs.

The change in the programme of girls' education along a number of lines indicates growth in effectiveness. Teachers are beginning to be aware that girls need other courses than the stereotyped programme required by an identical system for boys and girls. The difficulty of introducing new content in education becomes obvious from the fact that a girl in a civics class, working on a "Know your City" project, could not visit the post office, because girls are not supposed to go out and have no reason to see public buildings. In spite of difficulties new ideas are making headway. Physical education is, progressing, even though slowly because of the veil.

Physical education is now interpreted in the larger meaning as an emphasis on normal recreation-clubs, school excursions, and general creative activities. This represents an entirely new idea in education as a whole, but especially in the education of girls. The use of the school as the centre for entertainments, recreation, cinema and radio performance is being promoted.

The old Oriental idea of the crowds being entertained by the storyteller furnishes perhaps the germ for the new community usefulness of the school. Some teachers realize the need for vocational education for girls, but the time does not yet seem ripe for this emphasis.

Differentiation in girls' education, however, is emphasized through courses in home sciences, including homemaking, child care, sanitation and personal hygiene. With these new emphases the necessity for a closer relationship between the home and the school is obvious to thoughtful teachers, who realize that the real job of the modern school is social.

The Principal of the Baghdad Central College summed up the problem of the difference between the teaching of the school and the home thus: "Every Muslim girl who goes to the Baghdad School is exposed to two streams of influence which affect every act of her life—sleeping, dressing, and undressing at night, eating, walking, and thinking. The school teaches physical and mental activity; the home, passivity and fatalism. The school must seek to bridge the gap between its influence and that of the home."

This contrast between the ideals of home and school have led to a recognition of the need for adult education. There are some developments of adult education for the lower classes to raise the level of literacy, and also the higher level along the lines of social education. At the other extreme from adult education is the promotion of the modern kindergarten, an entirely new emphasis in Iraq. These kindergartens are in striking contrast to the Mulla schools for little children, where they sat all huddled up together before an old sheikh or an uneducated elderly Muslim woman, chanting the Quran in high shrill voices, swaying back and forth in rhythmic accompaniment.

The kindergarten in the Girls' School in Baghdad, which serves as a training centre for kindergarten teachers, would compare favourably in equipment with nine-tenths of modern American kindergartens. Another problem about which educators for girls in Iraq express concern is the question of social relationships. Under the regime of the veil the school does not encourage social contact, but the content of the teaching, as has been shown, lead toward the idea of unveiling.

Social change and education inevitably go together, since, as an Iraqi educator said, "You can't 'stagger' social advance" until the educational process is finished, and you cannot advance in education without some idea of social reform. The major difficulty in promoting a programme of modern education or even education along conventional lines in Iraq has been the securing of teachers. The steady development of a staff of trained women teachers in a decade has been accomplished to a large extent by the importation of Syrian teachers. The salaries paid by the Iraqi Government to these Syrian teachers have been very high, in comparison with salaries in Syria, but the need was urgent.

A real pioneering spirit and keenness for adventure together with their technical preparation for teaching, have been required of these Syrian teachers, who have been building a school programme for girls in a new country. This group of young Syrians has established the teaching profession in Iraq on a high educational level, has given prestige to teaching as a career and made it worthy of even the most conservative upper class. Their influence however has not been limited to the schools but has permeated the social environment.

Undoubtedly to the younger generation of Iraqi young men and women, the Syrian group of men and women teachers has presented, by their normal social relationships, a whole new way of life and inspired the desire in the younger generation of Iraq to be released from their traditional social restraints. The heyday of the Syrian teacher's opportunity, both for men and women—for there have been many of each has now passed.

The Syrian women teachers are now only in secondary and normal schools and are there much less than before. Eventually, perhaps in four or five years, they will be entirely replaced, as it is considered desirable, both because of national economy and national amour-proper, for Iraq to have her own teachers. The preparation of Iraqi girls for secondary schools is being accomplished by sending them abroad to Syria or elsewhere on Government scholarships. The extension of Government subsidies to girls in itself signalizes progress in girls' education.

Until 1928 these foreign scholarships were limited to men. Since 1928, when the first group of eight girls went to Syria, their number each year has steadily grown. Now thirty or more girls are studying abroad, mostly in Beirut at the American School for Girls and the British Syrian Training College, also in the American junior College for Women and the American University of Beirut.

Naturally, the problem of sending girls is more difficult than boys because of social conditions. Furthermore, there is less certainty of direct benefit to the Department of Education, since educating girls is something of a lottery because of the high probability of their marriage.

However, as an investment, not measured in direct returns to the schools, but to the community as a whole, this system of foreign scholarships has had great value. Especially worthy of note is the increase of Muslim girls on foreign scholarships. At first, only Christians were available, as Muslim parents could not think of sending their daughters abroad. The number of Muslim girls has increased; now about half the number or more are Muslims.

The attitude of Muslim parents has distinctly changed. Now training abroad is becoming every year a more natural thing, although it must still make quite a stir in a Muslim family to send a daughter five hundred miles across the desert, for ten months' study each year for several years, in a Christian Mission

School. Muslim girls now go abroad for study not merely on Government scholarships, but also on private funds to gain a higher education, as a few Muslims as well as Christians have felt the urge for something beyond the Baghdad School. These Muslim girls from Iraq who are studying abroad are already exerting a social influence in their home environment. They come back from Beirut each spring with new ideas showing Anglo-Saxon influence in points of view and clothes of the French style.

Often while abroad they have perhaps indulged in a vacation from the veil. All of these broader outside influences cannot fail to have their effects in Baghdad or in Mosul. Up to the present time the needs for higher education both for men and women in Iraq have been met by study abroad, in very large measure in the American University of Beirut, which has become the university for the Arabic speaking world. There has been some agitation in Baghdad for the establishment of a university but this is not considered probable for sometime, since this would involve an unwarranted expense for the small number of students who are as yet ready or desirous of higher education.

A medical college in Baghdad is, however, regarded as necessary to solve the most pressing national problem of health. The training of men and women in medical service is fundamental to the economic progress of Iraq and in the near future should be carried on in Iraq.

The admission of Muslim girls to the coeducational medical school in Baghdad would be an interesting parallel to the fact that the first university coeducation in Egypt was for women medical students. One of the special influences that has favoured the promotion of girls' education, especially in Baghdad, is the presence of a number of educated Turkish women, wives of prominent Iraqi officials. Their example has stimulated a spirit of competition in Baghdad mothers to have their daughters well educated and thus make a good marriage. The marriage motivation which is evident throughout the East in promoting girls' education, has thus an added force in Baghdad, because of the Turkish influence in the situation.

The group of advanced Turkish women has created a desire among some of the Baghdad women for social progress. The contrast between the freedom of Turkey and the social conservatism of Iraq has made a special impression because the Turkish women are Muslims. The combined effect of the Turkish and Syrian groups has undoubtedly been influential in creating in Baghdad a certain dissatisfaction with existing social conditions and in stimulating the urge for change. In the development of modern education in Iraq, Anglo-Saxon-British and American-influence has played an important role. British ideas furnished the basis of the educational system which was organized during the first years of the mandate.

American educational influence has been evident in the later developments in Iraq, largely due to the fact that most of the Syrian teachers were graduates from the American institutions in Beirut and a number of them also had studied in America. Moreover, the majority of the Iraqi students on foreign scholarships have also studied in Beirut in the American schools and hold key positions in the educational system of Iraq.

As a natural result of the predominance of Anglo-Saxon influence in Iraq, English is the second language. Compared with other countries of the Near East and Middle East, the work of foreign educational institutions in Iraq has been very limited. Girls' education, however has been directly affected by the three American Mission Schools for girls in Baghdad, Mosul and Basra.

These three institutions have contributed to a number of Muslim girls a sound educational preparation and have stimulated public appreciation of the value of girls' education. The primary impetus for general progress in Iraq and this, of course, affects the educational advance of women has come through the vigorous spirit of nationalism awakened since the World War. The example of Turkish nationalism, strong, aggressive, successful has been undoubtedly a stimulant for Iraq.

Leaders in Iraq repeatedly express the idea that the retarded development of women is a real handicap to the development of children and hence to the progress of the State. Iraq has adopted democratic institutions such as a constitution and Parliament, which are an anomaly in an illiterate country. Hence, the problem is to raise the whole educational level. The spirit of almost breathless nationalism of Iraq has stirred the public consciousness into a sense of need for education, and especially education for Muslim girls.

Education in Iran has always in the past been identified with religion, largely connected with the mosques and maintained by the clergy, created an unfavourable atmosphere for promoting the education of girls. The general public has always considered it useless to educate girls.

The idea expressed in Iranian philosophy that education should be highly selective for those who can profit by it, has always been the current opinion and has debarred girls from educational privilege as expressed in the saying, "Where the innate capacity is good, education may make an impression, but no furbisher knows how to give a polish to bad iron." Although the new spirit is overcoming the old prejudicial attitude toward girls' education, such a handicap is not soon overcome.

The number of Government boys' schools, primary and secondary, is about four times the number of schools for girls, and the total enrolment of boys in all schools in Iran is slightly more than three times that of girls. More than half the education of girls in Iran is carried on by private schools, which have contributed also very greatly to boys' education.

Teheran of course represents the high-water mark of interest in both girls' and boys' education. Rural education receives little attention and girls' rural schools are practically nil. The opening of ten primary schools of three grades for boys and girls is not only a numerical advance but also represents social progress in adopting coeducation. The teachers of these mixed primary schools are all women and over half the pupils are girls.

Education for the great majority of girls is limited to the elementary schools, which means a maximum of six years but often only a four-years' course. There are only a few middle schools and one normal school for girls, offering an eleven years' course and about thirty private middle schools, also of eleven years.

The American Mission institution for girls in Teheran, Nurbakush, with a course of twelve and sometimes thirteen years represents the top level of education for girls in Iran. Girls' education in Iran of any kind is the product of only about two decades and education on a modern basis is the result of only a decade. Viewed over a period of years there are distinct signs of advance. The fact that education for girls has begun is in itself the most hopeful evidence of progress. Apart from the growth in the extent of girls' education in Iran, it is worthy of notice also that education for girls has risen from the floor of the Quran school to the level of seats and desks of the modern primary school.

From the dull, damp room connected with some mosque with its crowd of little boys and girls huddled together on a mat in an atmosphere of disorder and all-talk-at- one-time casual heterogeneity under an old sheikh, whose method was to keep up an unbroken chanting of the Quran—from such a school it is a far cry to the present-day primary school with its well-ordered school room, its maps and blackboard, its orderly atmosphere, and young teachers, such as one finds in most of the schools in Teheran today. The fact, however, that some girls' schools are still held in private dwellings, ill-adapted for school use. And that many of the teachers are inexperienced, makes one, realize that schools for girls, even in Teheran, are of recent origin.

The eagerness of girls for education and the inadequacy of their facilities are also evident when one visited a Teheran primary school, and found three girls wedged tightly in each seat in a room with fifty children, which could not comfortably hold more than thirty or thirty-five. With girls clamouring for places in school, it is easy to understand the statement that the Parliament does not disagree over the necessity to expand education for girls.

When the first girls' school was opened there, a private venture of a wealthy Muslim woman, the key-bearded city fathers raised a strong opposition. "Why should there be a school for girls?" They said: "Who believes that they can learn?" The answer to their protest was a model small town school, an attractive new building, very spacious playground and an alert young teacher from Teheran, well trained according to the present standards.

Any doubt as to whether girls can learn is dispelled by the bright-eyed little Iranian girls, one hundred or more, learning the elements of modern education, and also the useful vocation of carpet weaving, if they choose.

The eager response of the girls must give deep satisfaction to the founder of the school, who herself is illiterate and therefore, perhaps, more keenly appreciates the value of education. She must feel that her annual expense for the school, the entire income from one of her villages, is a sound investment. But the city fathers doubtless still shake their heads at such rank and futile extravagance. In such a reactionary environment, modern education had been planted with great care.

The physical schools have been developed along the more formal type of gymnastic exercise. The creative forms of recreation through various extracurricular activities are scarcely known. New emphases, however, are being introduced by an American adviser to the Ministry of Education. A class of thirty-two young women in 1935 finished a course of three months in scouting as a preparation to develop this work in the girls' schools. Another group has been trained in sports to offset the programme of conventional calisthenics.

An effort is also being made to introduce more social plays, and games, and especially music, all of which are innovations. The programme of athletics in girls' schools has been given a great deal of newspaper publicity through frequent pictures of Girl Guide troops and girls in, active games and exercises. Thus, the public is being effectively educated to this new idea of girlhood. School hygiene is also receiving attention.

A special medical officer visits the schools, inspects the sanitary conditions, examines the children and sends those needing special attention to the clinic or hospital where free treatment is given. But since these visits are not very frequent, perhaps only once a month, the regular teacher is expected to emphasize the fundamentals of health. A distinctive feature of the teaching profession in Iran has been the work of the women inspectors. The system of having women inspectors, which was established when the private schools were brought under Government supervision, was necessitated by the fact that it was impossible because of the veil for men to visit girls' schools. Thus, a social handicap has led to a constructive educational benefit.

The women inspectors, many of whom are graduates of the American School for Girls in Teheran, represent a high type in the teaching profession. One of the best known of the women inspectors is Khanum Doulatabad, the pioneer in girls' education already mentioned, who was one of the first women from Iran to study abroad.

As Iranian girls at that time did not leave their own country alone, the ever watchful police held up at the border this eager student on her way to Paris, until verification could be received from Teheran. Today Iranian women students as well as men pursue higher education abroad. But women students have not yet received Government scholarships for foreign study. For over eighty years Iranian boys have been sent abroad for foreign study. Practically all of the present leaders of Iran have studied in Europe, the large majority in France.

An increasing number have been sent from the different ministries—Education, Health, Justice and others. Although, some of the other Ministries are still sending students abroad the Ministry of Education has now discontinued these foreign scholarships, at least temporarily, and is concentrating on the development of stronger institutions of higher learning in Iran. When a law was passed authorizing too foreign scholarships annually for five years for young men but making no provision for women students, the obvious inequality evoked a vigorous protest from some of the advocates of women's education.

Ten to twenty scholarships for teacher training were urged for women. The question became the subject of heated discussion carried on in the Press. The opponents argued on the basis of unpreparedness of girls and the danger of Western contamination, contending furthermore that Iran offered adequate training for girls.

The advocates of foreign scholarships for girls, among whom were several women, cited as proof of the capacity of girls the number of successful candidates in Government examination, and maintained that women would be less contaminated morally than men have been by foreign contact. They emphasized the necessity of training in Europe because of the backward conditions in Iran, which make adequate training impossible.

The discussion brought into sharp relief the conflict in Iran today between conservatism and progress. In spite of a strong tide in favour of foreign scholarships for girls, the opposition prevailed. No girls have been officially included on the Government lists, but a few, six or eight, have been partially helped by Government funds. However, quite a number of Iranian girls, perhaps sixty or more, are now studying abroad, mostly in Europe on private funds.

Recently, higher education in Iran for girls has been the subject of much public discussion. The conservatives in Iran as elsewhere East or West have advanced the argument that girls not only do not need advanced education but should not have it, since they are required for home life.

But quite aside from the opposition against higher education for women, there seems to be as yet on the whole very little demand for it in Iran. Nurbakush, Sage College, meets the needs as yet of the small minority who desire to go beyond the secondary school. The Government University will be eventually opened to women students in departments, beginning first with dentistry and pharmacy, for which courses several women students have already applied.

The prevailing lack of urge for higher education up to the present time is doubtless related to the fact that the interest in professional careers in Iran has not yet in any sense cut across the idea of marriage. Aside from teaching which, as has been said, is considered as an economic necessity rather than a career, there is practically no profession open to Muslim girls in Iran. Marriage is the main career. To ensure a good marriage, education up to a point is regarded as desirable. This explains in Iran as elsewhere the increasing number of girls in school beyond the primary and secondary stage. But higher education is not considered an additional marriage asset; perhaps this explains the lack of desire for it.

The fact that the education of girls is being extended, however, through the secondary stage is very important. The longer period of education and later marriage age point to the eventual solution of one of the major problems of Iran and of the East as a whole – the disparity between the literate husband and illiterate wife. Some few attempts are being made in private schools in Teheran to meet the problem of the present generation of illiterate wives, many of whom are pathetically eager to bridge the gap between themselves and their husbands. Some of them are beyond the schoolgirl stage and can only laboriously overcome the handicap of illiteracy.

Many are still the age of schoolgirls and eager to attend the regular schools, which, however, are already overcrowded and cannot admit married women or girls. A few private schools for married women have been started such as, for example, the one carried on by a Women's Association in Iran. These schools are small but significant, showing what should be done on a much larger scale to meet this important social problem.

The growing consciousness of this problem – the disparity in education between men and women – is one of the main secrets of the present awakening of interest in education for girls and women in Iran, whether it finds expression in the primary or secondary schools or in meagre adult education efforts. A few years ago there was not as at present this poignant awareness of the fact that Iranian women without education are under a terrific handicap.

The social and intellectual cleavage between men and women in Iran was not questioned. But today there is a growing consciousness of a need for change. The younger generation of educated men want educated wives in Iran as elsewhere. The Iranian mother desires to see her daughter well married, and enjoying an equality in marriage such as she, herself, has been denied. Perhaps just as in Baghdad the increase of foreign wives in the higher circles has made some Teheran mothers realize the desirability of educating their daughters.

Doubtless, Muslim women in Iran, especially in Teheran, have been affected also by a comparison of their social and educational position with that of women in other communities. The Armenians, in giving up the chaddur a number of years ago and availing themselves freely of educational opportunity have furnished a progressive example.

The Zoroastrian community with its freedom from social handicaps for women, and its active promotion of girls' schools may have also had an influence, although the forward movement of Zoroastrian women has produced no outstanding women leaders. More significant for Muslim women perhaps has been the example of the women of the Bahai community, who though still veiled, are quite free behind the veil, representing thus a halfway stage of progress.

The fact that in many communities the Bahai Girls' was the first and only school for a long time has undoubtedly stimulated Muslim educational effort, but the Bahaist influence is less important today than in the earlier period. The Muslim woman's desire for education and general advance has also been greatly affected by the social reforms in Turkey. A direct influence on the educational progress of Muslim women had also come from the Anglo-Saxon schools, the British and American Mission girls' schools in different parts of Iran and especially Nurbakush in Teheran.

These institutions had effectively presented to the community the highest value of education for girls. Without discussing freedom or apparently promoting freedom for women, they produced an atmosphere in which freedom is the natural result. At the commencement of Nurbakush in May 1929 for the first time the three Muslim unveiled graduates delivered their graduating 'addresses to an audience of eight hundred people, and were received with enthusiasm and applause.

The Mission Schools for Girls in Tabriz and Hamadan had deeply affected a whole area. The Shiraz Girls' School, formerly a Mission institution but now under private auspices has been a distinctive influence for education along modern English lines. It represents an adaptation of Anglo-Saxon ideals. Alborz College in Teheran, the American College for Men, has without question been a great force for the social and educational progress of women, in that it has given to its large student body of young men from all over Iran new social ideals.

The increasing penetration of Anglo-Saxon ideas, as represented in the British and American schools in Iran, is an interesting evidence of the new trend in Iran away from the European model of life and thought. For over eighty years French influence has been dominant. French is the second language; the educational system is modelled on French lines; Paris has always been the Mecca for Iranian students. But in the present period of awakening, a migration from French to Anglo-Saxon influence is evident, which is having a pervasive effect on the social and educational advance of women.

Although foreign influences, French and English, are exerting a subtle force toward change in various phases of Iranian life, the impelling motive of the present renaissance, of which the advance of women is a part, in Iran as in Iraq, is the newly aroused spirit of nationalism. This has for Iran the special meaning of a growth in the consciousness of national unity and a new appreciation of Iranian culture. The building of roads has facilitated travel and brought hitherto isolated cities into closer contact. The divided provincial loyalties of the past are being supplanted by a national loyalty and pride, which demands that Iran should not have an inferior position in the East. A few leaders in Iran recognize that the advance of women is a necessity for national progress and are therefore vigorously promoting girls' education. Even by the less thinking majority, education for girls is being accepted as a natural part of the new era. However, the situation changed to a great extent, following the Islamic revolution.

The obvious reason for the lack of education among Muslim women is purdah and general Muslim conservatism, an interrelated cause and effect. Purdah lays a detaining hand on the Muslim girl's education. It interferes not only after the veil is assumed, which is usually not until the age eleven or twelve years, but also before that age; the prevailing purdah psychology often prevents even little girls, not yet veiled, from attending the primary school, which does not have a woman teacher. Because of the dearth of women teachers in the primary schools many Muslim girls never cross the threshold of a school.

The direct effect of purdah on the number of girls in school is shown by the fact that in purdah-bound provinces like the Punjab and the United Provinces, the attendance of girls in school is lower than in other provinces. Apart from the fact that purdah undoubtedly curtails the school privileges of Muslim girls, it presents very practical difficulties in education. At the opening or closing hour, or in a smaller town like Bhopal, the covered bullock-carts lined up at the school door, and have watched the shrouded figures scuttle from the entrance of the school compound into the curtained safety of the conveyance.

In addition to the purdah conveyance, the necessity for a female attendant to accompany the girl to see to it that purdah is not broken on the way to school, and the elaborate precautions necessary for preserving strict purdah in the school, for example requiring even the elimination of all male servants from girls' schools — these restrictions have vastly complicated school life for a Muslim girl in India.

Other social customs characteristic of India, but not peculiar to Muslims, have prevented Muslim girls, as well as Indian girls of other communities, from having full educational privileges. Although child marriage is especially associated with Hinduism, early marriage among the masses of Muslims is also quite common.

In 1921 out of eight and a half million brides under fifteen years of age one and a half million were Muslims. This means that number of girls were cut off from any education beyond the early primary grades. With attention concentrated on early marriage for their daughter, the Muslim parents' chief concern naturally is to find a suitable son-in-law. Hence, attendance of girls in the primary school seems unnecessary and in the middle school is obviously impossible. As girls are withdrawn from school just at the time when they begin to mature in mind as well as body, this not only cuts off the majority from ordinary education but reduces to a minimum the number of Muslim girls who might become teachers.

The education of Muslim girls has been impeded not only by the specific handicaps of purdah and early marriage, but frequently by the conservatism of the Indian Muslim community. This conservatism has been strengthened by the Nationalist Movement. Muslim India in its fear of absorption by the Hindus, has shown a reaction similar to the attitude the Muslim community in Palestine in reference to Zionism. Some Muslim leaders have always insisted on having special privileges in schools for Muslims, unwilling otherwise to avail themselves of the regular facilities of education in India.

The general situation, of education for Muslim girls shows a very slow but steady advance both in the number of schools for girls and of girls in schools. After 1920 the curve of elementary and secondary schools begins to ascend. This period marks also practically the beginning of higher education for Muslim girls, although the number of Muslim girls is still negligible. Isabella Thoburn College in Lucknow, and Kinnaird College for Women in Lahore, which may be taken as valid criteria, show a steady increase of Muslims as also of girls from other communities.

The few Muslim women who are well educated often hold positions of unusual prominence.

A widely known Muslim woman in the Punjab, the first woman to take her doctorate, has an important post as an inspectress for girls' schools. She has maintained strict purdah and thus proved that in spite of the purdah, advance in education is possible. But it may also be questioned whether by such a policy she has not sacrificed an opportunity to exert greater influence for social advance, as the first highly educated Muslim woman in her part of India.

Of the widespread desire of Muslim parents for the education of their daughters there is no question today; even more evident is the eager response of Muslim girls themselves to these new opportunities.

The renaissance in education is affecting not only the extent but also the character of the Government programme for girls' schools. Under the old system the few girls who entered college found themselves well prepared for equal competition with men in professional careers; but preparation for marriage, the primary career for the great majority in India, as elsewhere in the East, has received little attention. The regular Government schools and the majority of private girls' schools have been bound by the straitjacket of the examination system.

Homemaking subjects, physical education, and hygiene have been only optional and difficult to promote, since the parents, as well as students, regard the school certificate based on the regular requirements as the final seal of education. There is, however, some loosening of the straitjacket bonds, through the beginning of vocational training and homemaking courses, and more physical education.

A certain amount of vocational education has been developed in connection with the regular schools. Some of the Mission schools have pioneered in this field attempting to coordinate girls' education more closely with the needs of practical life.

The most distinctive development in the Government system is the Government Zenana Industrial Schools in Lahore of which there are now fifteen. In addition to regular elementary education these schools offer courses in home arts and crafts along very modern lines. Although these schools are open to girls and women of different religions, and social levels, and different ages they especially serve Muslims and offer particularly the uneducated *purdahnashin* a belated opportunity to overcome her lack of earlier educational development by the right type of useful vocational training. The response of Muslim schoolgirls to education, keen as it is, perhaps is not as eager as is the desire of some young Muslim women, who were married at an early age and thus deprived of education.

The growing demand for more educational facilities for Muslim girls today reflects in no small measure the effect of some of the non-Muslim communities — the Parsees because of their social freedom of women; the Brahma Samaj community because of its aggressive social reforms; and the Christians because of their widespread facilities for education and the large number of Christian women pioneers in professional life have in different degrees helped to stimulate the social and educational advance of Muslim girls.

A few outstanding Hindu reformers, men and women, have also undoubtedly exerted a strong influence in the advance of Indian women as a whole affecting Muslims as well as Hindus. Undoubtedly one of the main forces that has steadily promoted the educational and social development of Indian women of all, communities, has been the Christian institutions for girls. These schools were very often the first school for girls in a community, and today they still constitute a large part of girls' education in India.

The study of progress in the education of girls and women

in India, is virtually a study of the educational efforts of Missions. Certain institutions have had a special effect on the education of Muslim girls, notably the two Christian Colleges in North India already mentioned Kinnaird College and Isabella Thoburn College, and the Women's Christian College in Madras. The increase in Muslim students in Kinnaird College is a special indication of a breaking down of conservatism since the Government College observes purdah strictly. A growing number of Muslim fathers desire the more liberal type of education.

In 1925 two Muslim girls, swathed in shroudlike white burqas were awarded their diplomas from Isabella Thoburn College which issues its diplomas at the convocation of the University of Lucknow. In 1929 three Muslim girls on the same platform received their diplomas, unveiled with all the other men and women students. Their names were read off in the alphabetical list and no one in the audience paid any attention to whether they were Hindu, Muslim, or Christian.

Since that time all Muslim students have received their diplomas publicly in the Lucknow University. In the liberalizing atmosphere of these colleges for women, such an advance is regarded as merely the natural result of a modern education. Some of the men's colleges are also exerting a progressive influence on women's education.

The major factor in the promotion of educational and social progress today is the influence exerted by Indian women themselves, both individually and through collective effort. A decade ago, only a few Indian women were conscious of their responsibility as a force for advance. Today there are a growing number of educated leaders who are devoting themselves to the crusade of education for the hundreds of thousands of uneducated women who, still behind the purdah, are voiceless to make known their needs.

In the small minority of highly cultivated leaders, who are

advocates of education, one can single out from different parts of India the few outstanding Muslim leaders who are devoting themselves untiringly to the promotion of woman's education and social reform.

A number of women's organizations in India have as their primary objective education and social reform, and through collective effort are influencing public opinion and official policy. Viewed in the light of statistics, the appalling illiteracy of Indian women, the comparatively small number of girls in schools, the withdrawal from school of many girls after but one year, the growing disparity in education between men and women, the dearth of women teachers—and with all of these facts intensified in reference to Muslim women the situation does indeed seem depressing. But the upward curve in the education of girls, Muslims as well as others, has begun. Official and private agencies are increasing the educational facilities for girls. The general public, including even the conservatives, has awakened to the need to educate girls as well as boys. The eager response of girls to these new opportunities is everywhere evident. Progressive influences, foreign and Indian, are working unitedly on this common problem of education for girls.

Due to the slow development of education, Egyptian women did not begin to emerge from illiteracy until after a spirit of nationalism asserted itself in 1919. Popular education, properly speaking, either for boys or girls, had its beginning in Egypt after that date. The previous unimportant position of education in Egyptian policy is shown by the fact that Lord Milliners's book *England in Egypt* devotes only a few pages to education and the *Encyclopaedia Britannica* gives it barely a page in small type. Up to this time popular education meant for the most part native schools, largely under untrained and even illiterate teachers, whose main qualification was their ability to chant the Quran. Under these conditions the figures for illiteracy and the disparity in education between girls and boys, are not surprising. Many of the women teachers could neither read nor write.

Anything above elementary schools for girls was obviously not considered. The Government in 1920 had only five primary girls' schools with 843 pupils. Since that time there has been a definite forward movement in education. The new Constitution of Egypt, proclaimed in 1923, provided for free and compulsory primary education, with 1935 set as the objective date for realizing this educational aim. Obviously this achievement has not been possible in such a limited period, but the country is moving toward that goal. There were in 1929 in contrast to 1919 almost twice as many elementary schools, and more than twice as many girls in elementary schools; almost three times as many higher elementary schools with almost three times as many higher elementary students; nine times as many schools for teachers' training for elementary schools with a little less than six times the increase in students; three times as many kindergarten schools and seven times the number of children; four times as many primary schools and four times the number of primary pupils.

This period marked also the beginning of secondary education for girls and the addition of a special college for girls; the transition from the old style makeshift school, often held in a mere hovel and taught by an illiterate teacher, to a well-organized modern school under a trained teacher; and the introduction of modern kindergartens on the Friable model. But the most significant progress of this first decade of the twentieth century lies in the fact that it marks the beginning of modern education for girls and its advance from the elementary grade to the college and university level.

The real landmark as regards girls' education is the year 1925 when girls' secondary education was officially established. Before 1925 a great gulf divided the status of boys' and girls' education. The fact that lower standards were required for teaching in girls' primary schools than in boys' schools, illustrated the inferiority of girls' education. Teachers for the boys' schools had to complete their secondary education before being admitted for teachers' training; whereas women teachers for girls' schools obtained the primary certificate after only four years' study in primary schools, and in addition the four years' course of a training college. Graduates of unusual ability were sent to England, but few won this opportunity, because of their short period of training and limited scope of knowledge. Girls not desirous of teaching suffered from the lack of general cultural values in the course.

Egyptian leaders, however, have recognized the inadequacy of the preparation for teachers of girls' schools and the resultant inequality of the educational status of boys and girls, and have accordingly promoted the addition of secondary schools for girls. To serve the two types of girls – those of the leisure class, desiring general education, and those preparing to teach secondary education was differentiated into two types of courses.

Some of the educators who are directing the policy of girls' education in Egypt, recognize the desirability of more differentiation in girls' education, especially in the secondary schools. The objectives of education for girls are not adequately met by the prescribed curriculum which was built to serve the needs of boys. Education of boys has been directed largely toward a Government Job and therefore based on the "white collar and clean hands" idea of education.

Such a system, which no longer fits the needs of boys, is obviously unsuited for girls. The difficulty of achieving differentiation in girls' education, however, is obvious because of the hidebound examination system. If equality in education for girls and boys means identical standards then differentiation in the girls' programme is impossible.

The important question is whether the special needs of girls can be met without sacrificing the principle of true equality. Opinion is divided on this subject. Some teachers advocate more attention to vocational education such as the industrial arts. An industrial Arts Course is offered in the Elementary Teachers' Training Schools, but as a whole, general vocational training is not yet considered necessary since the usual vocational lines, which constitute in the West the means of economic livelihood for the masses, do not exist for the Muslim girls. The girls' schools of Egypt are, of course, primarily geared to the needs of Muslims, because of the very large proportion of Muslims in the population.

Commenting on the question as to the need for vocational training for girls, the Director of Girls' Education some years ago said: "The public is not ready for economic liberty for women. It will be another twenty-five years before women will be in many professions in Egypt. We are pushing vocational training for boys, of course, as an economic necessity."

A gymnastics exhibition of two thousand primary schoolgirls under the supervision of the Egyptian Directress of Physical Education, illustrated the development of physical education for girls in Egypt. The complete freedom of the Egyptian girls at that time seemed refreshing in contrast with the veil-restricted life of schoolgirls in most of the other Muslim countries. This exhibition, the Second Annual Exhibition of the Physical Education Department in Cairo was held in the Gezireh sports grounds before a very large and representative gathering.

The children, with complete abandon and schoolgirl enthusiasm, carried out the varied programme, which showed incidentally the influence of the Supervisor's training in England – relay races and games, English country dances, drills and marches. The Muslim Director was assisted by a group of teachers, all Muslims, a fact which one recognized by their neatly bound scarf head-dress, which to the casual observer did not suggest a special Muslim style but gave only the impression of a distinctive fashion worn in preference to the hat. There was no suggestion of the veil or the psychology of the veil in their manner. And yet, one knew that it could not have happened a few years earlier in Cairo and at that time was possible in no other Muslim country except Turkey. Today Iran, as we have said, also endorses this full measure of freedom. Although the Islamic social customs have greatly changed, modernism in Egypt has not meant secularism in the schools. The teaching of Islam in the girls' schools is still being carried on but in a modern way by young teachers trained in the tenets of their religion.

The modern method of teaching religion in the Egyptian schools is appreciated in other countries. Palestine has occasionally turned to Egypt for a trained woman teacher of religion. The religious teaching in the training schools is given by sheikhs, not the elderly type as formerly, but often young sheikhs, some of whom have been trained in Europe. These younger sheikhs are the products of the new reforms of Al Azhar, the great intellectual centre of the Muslim world. The study of science and comparative religions in Europe can scarcely fail to have its effect.

Today the inclusion of the teaching of Islam in the school programme is a formal recognition of religion, one feels, rather than a vital endorsement of Islam, such as would characterize Muslim teaching in India. Girls in Normal School have always been supposed to keep their heads covered in classes taught by men, but this is no longer observed. Moreover, now they do not have the attitude of passive acquiescent deference before the sheikh as in the past. Sometimes the sheikhs have to call in a woman teacher to help in discipline.

The freedom of the Muslim schools of Cairo today is in striking contrast to the general conditions fifteen or twenty years ago, as related by one of the English inspectresses, who had taught for a number of years in a private school in Lower

Egypt. "Formerly the girls were always brought to school in covered conveyances; men clerks could not be employed.

The girls were all closely veiled, visited very little even in the homes of girls with whom they had been special friends in school, and after their marriage rarely saw each other. There was no need for more than primary schools as early marriage was the rule. Contact with foreigners was very slight; in fact, the Egyptians were afraid of foreigners." This, she explained, was not true of Cairo, but of Zagazig, a typical 'Large town in Lower Egypt. "When I opened the Girls' School in Zagazig twenty years ago," she continued, "the little girls were very much frightened.. One little girl especially would not allow me to do anything for her for three days. Then when she finally allowed me to undo the little Quran amulet to wash her neck, I knew that her fear had been broken."

What a striking contrast to that day of seclusion and fear of contact one finds in modern Egypt today with its crowded primary and secondary schools and its public gymnastics exhibitions. The social conservatism of the authorities does not in any way seem to retard the educational development of girls. The schools remain technically in the frame of Islam, but each year the frame is widened. The modern spirit dominates in spite of the adherence to certain traditions. Undoubtedly, one of the greatest difficulties in promoting rural education in Egypt is the placement of teachers. As in India and elsewhere the difference in living standards and in social mores makes it practically impossible for young women teachers to live in backward village areas.

Furthermore, trained women teachers are reluctant to leave the interests and amusements of the large city. There are few special inducements offered for rural service; quite the contrary, in fact, as positions in Cairo are often given as the reward for merit and students of lower scholarship are sent to villages. This problem is a subject for serious consideration. The most noteworthy advance in girls' education in Egypt during the last decade and a half has been the successful establishment of a trained teaching staff. The growth from two training colleges for women elementary teachers in 1920 to fifteen in 1934 with an increase in students from 447 to 1,132 shows that women teachers have been poured out in increasing volume.

In spite of the rapidity of the process, a high standard of training has been maintained by the English supervisors and English principals of the training colleges. The teaching profession has been made especially desirable. Egyptian women students in the training schools have received free board, and free tuition and sometimes even a stipend; whereas men in training have had only free tuition.

Women teachers have received better salaries in Egypt than teachers in any other part of the Near East, and often better than men in Government service. As a result, the supply has caught up with the demand, and in the elementary colleges even exceeded it. The definite Government endorsement of teaching has undoubtedly encouraged Muslim girls to enter the profession. Women have been given more official recognition in education than in any other field. A Muslim woman teacher some years ago was on the Government Education Board.

One of the inspectresses of women's education recently commented on the number of women teachers in evidence at the Ministry of Education and called attention especially to their complete freedom of expression. "There is no feeling of inhibition before the Director of Education; in fact, most of the women teachers would be quite free to express an opinion even to the Minister of Education."

The self-assurance and spirit of independence of Muslim women teachers in Egypt is especially worthy of comment because of the fact that Egyptian women have so recently entered professional life. Such an attitude is in sharp contrast to the hesitant attitude which is often characteristic of Muslim women of the old-fashioned type. The woman teacher typifies this new freedom of Egyptian women. In the establishment of the teaching profession for women, the system of foreign scholarships has been an important factor. From 1922 to 1930 the number of scholarships for women increased from ten to forty. The increase of applicants has made possible more careful selection, first from each school, then from the best from all the schools. Muslims, because of their larger number of applicants, have a practical though not theoretical preference.

Various lines of training are followed – Froebel kindergarten courses, Domestic Science, Art, Physical Training, and regular courses for the B.A. degree. These students are naturally sent to England because of the language and the general English basis on which education in Egypt is being developed. English headmistresses are now being replaced by Egyptian headmistresses, of whom a number have been chosen since the appointment of the first Egyptian headmistress, Mine Mansour Fahmy, a widely known educator. One of the distinctive forces promoting educational advance for women in Egypt is the Feminist Union of Cairo which, from its inception, has promoted as one of its primary aims, equality of educational opportunity for girls, requesting first the opening of girls' secondary schools, later the admission of women into the university, and the granting of foreign scholarships to girls. Through lectures, a woman's magazine, and in various other ways the Feminist Union has sought to promote the intellectual and moral advance of women as a necessary preparation for political and social equality.

The Feminist Union is also carrying on an interesting educational project – an industrial school where two hundred girls of the poorer class are given a general education, also domestic science, needlework and carpet making, as a means of earning a livelihood. There have been some interesting developments in adult education in Egypt. Several years ago a very ambitious programme of lectures for women was promoted by a movement called the Reconstruction Education Movement.

We have already referred to the lecture on the advance of women given by Madame Hoda Sharawi Pasha at the American University of Cairo. Lectures of this type are a regular part of the programme of the University Extension Department, which has as its objective the education of the public along lines that are of national interest.

There can be little question of the educational and social influence of having a Muslim woman deliver an address on the status of women before a mixed audience of perhaps a thousand people with two hundred women and a large number of white-turbaned sheikhs.

Foreign influence has had a more pervasive effect on educational and social advance in modern Egypt than in any other country of the Near East, exerting its influence with less shock. But French influence has been dominant ever since Mehmet Ali imported the body of French savants and Ismail followed a policy of conscious exposure of Egypt to French culture. The second language is French, the atmosphere and prevailing culture is French. As far as women are concerned, the upper class especially has been greatly influenced by French styles and French culture through private education, social contact and travel. It is interesting that British culture has not been the dominant influence in Egypt in view of the long period of occupation.

At the present time, however, there is a distinct increase in English influence, which is exerted primarily through the public school. English specialists in education, English methods of education. Egyptian students studying in England, the general use of English in the schools – all these are significant evidences and causes of the increase in English cultural influence. The Anglo-Saxon influence has been, in general, very favourable to a growth in social freedom and the educational advance of women.

Anglo-Saxon influence has affected Egypt not only through English, but also through American channels, especially through the American Mission schools. Many of these institutions antedate the Government schools and have been an outstanding educational force over a long period. The first girls' school in Egypt was opened by an American Mission seventeen years before the first Government school for girls was established by Ismail. The Assiut Mission School through educating a large number of Coptic women as well as a smaller number of Muslims had imparted education to girls in Assiut recognized as a necessity.

The American College for Girls in Cairo, a junior college, the most advanced institution for girls in Egypt, has demonstrated the value of higher education and prepared leaders for various professional careers and for lives of general usefulness. The College has for a long period had a large proportion of Muslim students.

The American institutions for men, Assiut College and the, American University at Cairo, which admits women to its courses, have played an important part in promoting the advance of women by educating young Egyptian men to a proper understanding of the position of women in society. One can scarcely speak of Syrian influence as foreign in relation to Egypt because of the cultural unity between the two countries established through the language, but as an outside influence coming into Egypt, Syria has played an important part. A number of early Syrian leaders, who have contributed greatly to the thought life of Egypt, have now become entirely identified with Egypt. Syrian influence is recognized as a definite element of progress.

The effect of modern Turkey on progress in Egypt, especially on promoting the development of women, has been less direct and obvious than in Iraq or Persia. Although the Turkish reforms have not been taken as a goal in Egypt as in other countries, there is, however, little question of the indirect effect of Turkey, as an example of a progressive Muslim country. The day has passed in Egypt when foreign influence is needed to promote either directly, or by example, the appreciation of girls' education.

National pride actuates modernists and reactionaries alike to promote education for girls as well as for boys as part of the programme of progress. Nationalism in Egypt is not merely a political passion. It has had the deeper meaning of a birth of national consciousness. This new spirit has generated the dynamic power for national advance. But unlike Turkey, Egypt has not considered advancement of woman as a sine qua non of national progress.

Under the Turkish regime very little attention was given to the education of Muslim girls. Some improvement began after 1908 with the opening of a few girls' schools by the Government. But as the language of the schools was Turkish, they had a limited effect in an Arabic-speaking country.

For the great majority of Muslim girls education was confined as elsewhere to the very heterogeneous Quran schools. A few girls of the upper classes received from the convent schools a somewhat sketchy education, consisting of a smattering of French, and a bit of handwork and embroidery. A smaller number was given instruction of sorts at home, but the foreign governess did not play as important a role in Palestine, as in Egypt and Turkey, in bringing the education and culture of the West into the harem.

Hence, comparatively few of the higher class Muslim girls in Palestine had any educational advantages. The situation for Christian girls was quite different because of the large number of Mission institutions in Palestine.

These Mission institutions practically left untouched the Muslim communities; hence, there was a great contrast in the educational advancement of Muslim and Christian women of the pre-war generation. This explains the fact that the literacy of women of the Christian community is approximately eighty per cent in contrast to five per cent for Muslim women. There is a similar difference in the literacy of Christian and Muslim men, of ninety per cent for Christians and ten per cent for Muslims. The post-war period marks the beginning of the new regime in education for all, but especially for Muslim girls. Since that time a Government programme has been vigorously promoted and the Muslim community also has undertaken education for girls as well as for boys.

The growth through the Government programme is clearly shown by the steady increase in the number of girls in attendance in schools since 1919. More than twice as many girls were in the Arabic public schools, the Government system, in 1932-33 as in 1920. This increase in the girls in Government schools marks primarily an increase in Muslim girls who are being educated, since the great majority of Christians attend private institutions.

The lack of education for Muslim girls, however, is shown by the contrast between the number of Christian and Muslim girls in school. In 1932 a little less than half of the total number of girls in schools of Palestine, both public and private were Muslims, a fact which has special meaning since seventy per cent of the population of Palestine is Muslim.

A further evidence of the lack of education for Muslim girls is the difference in the number of schools for Muslim girls and boys, and also in the enrolment of each sex. In 1932-33 there were almost ten times as many schools for boys as for girls in the Arab public system, and in rural Palestine, one girls' school for thirty boys' schools.

As to the enrolment the total number of Muslim boys in

school in both public and private institutions, was four times that of Muslim girls in schools of all kinds. The difference between the education of Muslim girls and of Muslim boys offers a significant contrast to the situation in the Christian community where there is practical equality in education for boys and girls.' Education for girls in Palestine is still in the primary stage. The Government policy has been to promote primary-schools throughout Palestine for the masses before raising the level of education for the few, who may be ready for the higher grades. In carrying out this policy of promoting primary education, the Government is developing village schools as rapidly as the villages will assume the cost of buildings.

The rural programme will benefit Muslims especially, as the rural population is very largely Arab. The great majority of rural schools, however, are as yet for boys. Muslim girls would receive more education if social conditions made possible co-education.

The policy of developing education in harmony with general needs is shown by the emphasis on practical subjects. There is as yet no vocational training except courses in domestic arts and homemaking. In several places practical instruction in infant welfare is provided through visits of the students to the infant welfare clinic under the supervision of the doctor and trained nurse.

Emphasis in the Government schools is also given to physical, education, singing and games, and drill. Interscholastic netball matches are held every year.

The Girl Guide Movement has been very popular in Palestine. There are over one thousand Guides—guiders, brownies and rangers. All of the companies except the Y.W.C.A. companies, are connected with schools. The Girl Guide displays and prize-giving programmes are limited to women and must be carried on under careful harem restrictions.

Training camps for leaders and small groups of girls which are held every year, make a marked appeal. A Western visitor to one of these camps finds it especially interesting to watch the arrival of Muslim Guides at camp; they arrive black-veiled and black-clothed and reappear from their tents completely different in their grey uniforms and picturesque white head-dresses. This transformation is a symbol of the effect of the Girl Guide Movement, which unites girls of different religions and gives them all a wider, freer outlook.

In developing the general system of education for girls, Palestine faced the common problem of the East—the dearth of trained teachers. In 1932-33 there were only 172 women teachers in a total of 827 teachers in the Government schools.

The special importance of the Teachers' Training College is, therefore, obvious and the growth of this college is an index of the steadily ascending curve of girls' education. This institution, which has always had an English Principal, has shown a continuous increase in the number of students and especially in the proportion of Muslim girls. Some years ago it was necessary to take the Muslim girls free of charge. Only girls of the middle class, and those merely because of economic necessity, were willing to enter.

Today the inducement of free tuition is no longer necessary; the applicants for admission include daughters of some of the best families in Jerusalem. Hitherto teaching has been considered as a respectable profession, but in the general public mind no girl would enter teaching except as an economic necessity, and certainly no girl of social position would teach. The Training College is successfully changing this idea. In the beginning trained Egyptian and Syrian teachers were enlisted for service in Palestine. Now they are being replaced by graduates from the Training College.

The need for primary teachers was so urgent that the requirements at the beginning could not be too high nor the selection of candidates too rigid, but now higher standards for admission are required and greater care can be taken in selecting candidates for training. A more advanced course has also been developed, in addition to the regular teachers' training, in order to meet the need for a secondary school for paying pupils.

In promoting this programme of steady growth the Teachers' Training College has been very careful to stay within the conventions of the veil, which are still widely observed in Palestine. There are of course Christian students who do not observe Muslim customs but the general atmosphere of the school is in harmony with Muslim ideas. By its distinctly harem conditions the Training College has achieved its primary objective of winning the confidence of even conservative Muslim parents, and attracting Muslim girls for training.

Apart from the Director of Education, who visits the school freely, no men are allowed. But when the Director later visits the schools where the training students teach, often the teachers veil. This is an interesting contrast between Egypt and Palestine, as Egyptian teachers have never veiled before the Directors on their visits to the schools. When other men visitors come to the Training College, the girls are told in advance and given the opportunity of veiling. The girls are not allowed to receive any male visitors except the immediate family or relatives.

The commencement exercises, sports, contests, and other school gatherings have only women audiences. For the classes in the Quran the girls all have their faces covered even though the sheikh is often an elderly man. In the Training College these elderly religious leaders have not been replaced by young sheikhs as in Cairo. But some of the girls' schools now have women teachers. It is safe to surmise that no ethical teachings along modern lines are injected into these Muslim classes in religion.

Although the Training College carefully avoids promoting modern social or religious ideas, it is steadily laying the foundation for a future social freedom which seems inevitable. The impact of modern ideas is irresistible so that the individual girl is unconsciously being led toward social change. In order that the excellent training given at the College may not be lost, a careful plan of supervision during the first year of teaching is followed and the final certificate is withheld until after that apprenticeship is satisfactorily completed.

The allocation of graduates from the Training College to their teaching posts presents in Palestine as elsewhere a serious problem. Prevailing social attitudes make it difficult and often impossible for a girl to teach outside of her own village. Christian as well as Muslim teachers insist on teaching at home, or perhaps the parents insist. For example, the parents of a girl living in Safe were unwilling to have her teach in Tiberias, less than an hour's distance away.

Muslim communities that are especially reactionary such as Hebron and Nablus, demand a Muslim teacher but social conditions make it difficult for a Muslim woman from outside to live in these places. Christian teachers often find difficulties in teaching in an entirely Muslim town where social conventions make life very restricted. For what might pass as harmless in Jerusalem is often considered to be questionable morals in a centre of greater conservatism. To meet the need for teachers in the village schools, the Training College in Jerusalem has established a Rural Training Centre in Ramallah which is about twelve miles from Jerusalem. The curriculum includes mainly practical subjects-Domestic Science, Needlework, Gardening and Care of Poultry.

All of the students for the first year, thirteen in number, are Muslims. The standard of living in the school is that of a village, with the same type of convenience but with an emphasis on health and cleanliness. The Department of Education has established a small number of foreign scholarships for girls. Several have had training in Egypt, in the American University of Beirut, and in England. Palestine has not, however, promoted the foreign scholarship plan as vigorously as have Iraq and Egypt.

The major task has been the training of women teachers for the primary schools, which is being achieved in the Training College in Jerusalem. Secondary education has not been undertaken and therefore the preparation of secondary teachers by training abroad has not yet been promoted.

In spite of evidences of conservatism, which one finds with interesting variation in different places, and in reference to different questions related to girls' education, there is today a general acceptance of the idea of education for girls as well as boys.

Even in reactionary centres like Hebron a distinct change is evident as the demand stage had already begun in 1930, when the pressure for a new school was being felt. The keen interest in girls' education in Jerusalem represents the other end of the scale from Hebron. The Directress of the Mamuniya School, a Syrian Christian, commented on the increase of Muslim girls in the upper grades, as shown in this leading Muslim girls' school in Jerusalem. Interest is also growing in education for girls beyond the elementary stage. As has been said, the Government has not as yet provided secondary schools for girls. But the Teachers' Training College has a two years' course and the Jerusalem College for Girls and also the Friends' School at Ramallah offer secondary education. These two institutions represent Christian effort of a very high type; the Friends' School is a Mission institution, the Jerusalem College for Girls, a private Christian enterprise with missionary cooperation, and some Government support.

The latter, founded in 1918, is the highest institution for girls in Palestine, offering a fourteen years' course, which extends from the kindergarten through the secondary grade to teachers' training and the first year of university. The American

Friends' School for Girls in Ramallah, the first school for girls in Palestine, which was founded in 1869, has been a most convincing argument for girls' education.

As a boarding school with girls from all over Palestine, its influence has been widespread and very beneficial. Obviously these two private schools cannot long satisfy the demand for secondary education of girls in Palestine. In the last decade of Government primary schools the number of Christians who have attended Government primary schools has increased and therefore the demand for free secondary education has grown steadily.

Through the Government schools, moreover, an entirely new Muslim client for girls' primary and therefore also for secondary schools has been created. Today Palestine has passed beyond the period in which private schools can adequately meet the needs for girls' education. The growing demand for both primary and secondary schools is the real criterion of progress in girls' education in Palestine.

Apart from the educational facilities for girls, provided by Government schools and private Christian agencies, girls' education in the elementary stage is also being advanced by the Supreme Muslim Council, through funds from the mosque endowments. More money is expended for boys' schools, but the necessity for girls' education is recognized, and also the need for education on modern lines, which is shown by the effort to secure well-trained Muslim and Christian teachers from Syria.

In addition to the regular Government programme these schools of the Supreme Muslim Council stress especially Arabic and Islamic teaching. The objective in these schools, both for boys and girls, is to strengthen the Muslim influence and safeguard Islamic culture, which Muslim leaders have felt to be endangered by the, Zionist influx since the Mandate. "Strictly Muslim education is necessary," as the secretary of the Supreme

Muslim Council explained, "because the Government cannot give the Arabic language adequate emphasis; nor Muslim tradition its full value." Although the veil is carefully maintained in these Muslim schools under the Supreme Council, the need for a modern programme and for modern methods of education is fully realized.

Whatever may be the reason, well-trained teachers are employed in these Muslim schools; games, guide activities, dramatics are all encouraged as a part of the programme. The Supreme Muslim Council has also taken a very advanced step in establishing a number of foreign scholarships for Muslim girls; four in Helouan Training College in Cairo, and one in the Sidon Mission School for Household Economics in Syria, the only school of its kind in the Near East. In addition to these foreign scholarships, a scholarship has been granted for nurses' training in the Jerusalem hospital. The influences which are producing an active interest in girls' education on the part of Muslim leaders are an interesting complex of conflicting tendencies.

Undoubtedly the presence of an aggressive Zionist minority, which is increasing in numbers and power, has affected the Muslim attitude and strangely enough along two opposing lines. The necessity for competition on an equal basis and consciousness of a lack of education and general Muslim lag, have spurred the Muslim community to progress.

The contrast between the educational development of Muslim women with that of the women from other communities, also furnishes the urge to promote education for Muslim girls as a necessary part of their general advance. On the other hand, the presence of an entirely different civilization nothing could be more different than the conservative Muslim and the modern Zionist—has aroused a fear of absorption, and has therefore produced a defence psychology that tenaciously protects Arab and Islamic culture; hence the extreme social conservatism of the Arab community in Palestine, which adversely affects the position of women.

A leading citizen of Jerusalem who voices the policy of the Supreme Muslim Council expressed very clearly this double motivation of progress and conservatism: "Zionism brought an awakening of national consciousness and a sense of necessity for social uplift which must affect women. To oppose Zionism we have realized the necessity for the same weapons that the Zionists have. The Jews maintain a high educational level both for men and women. Hence, to bring up the Arab level we must educate Muslim women."

The inner life of Palestine, until after the World War, was singularly unaffected by foreign influence. The Christian groups from abroad which were concentrated in Jerusalem did not fuse into the life of the country as a whole. The very fact that Jerusalem is the sacred city of three great faiths has always divided the community into compartments.

The adherents of each religion leading segregated lives, Muslims and naturally most of all Muslim women, were quite isolated from the other currents of life, practically cut off from contact with the outside world. But the post-war period has brought Palestine as a whole, and especially Arab life, sharply into contact with modern forces.

The impact of foreign influence has not aroused as keen a desire for change as in Iraq. But the insistent exposure to modern life is undoubtedly having its effect. The promotion of school's for girls as for boys by the Government has presented the opportunity and thus stimulated the desire of the Muslim community to .advance. Education for girls will doubtless develop more slowly than boys' education, but the forward movement seems assured.

The fact that in Trans-Jordan education is the third item in the Government expenditure is an evidence that it is of primary interest in this newly formed political entity but very old country. Schools in Trans-Jordan under the Turkish regime were few and far between- seventeen schools for boys, four for girls, the traditional Quran schools. Practically all that remains of the Turkish school system now is the war-wreck of a rather good school building in Kerak, the former Turkish seat of government.

The rest of the country seems to have been untouched by education save for a few Mission schools, which were and are very meagre in comparison with Mission schools elsewhere. But the postwar period has brought to Trans-Jordan, along with cinemas and automobiles, the development of education both for boys and girls. For girls especially, the present period represents a clear gain over the pre-war period, and steady progress in overcoming the disparity between girls' and boys' education. Fortunately Adib Wahby has remained Director of Education for a number of years and has been able to witness the results of his efforts. In 1930 there were eight times as many boys' primary schools as primary schools for girls; today the proportion is three to one. There is as yet, however, no girls' secondary school but four for boys.

In the beginning it was necessary to import women teachers from Syria and Palestine and pay them higher salaries than were paid to men teachers. The lure of the desert —Amman is just on the edge of the desert—did not appeal to the girl from Beirut or Jerusalem, accustomed to more "civilization." Today over half the women teachers are from Trans-Jordan, and their salaries are no longer higher than those of men. Progress in education has equalized the salary standards so that the women teachers have lost their advantage. To attract Trans-Jordan girls of the better class into teaching has apparently not been very difficult, as there is less prejudice to break down in this breezy town of Amman on the desert's edge than in many more sophisticated cities. Moreover the well-paid young teachers from outside, representing the latest styles of Beirut or Jerusalem, doubtless have made the teaching profession singularly attractive for girls of the first families.

The difficulty in training Trans-Jordan girls has been, until the present time, solved by scholarships in Jerusalem or Syria. Six girls are now studying in Jerusalem. But eventually there will doubtless be a training school for women teachers in Trans-Jordan. The danger of a purely academic education, unrelated to the simple environment of Trans-Jordan girls, is recognized. But a special Arts and Crafts school for girls, corresponding to the very modern Trade School for Boys, although frequently discussed, has not yet been achieved.

In the promotion of the new educational programme Trans-Jordan presents an interesting contrast to Palestine. In Trans-Jordan the programme depends entirely on local initiative. The English Adviser for Trans-Jordan has no direct relationship to internal affairs; such as, health and education. The primary interest of the Mandate in Trans-Jordan is in the problem of security, without which, of course, there could be no constructive development along any line.

The attention of the Mandate is centered in the air over Trans-Jordan, rather than on the land itself, as the maintenance of the air route across the desert through Trans-Jordan and Iraq is vital to the route to India. The English Adviser, although personally interested, assumes no direct responsibility for social or educational developments.

In Palestine, education is directly promoted and administered by the Mandate under a more direct foreign administration than in any other country of the Near East. Efficiency of method and speed in promotion are the result. The desire of the people, however, under the direct foreign promotion in Palestine is no keener than in Trans-Jordan.

In Syria there is a lack of any united system of education

and therefore a divergence of cultures and educational trends. This means that there is not merely a difference between the backward and progressive sections as in other countries, but also a distinct variation in the type of education and culture in different parts of the country and even in the different communities in the same section. The lack of a single educational system has retarded the education of Muslim women much more than the Christian, especially in the Lebanon, since Muslim girls for the most part have not taken advantage of the many Christian schools. Before the war, a few Muslim girls of the upper class in the Catholic convent schools and the Protestant schools, were the great exception.

Since the war the number of Muslim girls in foreign schools and in Muslim schools has increased but they represent a selected class, which are less conservative and not averse to foreign influence. The great middle class of Christians as well as Muslims has felt a lack of free public education, since the middle class in any country is cut off from educational advantages as long as there is no public system. During the war, an interesting attempt was made to lay the foundation for a school system on definite national lines. The leading educator from Istanbul, Halide Edib, was sent to Syria with a staff of fifty or more teachers to establish primary, secondary and normal education for girls. Schools were opened in Beirut and Damascus on very modern lines, with Arabic as the basis for instruction and French and Turkish as additional languages. This excellent effort, however, was brought to an abrupt close by the fortunes of war, but has left permanent results, as the present Government system is based on these schools.

Under the French Mandate, schools have been promoted through the local governments, on French and Arabic lines. An attempt is being made to standardize courses and certificates according to the French system. There has been no interference with the programme of foreign schools, although it is to the advantage of their students that the foreign schools meet the requirements of the French school certificates for different grades.

The foreign schools have remained practically autonomous and constitute as a whole the major educational influence in Syria. The Government schools do not compete with the foreign schools; the main value of the Government system consists in its extension of education to the masses.

The Muslim Philanthropic Educational Society has been recently developing facilities for secondary education of girls. Thus, education on modern lines is reaching down further into Syrian life. Muslim girls especially are profiting from the development of Government schools. It is estimated that at least ninety-five per cent of the girls in Government schools are Muslims; since the girls and also boys of the Christian population, especially in the Lebanon, are educated in the various Christian schools, local and foreign. Hence the Government schools have had their primary benefit in reaching the Muslim community.

That this extension of education for Muslim girls is greatly needed, is obvious. Although the Muslim population of Syria is over one-half the total, the proportion of Muslim girls in schools was only a little more than one-fourth of the total enrolment in 1928. The hopeful feature in the situation, however, is the trend of increase. The number of Muslim girls in both the Government and private schools is practically a clear gain in view of the meagre pre-war Government facilities and small pre-war attendance of girls in private or public schools. A distinctly constructive new factor in the situation is the active promotion of girls' education, both primary and secondary by the Muslim Philanthropic Education Society.

In addition to promoting primary education for girls, the Government has provided a certain amount of secondary and higher education for girls; in the Lebanon the New School with secondary grades and two years of normal training; in

Damascus, a normal school and the Syrian University open to women; in Aleppo, a secondary school and normal school. Secondary education for girls in Syria is largely provided by foreign institutions, the majority of which are in Beirut. The beginning of secondary education in the Government school in Beirut is a hopeful trend, as it is primarily intended to provide secondary education for girls of the middle or poorer class, who cannot afford the private school.

The Government schools for girls in Syria give the impression of a decided mixture of French and Arabic. The atmosphere is distinctly French with Arabic as a second language and culture. In the kindergarten the picture of a French kitchen, a French home, a French barnyard, build up the child's vocabulary in a French atmosphere. The group of little five-year olds sing with great enthusiasm C'est la musique du Moulin. But they also sing with equal fervour the anthem of the Lebanese Republic, a good example of Syrian adaptability.

Muslim girls after leaving school, which is usually not later than the fifth grade, are cut off from any educational influences. The eager and grateful appreciation of some of these ex-primary schoolgirls throws light on the empty veiled leisure of the average Muslim girl's life. Those who are in touch with the problem of girls' education in various, parts of Syria, it is interesting to note, find certain similar signs of progress, however different the actual situation may be. There is little question that the best educational facilities for girls in all stages—primary, secondary and college—are afforded by foreign institutions.

Before the war these schools were largely attended by girls of the Christian community; since the war there has been a marked increase in the attendance of Muslims. Schools such as these offer an interesting index of the present attitude toward secondary education for girls. The need for higher education for girls, Christian and Muslim, is being met by the American

Junior College for Girls, and by coeducation in the American University of Beirut. Originally a part of the American Girls' School, the Junior College is now an independent institution, preparing girls to enter the Junior Year of the University of Beirut. Its influence is steadily increasing.

As the highest institution for girls in the Arabic-speaking countries, exclusive of Egypt, the Junior College attracts students from Iraq and Palestine on Government scholarship and also on private support. Of the twenty-five Muslim graduates from the Junior College, a number are holding important teaching positions. Aside from the regular academic college course, the Junior College stresses homemaking, health, recreation and community service, such as a special club project for a group of forty to fifty homeless Muslim boys.

Summer programmes of village welfare carried on in the Lebanon villages, by groups of Muslim and Christian students under faculty supervision, illustrate a creative approach to major problems of rural education. Such attempts to bring students in direct contact with backward village life, may have a helpful bearing on the problem which is caused by the growing cleavage between the educated urban minority and the underprivileged rural population, one of the critical problems of the East as a whole.

Co-education at the American University of Beirut has met with a favourable response as is shown by the increase in numbers each year, although the demand for higher education for women is still very limited. Of the twenty eight women students in 1934, two were Muslims. The first Muslim woman graduated in 1929, Madame Ihsan Shakir el Kousy, an Egyptian, whose example doubtless encouraged other Muslim women students to enter a coeducational university. The fact that she was studying with her husband, prevented any adverse reaction to the idea of an unveiled Muslim woman attending classes with men.

Co-education for Muslim girls is still distinctly in the pioneering stage in Syria. There is perhaps little awareness of its significance; in some quarters there may be active opposition. But the student body has accepted co-education as an established fact, recognizing women students on an equal basis, as members of the same classes with men, and in the normal relationships of study and discussion group contacts. Women share also in student activities and also hold student offices; for example, a woman student, the only one in a class of fifty, recently was elected class president. Viewing the present situation of education in Syria with special reference to Muslim girls, one is conscious of a general awakening of interest, not only in advanced but in backward areas, and a slow but sure advance from the primary school to the university.

Foreign influences have played a larger part in this advance in certain areas of Syria than in any other Eastern country. The absence of foreign contact in some parts explains perhaps in large measure the greater divergence in Syria in the development of different sections than is characteristic of other countries of the East.

The growing awareness of the disparity in education between men and women; the marriage motif, which causes parents to realize the impossibility of their daughters' making a good marriage unless educated; the presence of the more advanced educated Christian community, especially in the Lebanon, which stimulates in Muslim girls and women the desire for progress; the urge to adopt modern ideas, due to the irresistible pressure of Western life; and finally the spirit of keen nationalistic self-determination and aroused self-respect these are the conscious and unconscious motivation, for progress in Syria.

A composite of progressive influences and personal desires is thus actively operating in favour of the educational advance of Muslim women of Syria. The forces for education are not, however, *pari passu* leading to an immediate social transition as symbolized by unveiling. Nationalism under a Mandate Power is driven back into itself and seeks defence for its own traditions. The assertion of self-determination which is politically discouraged finds its outlet in the insistence on its own social conventions. The Muslim community in Syria and Palestine, in the presence of foreign influences, tends to become socially conservative; and social conservatism in Islam is not conducive to a change in the social status of Muslim women.

Education for girls in Turkey was the sudden product of the new regime. The almost passionate drive to educate the masses is the distinct result of the new republic, but a period of preparation came before. A few Turkish women of the upper class began to receive the private cultural education of the home soon after Turkish men came under the influence of French ideas, even as far back as Mahmud the Great (1809-39). Later, during the period of the Tanzimat reforms (1839-79) foreign governesses were introduced into the harem for the privileged few. Even the severity of Abdul Hamid could not stop the flow of Western influence, although it dammed up the outlet and made the open acceptance of Western ideas and attendance at Western schools difficult, especially for girls.

For the great majority of Turkish women, however, aside from the Quran schools and a girls' normal school for training elementary teachers, attended primarily by orphans and poorer girls, there was no real educational provision for girls, until after, the Constitution in 1909. The first serious efforts at more than mere elementary education for girls came in 1913 with the establishment of a coeducational or secondary school for girls by Bayan Nakiye Elgun, for over thirty years the outstanding educational leader of Turkey, now a Deputy in the Grand National Assembly.

The extension of primary education followed, and also the reorganization of the Evkaff (Mosque Foundation) schools was undertaken and effectively carried out by Halide Edib and Bayan Nakiye. These schools were consolidated in 1916 under the Ministry of Public Instruction. The adverse fortunes of the World War—the period of despair and defeat that followed, the Allied Occupation, the Turkish struggle and triumph in the Greek War constitute the all-absorbing, later sequence of events, in which the interest in education was lost in major issues. Then came the birth of the New Nation, and the realization of the necessity for strengthening its foundations.

Under the new regime, education has been assumed as a vital national responsibility and, as a consistent part of the promotion of general education, girls' education has moved steadily forward. The decade between 1913 and 1923 shows a gradual development and improvement of girls' education but with no distinctive change in direction. The next decade between 1923 and 1933 reflects not only the strenuous drive for increasing girls' education, but also the introduction of coeducation.

Most of the elementary education for Turkish girls is now provided through mixed schools. As a primary mean of solving the tremendous problem of the disparity in education of girls and boys, Turkey adopted co-education in 1925, beginning with the elementary schools, later introducing it to a certain extent in other stages. The success of co-education, as a national programme is shown by the rapid increase of girls in primary schools, an achievement which would have been obviously impossible under the system of separate schools because of the double expense as well as the lack of teachers.

In the adoption of co-education, Turkey differs from all other Eastern countries, which have not yet cut the Gordian knot of their difficulty in promoting general education and especially education of girls. A trip through Asia Minor from Marash to Marsovan several years ago revealed how widely co-education is being extended. Strangely enough or perhaps naturally enough, co-education has been introduced especially in the Interior rather than in Istanbul. The primary reason is doubtless economic. The only possibility of extending education has been through the economy of mixed schools. Hence, not only primary but also some middle schools and lycees in the Interior are co-educational; whereas in Istanbul there are separate girls' middle schools and lycees, and co-education has not replaced the already well-established system. But if new schools are built in Istanbul as elsewhere they will doubtless be co-educational.

In addition to its economic value, co-education is serving a definite purpose as a leverage in lifting social conditions, especially in the Interior. Since one still sees veiled women in Asia Minor, the idea of co-education may seem strangely incongruous, but the very fact that the veil has not entirely disappeared in the Interior is a logical social reason for co-education. The present generation of women in Asia Minor may not all discard the veil, although there are indications that unveiling may be more aggressively promoted.

In order, however, that the best social as well as educational values may be safeguarded in the co-education system, certain wise precautions are being taken. Only mixed activities that belong properly to the school programme are encouraged. Mixed dramatics and mixed recreation are under careful guidance and subject to certain restrictions; for example, in school plays no girls can take boys' parts, or vice versa. Moreover, care is taken that teachers shall not present extremes in modern social customs. Rouge and lipstick and lurid fingernails are frowned upon, and a frown often equals an order. Teachers, moreover, are not allowed to enter the Turkish beauty contest. The need for careful social guidance of co-education in order to meet its inherent difficulties and avoid possible social dangers, is fully recognized by thoughtful Turkish teachers in mixed schools.

One of the major problems in Turkey, in the extension of

schools in rural areas, is the provision of trained teachers. To allocate an individual teacher to rural schools is always difficult, because of the social adjustment to an isolated village life. This problem is being met in some places in Turkey by the appointment of a married couple to a village. The married couple conducts the school on modern lines, creates a modern home, which invites imitation, and adds greatly to the general community life.

As a further effective use of teachers in rural areas, to facilitate the spread of rural education, the idea is being developed of establishing a school with a number of teachers and a boarding home for students in a central village, perhaps also a clinic and small hospital, the whole unit thus serving the needs of the surrounding area.

The boarding school is required as a modification of the usual consolidated school because of the lack of bus lines and the great distances between the villages. A very interesting demonstration of this concentrated plan of rural reconstruction in education and health has already been achieved in Etemetsu, a model village half an hour's distance from Ankara. To see the very up-to-date, small, but adequately equipped hospital with a keen young doctor in charge, and an attractive midwife, and to visit the modern school and boarding home near by, staffed by several young married couples, was like catching a glimpse into the future of rural Turkey, if such a plan could be carried out more widely. The alternation of the regular school programme with practical work for boys, several hours each day in the garden and fields, and for the girls, the same amount of time spent in weaving and sewing, showed that this modern school was avoiding the danger of educating village children away from village life.

The boarding home for more than a hundred children, some of them under the special support of the Child Welfare Society, showed that the influence of the school was extended into villages beyond walking distance. Adjoining the school, but with a separate entrance and a small garden, was an attractive building for the teachers, in which each married couple had a little private apartment.

Such a plan undoubtedly ensured the continuity of the teaching staff and their full contribution to the community life. Between this small group of teachers and the people of the village evidently there is an intimate contact, as a visit to several homes clearly showed. The way one of the young mothers proudly displayed her baby to the midwife for her approval was an evidence that the home and hospital are closely related. The promotion of education in the new Turkey has meant the modernization of the whole educational programme.

Of central importance in this process of building Turkish education on a modern basis is the policy of secularization of schools. The starting-point for all of the reforms in education was the elimination of the power of the ecclesiastic authorities. For example, co-education, which has increased especially the education of girls, could scarcely have been accomplished under the old regime, when schools were dominated by religion. Following out this policy, the schools have been completely secularized.

The Turkish girls of today, therefore, have no formal religious instruction in the school. The chanting of the Quran, the teaching of the Islamic formula, the proper ritual and prayers, as far as the schools are concerned , are all things of the past, since definite religious instruction is regarded as the function of the home, not the school. Religion as such is not repudiated, but is regarded as an entirely individual matter. Not only in reference to religious teaching but in general because they did not assert complete independence, there is a distinct trend in education away from the old traditional ideas.

One of the most important developments is the introduction of physical education on modern lines, given by well-trained teachers. Mild calisthenics directed by the regular class teacher in high-heeled shoes, giving her commands passively in a colourless voice, constituted the physical education of the earlier period.

Today one finds a vigorous young Turkish Physical Director, well trained, conducting her class in a regular uniform and flat-heeled shoes, issuing commands in vibrant tones and actively leading the gymnastic exercises. The present teachers of Physical Education are graduates of the course given in Ankara at the Men's Normal School, or at the Istanbul Normal School.

The course in Ankara is one of the most recent developments in co-education. The lectures in theory for men and women students are held together; the courses in practical gymnastics are separate. The men and women students use the same gymnasium, but at different times. At one end are the dressing-rooms and showers for men; at the other, those for the women. The freedom of this joint physical education training course for men and women is the natural result of the new social attitude in Turkey.

Another significant emphasis in the education of Turkish girls is the promotion of vocational education. A number of excellent vocational schools have been established to teach practical arts, as their name Sanat schools signifies.

The Ismet Pasa Institute in Ankara serves as a model for the rest of Turkey for schools of this type, with its fine modernistic building, its excellent classrooms and laboratories, its splendid equipment, adequate dormitory facilities, and well-trained staff. In addition to regular middle school subjects, a primary certificate is required for entrance-two main courses are offered, household economics and a clerical course.

The Household Economics Course is very complete, including home arts, sewing, tailoring, embroidery, cooking, laundry and millinery, which has a rather special interest in

Turkey, because of the discarding of the veil. As the veil was less expensive than the hat, there is a distinct economic value in having Turkish girls learn millinery. Two enterprising graduates of the school have set up hat shops in Ankara and are doing a flourishing business.

The Clerical Course also meets a timely need in view of the recent entrance of Turkish girls into business life. In addition to one of these two special courses, Home Economics or Clerical Training, all of the students have a simple course in Home-making and Child Care, taught by a well-known young Turkish woman doctor, a specialist in child welfare. This Institute offers an interesting illustration of the consistent year-by-year growth of education in Turkey.

In a five-year period it has become established in its very spacious new building. The French Directress has been replaced by a Turkish Director, with a Turkish woman assistant, both of whom have studied in Europe. Turkish teachers, several trained abroad, have replaced all of the foreign teachers except one, the French specialist in millinery. In addition to the clerical course at the Ismet Pasa Institute, training along commercial lines is offered for girls in the very up-to-date Ankara Commercial School, a co-educational institution under a Russian Principal. This school has a number of modern emphases in education; such as student cooperatives, student savings department, a student shop and the student management of the library.

In the development of Turkish education along modern lines, the problem of the training of women teachers is receiving serious consideration. Training for primary teachers is provided in a number of normal schools throughout Turkey; training for secondary teachers is given in the Higher Normal School in Istanbul, connected with Istanbul University. The requirements for teaching have been advanced: to teach in a lycee, a diploma from the university is necessary; for the primary or secondary grade, a normal school certificate. The relationship of the teacher to the community is a vital question for Turkey today.

The young normal-school graduates from Istanbul, fully emancipated young Turkish women wearing hats, fond of dancing and a normal social life, face a difficult problem of social adjustment when they find themselves planted in backward communities, where perhaps some of the women are still veiled and old social customs are still observed. Moreover these young teachers in the Interior have the responsibility of interpreting by their own example the meaning of social freedom. For all this they must be adequately prepared. Hence, the task of the normal schools is not merely to give academic training in methods of teaching, but to socialize education and interpret the career of teaching on a very high moral level. Some of the directors of the normal schools and teachers have grasped the significance of the problem, and are working creatively to develop in every way possible the social values in education.

The young graduates on their part, eagerly take advantage of all opportunities, especially extracurricular activities, such as folk-dances and games for recreation, in order to prepare themselves for the varied demands of teaching service in the Interior. In addition to the regular training courses in normal schools, which are given on a Government scholarship for a contract of five years, obligatory service in the interior, the plan of short-term summer training courses, especially designed for the untrained village teachers, of whom there are still many, has been developed within the last few years.

For foreign scholarships to prepare for teaching along special lines, women students compete on equal terms with men. The competition for foreign scholarships is open primarily to lycee students both boys and girls, but in some special cases, students in the orta mektep, junior high school, also compete. The principle of equality of boys and girls for foreign scholarships does not necessarily mean that the same number of Turkish men and women students receive foreign scholarships. The needs of Turkey for special types of service naturally have a direct bearing on the situation.

Higher education in Turkey is open to women on a basis of full equality with men. Women were admitted to the university in 1915 during the World War, but attended at first as quite a separate section; the men's classes were held in the morning, the women's classes in the afternoon. This involved a duplication of time and effort on the part of the faculty, and hence a double expense.

In the summer season of 1921 accordingly mixed classes were begun, with men and women students on different sides of the room and with no contact outside of classes. The women students entered the classes veiled, raised their veils during the class, and lowered them when leaving.

The fact that this first group of pioneer women students was in a conspicuous and difficult position, was shown by their extreme care in the details of veiling. These early days of co-education in Turkey are typical of the present situation in some countries in the Muslim East, where co-education is regarded as a doubtful social experiment.

Since 1922, when the Medical Faculty was opened for women, there has been a continuous increase in the number of Turkish women in the University of Istanbul, studying law, science, letters, medicine, dentistry, pharmacy, and even engineering. In 1934 the total number of women students was over one-fourth the number of men students.

An interesting evidence of the increasing response of Turkish girls to the opportunity of a higher education is the number of out-of-town students now attending Istanbul University. It is a distinctly new development for a hundred or more Turkish women students to come from the Interior to Istanbul for higher education. Many of these non-resident women students live with relatives or friends, but soon a regular dormitory provision for them will doubtless be needed.

Apart from the opportunities for higher education offered at the university, facilities for cultural studies are provided in special schools in which women students are registered together with men. A Government school for the training of teachers of music in Ankara usually has an equal number of men and women. This school of music is of interest because it shows the present effort being made to westernize the music of Turkey. The students from this school will fill positions in teaching music all over Turkey.

The study of art, also on Western models, is offered in the Beaux-Arts School in Istanbul, situated in one of the palaces on the Bosphorus, which shows the way the old regime serves the new. There is a fair proportion of women students in the various departments. Girls from the lycees compete for entrance. Commercial art, poster making, interior design are all given special attention. In addition to promoting regular education in all its phases, Turkey has vigorously attacked the problem of general adult education.

The illiteracy of Turkey some years ago was estimated at eighty-five per cent; the general illiteracy of women was higher than men, as is usually the case. The adoption of the new Turkish script in 1928 presented the opportunity and drastic necessity for a nationwide drive for literacy. The change from the old to the new letters meant for the time being that the whole nation was reduced to the level of illiteracy. It was immediately necessary for all-the learned and the unlearned-to go to school.

Consequently, a campaign for literacy, unparalleled perhaps in world history, was launched. In October 1928 the nation's schooling began, including Kamal Ataturk, Cabinet ministers, officials, teachers, peasants, men, women, and children of all classes. Attendance at these National Schools in the first year was compulsory for everyone between the ages of sixteen and forty. As soon as the student learned to read and write and could pass an examination, a certificate was issued which served as exemption from further study.

Enforcement of the law was vigorously prosecuted by the Turkish police. The course was taught by regular teachers, who received a small supplementary salary for this extra teaching. School buildings and other public buildings were utilized. The courses were held outside of regular school hours, classes for women for the most part were held in the daytime; and for men, at night.

The courses during the second year were of two types: the simple course for literacy, and a more advanced course including geography, higher arithmetic, additional reading, letter writing and civics. Women constituted over half of the million students in the National Adult Schools, which were established in September 1928, when the new language was officially adopted, and continued during two years.

According to reports, women made equal progress with men. Women of all classes took advantage of the opportunity to learn to read, even mothers attended classes with babies in their arms. The upper class of women, highly educated in the old Turkish language, entered into this pursuit of literacy in new Turkish with zest as in a game, studied at home or in one of the national schools, passed their public examinations along with the masses, and proudly received their diplomas with their pictures attached as on a passport.

The women of the people especially have profited by this drive for learning the new letters. Illiterate before, with little thought of ever learning to read and write, they have suddenly, through the national schools, been awakened to an idea of their ability, hitherto unknown.

The number of women reading newspapers on the trams and boats is a visible proof of their new literacy.

Foreign influence has permeated the life and thought of the country. It is difficult to estimate what was the full measure of this foreign influence silently pervading the Turkish harem, and bringing glimpses of a different world, for such subtle influences are not summed up in statistics. In the later period foreign schools began to play their part in the education of Turkish women.

Throughout the Interior of Turkey the American Mission Board has had a chain of girls' schools for a considerable time, until recently when their number has been reduced and their influence concentrated in a few selected centres. Although these schools have been attended primarily by girls of the non-Muslim population, they have undoubtedly benefited the cause of education in Turkey as a whole, giving a successful demonstration of modern girls' schools at a time when the need for education for girls was not generally recognized.

The French and Italian convents have contributed primarily to the education of girls of their religious community with also a limited contact with the Turkish population. The influence of the convent schools has been mainly along the lines of home-training and culture. None of the foreign institutions perhaps has exerted a greater influence on the education of girls over a longer period than Istanbul Women's College, which was founded as a high school in 1875 and became a college in 1910.

Through its general influence and through the individual example of some of its distinguished graduates, this college represents one of the major educational forces which has prepared for the forward movement of the Turkish women. The last decade shows an increased number of Turkish women students in the College, a fact which indicates the growing interest in higher education for Turkish women. The Turkish graduates and former students at the College are contributing in many ways to the life of Turkey; as homemakers, women in business and professional life, in public affairs, and more recently in the Councils of the State, as the recently elected group of Turkey women deputies includes several graduates of the College.

In the promotion of higher education for women, Istanbul Women's College has exerted an influence not only in Turkey but widely throughout the East. In relationship to the work of Istanbul Women's College, Robert College for men has had a direct effect on the education of women in Turkey, through creating an understanding of modern social values and an appreciation for the necessity of a higher educational and social status of women.

Foreign educational influence in Turkey are working in close relationship with the Turkish Ministry of Public Instruction, seeking to make their distinctive contribution in accordance with the educational policy and ideals of Modern Turkey.

The national system of Turkish education, highly centralized and closely integrated in all of its branches, determines the general trends as well as specific emphases of the present programme. Turkey differs from other countries in the East in its general attitude toward foreign influences.

In contrast to the *laissez-faire* attitude in Syria, or the unconscious absorption and assimilation of foreign influence in Egypt, or the acquiescent acceptance of foreign educational benefits in Palestine, the New Republic follows a policy of careful selectivity and appraisal of foreign influences. There is little question that Turkey recognizes certain values in the educational systems in Europe and America.

The presence of foreign educators in the Turkish school system is ample proof of this fact; for example, an American woman specialist in primary education, made a practical demonstration of modern methods in a Turkish primary school; an American specialist in teaching English to foreigners gave a series of courses to Turkish teachers of English; several American teachers of English are at present in Ankara schools, and a few in Istanbul.

A large group of noted German professors are aiding in the re-establishment of the University of Istanbul on advanced modern lines. French and Russian specialists are contributing in their special technical and cultural fields to the educational development of Turkey on modern Western lines.

But modern Turkey today does her own shopping for education and culture and for scientific progress—it may be in Berlin, or Paris, Moscow, London, or New York. It has been of special significance to the education of girls that this process of selecting foreign values has indicated a definite interest in Anglo-Saxon and perhaps especially in American methods.

In speaking of European culture and education, a former Minister of Public Instruction said in a personal conversation that the culture of Europe was more suited to the old regime than the new. Turkish girls have come out, of the harem and need now an education of practical emphasis and social value, so that they may be better fitted for civic and national responsibility. It is important, however, that one should remember that the choice of foreign values is only a means to an end. The primary basis of Turkish education and culture is not foreign but Turkish. The sense of direction in Turkish education as in Turkish life is singularly clear.

Lessons from Past : Before the advent of Islam, Arabs were groping in the darkness of ignorance. There was no importance of life for them. Their main aim was to acquire more and more material progress for worldly pleasure. The realities of life were beyond the range of their thinking.

Islam, explained to them the real philosophy of life and

provided the complete code which included moral restrictions and the principles of right and wrong. It gave them the clear concept of Heaven and Hell. It taught them to obey Allah and His Messenger, Muhammad (S.A.W.).

When these Arabs gradually accepted the teachings of Islam, a new society came into existence. It was refined and free from all vices. During the evolution of Islamic Society, a commandment of Allah was revealed:

> "O Prophet, if believing women come unto thee, taking oath of allegiance unto thee that they will ascribe nothing as partner unto Allah, and will neither steal nor commit adultery nor kill their children, nor produce any lie that they have devised between their hands and feet, nor disobey thee in what is right, then accept their allegiance and ask Allah to forgive them. Lo ! Allah is Forgiving, Merciful." (60 : 12)

In this verse of the Holy Quran, woman has been directed to follow certain principles of Islam. However, it becomes essential for woman to educate herself in order to understand and follow the principles in letter and spirit. She has been categorically instructed to obey the Holy Prophet (S.A.W.). This commandment made women to think and seek the knowledge of Islamic teachings. The Muslim- women practised the principles of Islam and acquired honourable status in the society. Hadrat Aishah (R.A.A.) says:

> "The Ansari women were wonderful ! Nothing could check them from understanding of Islam." (Muslim)

The women during the times of the Holy Prophet (S.A.W.), acquired profound knowledge of teachings. Hadrat Aishah (R.A.A.) says:

> "We used to memorise, not only but injunctions of every verse of the Holy Quran revealed to the Holy Prophet (S.A.W.). (Al Iqdul Farid)

The real place of woman's education is her home. Therefore, Islamic Shariah directs the parents to educate their daughters so that they may be able to distinguish between right and wrong.

It is the duty of the parents to educate their daughters in order to provide them an honourable status in the society. Without education, it is not possible for a woman to understand the teachings of Islam and mould her life accordingly. The Holy Prophet (S.A.W.) has encouraged the education of women and thus earn the pleasure of Allah, in these words:

> "Whosoever brought up three daughters, taught them manners and etiquette, got them married and treated them well, Heaven is for him." (Abu Daud)

The foundations, of the family in Islam are blood ties and marital obligations. No other type of relationship, like "Adoption" "Mutual Alliance", "Common Law", "Trial Marriage" or "Mutual Consent" to sexual intimacy, will constitute family in the Islamic sense. Islam appreciates the religious virtues, the social necessity and the moral advantages of marriage. There are many verses in the Holy Quran and sayings of the Holy Prophet (S.A.W.) which go as far as to say that when a Muslim marries, he has thereby perfected half of his religion; so let him be conscious of these religious obligations and be careful with the other half.

There are many statements of the Holy Quran and traditions of the Holy Prophet (S.A.W.) that prescribe kindness and equity, compassion and love, sympathy and consideration, patience and goodwill. The Holy Prophet (S.A.W.) goes as far as to declare that the best Muslim is the one who is best to his family, and the greatest, most blessed joy in life is a good and virtuous wife.

These ethical principles allocate to the wife certain rights and corresponding duties. It is the husband's duty to behave with his wife in an equitable and kind manner. He is bound for the full and adequate maintenance of his wife, a duty which he must discharge cheerfully, without reproach, injury, or bickering.

The Holy Quran says:

"O ye who believe ! Ward off from yourselves and your families a fire whereof the fuel is men and stones, over which are set angels strong, severe, who resist not Allah in that which He commandeth them, but do that which they are commanded." (66 : 6)

Malik-bin-Huvairis says that he, alongwith some other youngmen, stayed with the Holy Prophet (S.A.W.) for twenty days to acquire the knowledge of Islam. When he (S.A.W.) realized that we were anxious to go home, he (S.A.W.) said, "Go to your wives and children and live with them and teach them the principles of Islam and order them to practise." (Bukhari)

Hadrat Umar Farooq (R.A.A.) wrote to the people of Koofa "teach them Surah Noor."

The Holy Prophet (S.A.W.) said, "There are three types of men who will be rewarded twice as such. One of them is that man who has a maid and teaches her good manners and imparts her better education and after freeing marries her." (Bukhari)

Once, the Holy Prophet (S.A.W.) got a woman married to a very poor man. The Holy Prophet (S.A.W.) asked him to teach the Surah of the Holy Quran that he knew to his wife in lieu of dower. (Bukhari)

Sometime, the Holy Prophet (S.A.W.) instructed the men to teach particular portions of the Holy Quran to their wives. For instance, he (S.A.W.) said, "Undoubtedly, Allah has completed Surah Baqarah

(The Cow) with two verses which have been given to me from the treasure which is under Heaven. So you learn and teach them to your wives also." (Darmi)

A daughter of the Holy Prophet (S.A.W.) says that while teaching her, the Holy Prophet (S.A.W.) used to say, "When you rise in the morning say that Allah is Holy and that He alone can provide the power to praise Him. Whatever Allah wishes it happens and whatever He wishes not, it happens not. Remember, Allah commands everything and He is the Knower of everything." (Abu Daud)

The Fundamentals

The well-known Maliki scholar and jurist Allama Ibn Alhaj has written:

"If woman demands her right in respect of Deen (Islam) from her husband and approaches the 'ruler of the time for the issuance of an injunction in her favour for the acquisition of religious education which is her legal right, that is, either the husband himself should educate her or allow her to go out and study, then it is obligatory upon that ruler to order her husband to fulfil her wishes, as he (The ruler) does in case of worldly rights. Because the religious rights are more important than the material."

(Al Mudkhal Ibn Alhaj)

Imam Fakhruddin Hassan Bin Mansoor Hanafi (d. 295 A.H.) in his famous fatwa, says, "A woman has no right to participate in any literary sitting without the prior permission of her husband, when any problem arises, she should consult her husband. If the husband is not a learned man, he should solve the problem with the help of other learned men, then she must not leave her house without his permission.

> However, if the husband fails to make research and solve her problem, then she can visit any educational institution without his permission and get the problem solved. Because it is incumbent upon both, man and woman, to acquire knowledge. Specially, when the wife is helpless, her right to acquire knowledge will have priority over the husband's right."
>
> (Fatawa Qadi Khan)

The Result

Islamic Shariah provides all facilities to woman to acquire knowledge. It intends to develop her mental powers in order to become a useful member of the society. Islam emancipated woman from ignorance and made her position dignified and honourable. 'Urwah bin Zubair, (R.A.A.) says about Hadrat Aishah (R.A.A.) :

> "Hadrat Aishah (R.A.A.) knew more about the injunctions of Holy Quran, poetry and literature, the History of Arabs and their hierarchy than any other person."

Moosa bin Talha says:

> "I have not come across any other person more eloquent than Hadrat Aishah (R.A.A.)." (Tirmidhi)

Ibn Abee Malkah (R.A.A.) asked Hadrat Aishah (R.A.A.), "We are not much surprised by your knowledge of prose and poetry because you are the daughter of Hadrat Abu Bakr Siddique (R.A.A.) whose literary status is well-known. But from where did you learn the medical science?" She replied, "Whenever the Holy Prophet (S.A.W.) fell sick, the medical team prescribed medicines for him. I learn the use of these medicines from them." Hadrat Aishah was so apt in accounts that the senior companions of the Holy Prophet (S.A.W.) used to consult her on matters of inheritance.

Umrah bint Abdur Rahman was one of the students of Hadrat Aishah. (R.A.A.). Ahmad Ibn Hanbal says about her, "The Jurist, Umrah bint Abdur Rahman was brought up by Hadrat Aishah (R.A.A.). She related a great number of Hadith through her which are authentic. Her memory is sharp." "Ibn Habban testifies about her, "She has learnt most of the hadis from Hadrat Aishah."

Allama Ibn Abdul Birr (R.A.) says about Hadrat Zainab (R.A.A.), "She was a great jurist of her time."

Abu Rafay Saigh says, "When I talk of any woman jurist of Medina, I at once remember Zainab bint Abi Salma."

Ummul Hassan, a maid of Hadrat Umme Salamah (R.A.A.) was a great scholar who preached and delivered sermons to women. About Ummul Momineen Hadrat Safiyah, Imam Navavi says, "She was one of the wise and intellectual women."

It is said that Fatima bint Qais (R.A.A.) argued with Hadrat Umar (R.A.A.) and Hadrat Aishah (R.A.A.) over a juristic problem for a long time but they could not change her view. The other scholars also gave preference to her thought. Imam Navavi has said about her, "She was one of those who migrated in the earlier period and was a versatile genius."

Hafsa Bint Seerin (R.A.A.) of Basra completed the study of the Holy Quran when she was just twelve years old. The famous Judge of Basra, Ayas-bin-Muawiya says about her:

> "I did not come across any other person whom I could give superiority over Hafsa Bint Seerin."
>
> (Tahzib-al-Tahzib)

Sayeed bin Musayyab had married his daughter to his pupil. The next day her husband was preparing to attend the literary sitting of her father. She said to him, "Be at home, what Sayeed bin Musayyab can teach you there, I can teach you here."

Similarly, the daughter of Imam Malik (R.A.) was a learned lady. If a student made a mistake while reading Moatta, she used to knock at the door of her room from inside. Imam Malik had full confidence in her knowledge, therefore, he used to ask the erring student to repeat it correctly.

About Umme Varaqa Bint Naufil (R.A.A.), it has been said, "She had studied the Holy Quran, therefore, the Holy Prophet (S.A.W.) had allowed her to lead the prayers of the female members of her family."

> A famous Maliki Imam, Ashhab (R.A.) once bought some vegetables from a maid. In those days it was a custom to give bread to the seller in lieu of money. Ashhab (R.A.) had no loaf at that time. Therefore, he asked the maid to come and collect the loaf from him in the evening when he' would get it from the baker. She replied that it was not fair because according to the Shariah, the exchange of commodities must take place on the spot. (Al-Mudkhal, Ibn Alhaj)

The history shows that most of the Muslim women not only knew reading but they were well versed in writing as well. They were competent to write letters and note down various problems.

Educated Muslim women made great contribution to the cause of education and learning. They became the source of guidance and enlightenment for the society. Imam Ibn Qayyim says:

> "The Companions of the Holy Prophet (S.A.W.) who were competent to issue religious decrees (fatwas) were about one hundred and thirty. This number includes men and women both." The persons who issued most of the Fatwa included Hadrat Aishah (R.A.A.) and Hadrat Umme Salama (R.A.A.).

The other women who issued few Fatwa are:

Umme Atiya, Hadrat Hafsa, Hadrat Umm Habiba, Hadrat Safiya, Laila bint Qaiyim, Asma bint Abi Bakr, Umme Sharik, Khaula bint Towait, Umm Darda, Atika bint Zaid, Sahla bint Hadrat Juwairia, Hadrat Maimoona, Hadrat Fatima bint Qais, Hadrat Umme Salama, Zainab bint Umm Salama, Umm Aiman, Umme Yusuf and Ghamadiya (R.A.A.).

These wise and learned women made a great contribution to the cause of Islamic teachings and helped in the uplift of the society.

Hadrat Aishah (R.A.A.) was a renowned scholar of Ahadith She has narrated two thousand, two hundred and ten Ahadith ' Her knowledge was so apt that sometimes she corrected Hadrat Umar (R.A.A.) and Abu Hurairah (R.A.A.) Hafiz Ibn Hajar says :

"Hadrat Aishah (R.A.A.) had learnt a great many things from the Holy Prophet (S.A.W.) and lived for fifty years after him (S.A.W.). People were greatly benefitted by her. Many principles were related through her and it is said that one-fourth of the laws of Shariah were related by her."

Suhairah bint Huzair has said about Hadrat Safiyah (R.A.A.), "I, alongwith some other women, went to Medina after Hajj and visited Hadrat Safiyah (R.A.A.). There were already some women from Koofa. We requested her to explain to us the laws regarding the relation of husband and wife and other relevant topics."

The knowledge of the Holy wives of the Holy Prophet (S.A.W.) greatly helped in the solution of the problems which puzzled the Companions of the Holy Prophet

(S.A.W.). Imam Ibn Qaiyim (R.A.) says : "When there was any difference of opinion amongst the Companions of the Holy Prophet (S.A.W.) and any of the Ummahatul Momineen quoted any hadis, then they accepted it and forgot their differences."

(Zadul Maad Vol. 4, Page-221)

About Umme Atiya (R.A.A.), Allama Ibn Abdul Bir (R.A.) has said : "She attended the after-death bathing ritual of the daughter of Holy Prophet (S.A.W.) and she explained the principles of bath (Ghusl) very efficiently. Her hadis regarding bathing of dead body has become the fundamental principle (for Muslims). The Companions of the Holy Prophet (S.A.W.) and their disciples in Basra learnt the rules of the bathing of the dead body from her; and there are many other Ahadith also, which have been related through her by Ans-bin-Malik, Muhammad bin Seereen and Hafsa bint Seereen." (Al Istiab)

Bibliography

Adams, C.C. : *Islam and Modernism in Egypt,* Oxford University Press, New York, 1953.

Ahmad, Bherhan : *The Mujaddid's Conception of Tauhid,* Feroz Pub., Lahore, 1940.

Ahmad, Imtiaz : *Divorce and Remarriage among Muslims in India,* Manohar Publishers, New Delhi, 2003.

Ahmad, K. N. : *Muslim Law of Divorce,* Kitab Bhavan, New Delhi, 1988.

Ahmad, Manzuruddin : *Islamic Political System,* Kitab Bhavan, New Delhi, 1991.

Ali, Chiragh : *The Proposed Political Legal and Social Reform under Muslim Rule,* Popular Prakashan, Bombay, 1883.

Badrul, S. : *Muslim Behaviour,* Kitab Bhavan, New Delhi, 1991.

Bahedur, Kalim : *The Jamaat-i-Islami of Pakistan,* Progressive Books, Lahore, 1978.

Baksh, S. K. : *Politics in Islam,* Kitab Bhavan, New Delhi, 2003.

Bawer, Raymond : *The New Man in Soviet Social Psychology,* Oxford, New York, 1990.

Berger, M. : *Islam in Egypt Today : Social and Political Aspects of Popular Religion,* MacMillan, London, 1970.

Bernier, Francois : *Travels in the Mogul Empire*, MacMillan, London, 1916.

Bukhsh, S. K. : *Contribution to the History of Islamic Civilization*, Kitab Bhavan, New Delhi, 2000.

Charles, Howard : *The Constitutionalism*, Great Seal Books, New York, 1947.

Chave, F. : *Islamic Histroriography*, Cambridge University press, New York, 1990.

Davids, Waines : *An Introduction to Islam*, Cambridge University Press, New Delhi, 1995.

Durrani, F.K.K. : *Muhammad (PBUH) the Prophet*, Oxford, New York, 2001.

Enayat, Hamid : *Islam in the Political Process*, Cambridge University Press, Cambridge, 1993.

Engineer, Asghar Ali : *A Rational Approach to Islam*, Gyan Books Pvt. Ltd., New Delhi, 2001.

————: *Islam : Challenge in Twenty-first Century*, Gyan Books Pvt. Ltd., New Delhi, 2004.

Guillaume, A. : *The Traditions of Islam*, Khayats, Beirut, 1966.

Hassan, Ali : *Observations on the Musulmauns of India*, Macmillan & Co., London, 1832.

Helmut, Reifeld : *Islam in South Asia : Adaptation, Accommodation and Conflict*, Social Science Press, New Delhi, 1999.

Houtsma, T. : *Encyclopaedia of Islam*, Macmillan, London, 1934.

Irfan, Habib : *The Agrarian System of Mughal India*, Popular Prakashan, Bombay, 1963.

Jafar, Sharif : *Islam in India*, Oxford, New Delhi, 1972.

James, Burges : *The Muhammadan Architecture of Ahmadabad*, Bernard Quaritch, London,1900.

Jha, V. : *Indian Society: Historical Probings*, Rawat Pub., Delhi, 1974.

Joseph, and Bosworth, C.E. : *The Legacy of Islam,* Oxford University Press, New York, 1979.

Karl, Jaspers : *Man in the Modern Age,* Routledge & Kegan Paul Ltd., London, 1997.

Katharine, Scarfe : *Perception of the Islamic Word,* Cambridge University Press, New Delhi, 1992.

Lewin, Roger : *In the Age of Mankind,* Simithsonian Books, Washington, D.C., 1956.

Lewis, Richards : *Universe,* Harmony Books, New York, 1973.

Martin, Lings : *A Sufi Saint of the Twentieth Century,* Century Pub., London, 1971.

Mirza, Waheed : *The Life and Works of Amir Khusrau,* Kaveri Pub., Calcutta, 1935.

Mortimer, Edward : *Faith and Power, the Politics of Islam,* Oxford, New York, 2002.

Muhammad, Iqbal : *Six Lectures on the Reconstruction of Religious Thought in Islam,* Royal Pub., Lahore, 1930.

Nabith, A. : *The Foundations of the Articles of Faith,* Feroz Pub., Lahore, 1963.

Nasr, Seyyed H. : *An Introduction to Islamic Cosmological Doctrines,* Cambridge, 1964.

Nicholson, R.A. : *Literary History of the Arabs,* Kitab Bhavan, New Delhi, 1994.

Nusservanji, D. : *Zoroastrian Civilization,* Oxford, New York, 1922.

Oage, Charles H. : *The Society,* Macmillan & Co., London, 1959.

Padwick, C.E. : *Muslim Devotions,* MacMillan & Co., London, 1960.

Phillips, O. Hood : *Reform of the Constitution,* MacMillan & Co., London, 1970.

Pierce, R.A.: *Russia in Central Asia, 1867-1917,* University of California, Berkeley, 1960.

Qadir, Abdul, : *Criminal Law of Islam,* Kitab Bhavan, New Delhi, 1999.

Qazi A. Qadir : *The Changing World of Islam,* Royal Pub., Lahore, 1992.

Rizvi, Hasan Askari : *Islami Reassertion : a Socio Political Study,* Progressive Publishers, Lahore, 1981.

Robert, D. : *Exploring our Living Planet,* National Geographic Society, Washington, 1989.

Saukat, S. : *Human Rights in Islam,* Kitab Bhavan, New Delhi, 2001.

Sharma, Arvind : *Women in World Religion,* New York Press, New York, 1990.

Syed, M. H. : *History of Muslims in India,* Anmol Publications, New Delhi, 2003.

———— : *Islamic Terrorism : Myth or Reality,* Gyan Books, New Delhi, 2002.

Tarn, W. W. : *The Greeks in Bactria and India,* Cambridge, London, 1938.

Thomas, Arnold : *The Legacy of Islam,* Oxford University Press, New York, 2000.

Thompson, H.R. : *Sculptures and Inscriptions of Darius the Great on the Rock of Behistan,* Oxford, London, 1907.

Tritton, A.S. : *The Caliphs and their Non-Muslim Subjects,* Oxford, New York, 1930.

Tutsch, Hans E. : *Facets of Arab Nationalism,* Wayne State University Press, Detroit, 1965.

Underhill, E. : *Mysticism : a Study in the Nature and Development of Man's Spiritual Consciousness,* Oxford, New York, 1956.

Usmani, J.M. : *The Authority of Sunnah,* Kitab Bhavan, New Delhi, 1998.

Von, Edmund : *Modern Islam,* University Press, Los Angeles, 1952.

Von, Grunebaum : *Unity and Variety in Muslim World,* Oxford, New York, 2003.

Waheed, Akhtar : *Sufi Approach to the Problem of Alienation,* Wilson & Co., New Delhi, 1975.

Weiner, Myron : *Sons of the Soil : Migration and Ethnic Conflict in India,* University Press, Prineton, 1978.

Williams, Michael : *Outlines of World Military History,* Oxford, New York, 1996.

Wilson, Lambron : *Traditional Modes of Contemplation and Action,* University Press, Tehran, 1977.

Wolfson, H.A. : *Glimpses of Medieval Indian Culture,* Popular Pub., Bombay, 1959.

Yahanan, Friedmann : *Tolerance and Coercion in Islam : Interfaith Relations in the Muslims Traditions,* Cambridge, New York, 1990.

Yazbeck, Haddad : *Islamic Values in the United States,* Oxford, New York, 1997.

Zaehner, R.C. : *Hindu and Muslim Mysticism,* Oxford, London, 1960.

Zahid, Malik : *Subjects of Quran,* Kitab Bhavan, New Delhi, 1998.

Zahurul, Hasan : *Tarikb-i-Sufiya-i-Gujarat,* Jamil Academy, Ahmadabad, 1981.

Zaki, Azam : *The Ideas of Arab Nationalism,* Cornell University Press, New York,1956.

Index

Q

R

S

❑❑❑